My AMERICAN DREAM

To Jennifer —
Enjoy!
B Feigin

My
AMERICAN
DREAM

A JOURNEY *from* FASCISM *to* FREEDOM

BARBARA SOMMER FEIGIN

FIVE STAR
PRESS

Copyright © 2024 Barbara Sommer Feigin

All rights reserved.

No part of this book may be reproduced, or stored in a retrieval system, or transmitted in any form or by any means, electronic, mechanical, photocopying, recording, or otherwise, without express written permission of the publisher.

Published by Five Star Press, New York
www.barbarafeigin.com

Edited and designed by Girl Friday Productions
www.girlfridayproductions.com

Cover design: Rachel Marek
Project management: Sara Spees Addicott
Editorial: Laura Dailey
Map source: Porcupen/Shutterstock

All photos are from the author's private collection.

ISBN (hardcover): 979-8-9886261-0-7
ISBN (paperback): 979-8-9886261-1-4
ISBN (ebook): 979-8-9886261-2-1

Library of Congress Control Number: 2023915739

This book is for those who mean everything to me:

My parents, Eric and Charlotte Sommer

My husband, Jim

My sons and daughters-in-law, Michael and Annelise, Peter and Natalia, Daniel and Stephanie

My grandchildren, Erica, Elle, and Charlie, Alexandra and Thomas, Jackson and Dylan

MY FAMILY'S JOURNEY

from FASCISM to FREEDOM

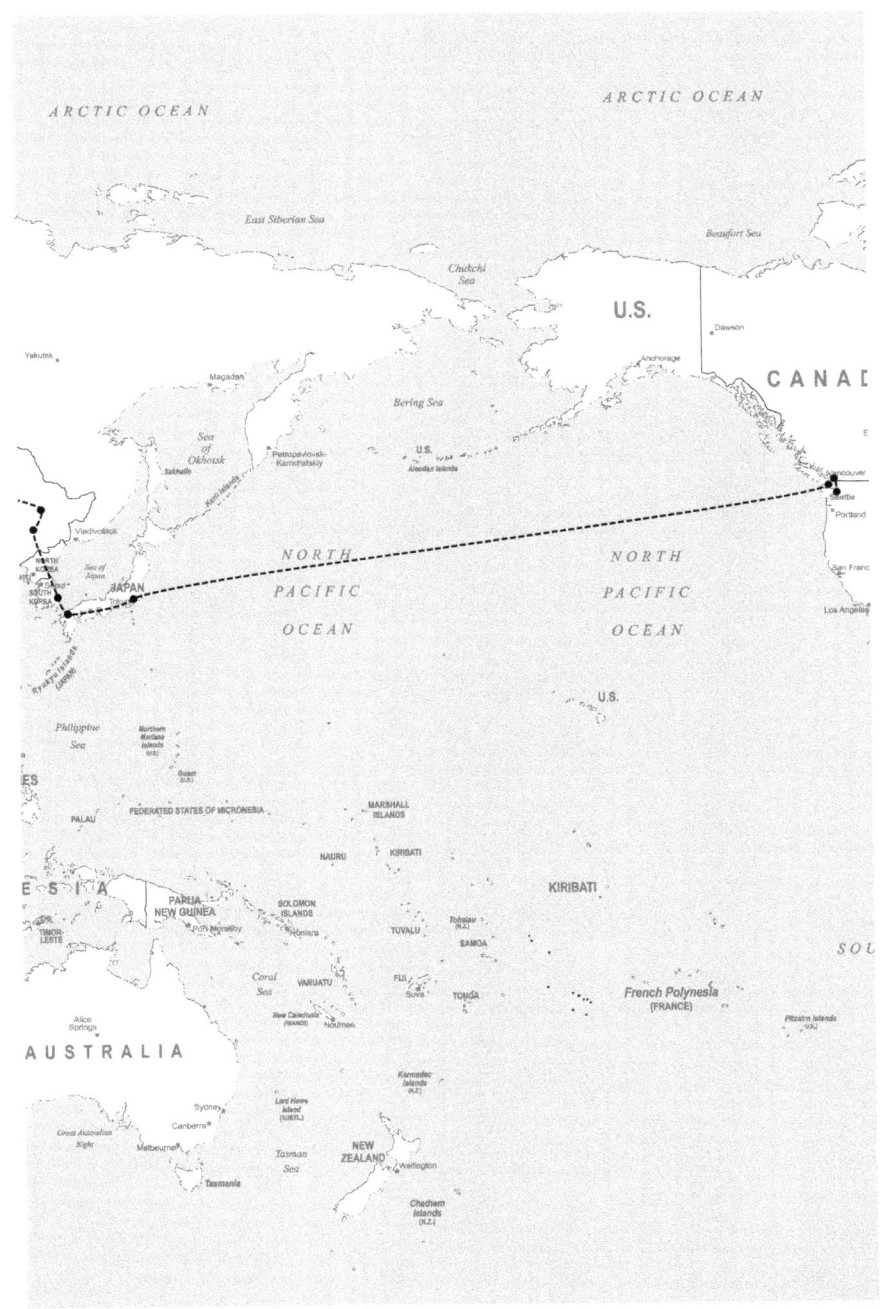

CONTENTS

INTRODUCTION xi

PART ONE
    Chapter One: Before We Left Berlin 3
    Chapter Two: The Journey 8
    Chapter Three: The Story As Told by My Father 11

PART TWO
    Chapter Four: Becoming an American: My Early Years 31
    Chapter Five: Becoming an American: My High School Years . . 53
    Chapter Six: The Whitman Years 61
    Chapter Seven: Program Girl 67
    Chapter Eight: New York, New York 79
    Chapter Nine: Jim 82
    Chapter Ten: More about My Mother 96
    Chapter Eleven: Welcome to the World of Advertising. 99
    Chapter Twelve: This Is the Year That Was 108
    Chapter Thirteen: Mad Woman 120
    Chapter Fourteen: Our Crazy Balancing Act 140
    Chapter Fifteen: More about My Father 155
    Chapter Sixteen: My Charmed Life, No More 158
    Chapter Seventeen: Mad Woman Redux 166
    Chapter Eighteen: The Ties That Bind 182
    Chapter Nineteen: Turning Points 191
    Chapter Twenty: Exploring My Roots 200
    Chapter Twenty-One: The Long Goodbye 204
    Chapter Twenty-Two: The Aftermath 215

CONTENTS

Chapter Twenty-Three: New Beginnings 219
Chapter Twenty-Four: Whitman Revisited 223
Chapter Twenty-Five: Travels with Nancy 228
Chapter Twenty-Six: My Proudest Accomplishment 232
Chapter Twenty-Seven: Legendary Pioneer 244
Chapter Twenty-Eight: We Are the Champions 246

EPILOGUE 251

ACKNOWLEDGMENTS 255

ABOUT THE AUTHOR 257

INTRODUCTION

One morning in 2013, when I'm in my office in New York City, my phone rings. It's my sister, Carolyn, calling from Annapolis, Maryland, where she and her family have lived for many years. Carolyn and I speak regularly to post each other on family happenings, and I'm expecting this call to be a routine catch-up call. But it's not; this call is different.

Carolyn tells me she has amazing news for me. She says she's found a detailed journal among my late father's papers, one he wrote before and during the terrifying escape our family—my Jewish father, my mother, and I, at two-and-a-half years old—made in 1940, at the onset of World War II, from Nazi Germany to Yokohama, Japan, and then across the Pacific Ocean to Seattle and finally to Chehalis, a small farming and logging town in southwest Washington State, where we settled.

I am dumbfounded—shocked, to learn this journal exists. Of course I've always known that our family made this escape, but not a single detail beyond that. I remember nothing, and my parents never spoke of it. For me, though I was born on November 16, 1937, in Berlin, it was as if our family's life began when we arrived in America. For years I've talked with Carolyn about having a gaping hole in our history. And now at long last, when I'm seventy-five years old, I'll be able to fill that hole.

Carolyn sends me a copy of the journal, a folder of loose-leaf papers with my father's recollections translated into English. Some of the translation is in my father's familiar handwriting and some is on typed pages. The folder also includes a trove of typed copies of letters my parents wrote to their parents, still in Germany, telling of their early days in America and their elation at being in the land of the free.

My grandparents on my mother's side, the Demmers

My grandparents on my father's side, the Sommers

INTRODUCTION

When I receive the journal and hold it in my hands, an electric shock runs through my body and into my brain. I'm very conscious that reading it will change my life. As I turn the pages, I'm rapt, emotionally overwhelmed, and nearly incredulous. I think anew about how ignorant I've been of so much that shaped the lives of my parents and, in turn, of me.

All I'd really known about my parents were a few of the basic facts I'd observed or had been told. My mother, Charlotte Augusta Martha Demmer, was born in Berlin in 1902, to Elizabeth and Fritz Demmer. She had two sisters, Edith and Kate. She and my father, Eric Daniel Sommer, met as young adults when both of them belonged to a rowing club in Berlin. My father was born on May 3, 1900, to Julius and Elise Sommer and was brought up in Regensburg, Germany. He had two younger sisters, Friedl and Erna. My parents were married in 1932 in Berlin.

My father's journal presents a story of intrigue, of the terrifying fear of the unknown and of death, and ultimately of the elation of finding freedom. Our escape marked a historical turning point for us, one that was life changing and life affirming and that affected not only the three people involved, but their children, their children's children, and all generations to come. The story is riveting; my father brings us all into the experience with vivid, evocative descriptions of everything he saw and heard and did, and with powerful and poignant descriptions of the emotions he felt.

The words of my father told me a great deal about my parents, things I'd never even thought about as I was growing up. I began to understand them and to understand myself more fully as I developed a highly raised consciousness not only about their terrifying, death-defying escape but also about their great strengths of character: their courage and bravery, their perseverance and determination, their optimism through incredibly stressful times, and their resilience when they were faced with nearly insurmountable obstacles. I was also amazed to learn of my father's creativity—his evocative and emotional story-telling ability—and of my mother's strategic ability to solve the complicated puzzles of life. Underpinning everything was my parents' deep love of family.

My father, Eric Sommer

    Having gone through most of my life knowing nearly nothing of my parents' background and experiences and how all of this shaped their lives, I vowed that this would not be the case for my own children and grandchildren and future generations. I want them to know my own story.

    As I began writing this memoir, I came to realize my story is actually three intertwined stories. The first is of a young, German-speaking refugee girl in a small town yearning to become an authentic American. The second is of a trailblazing woman executive who forged a successful career in a male-dominated business—advertising—in a time when career-building opportunities for women were virtually nonexistent. And simultaneous with building a career, the third story is of a wife and mom of three sons, fiercely dedicated to building strong family bonds during sometimes-turbulent times, including twenty-five years

My mother, Charlotte Sommer

when I was a caregiver for my husband, who suffered two very serious strokes when he was quite young.

Reflecting back over the arc of my life, it strikes me that maybe it was my outsider's perspective growing up and the powers of observation and insight I developed that gave me an edge over the course of my career. I'm sure it was my parents' devotion to family and their resilience that became a model for my own fierce dedication to being a wife, a mom, and a caregiver and my ability to bounce back when I hit bumps in the road. At a time when our country has arguably never been more compromised by divisiveness, hate, even violence, the ravages of the COVID pandemic, systemic racism, xenophobia, economic hardship, and despair, it occurs to me that my story might serve as more than a family record. I hope it will remind us—as Americans—who we are at our core, when we try to be the best we can be.

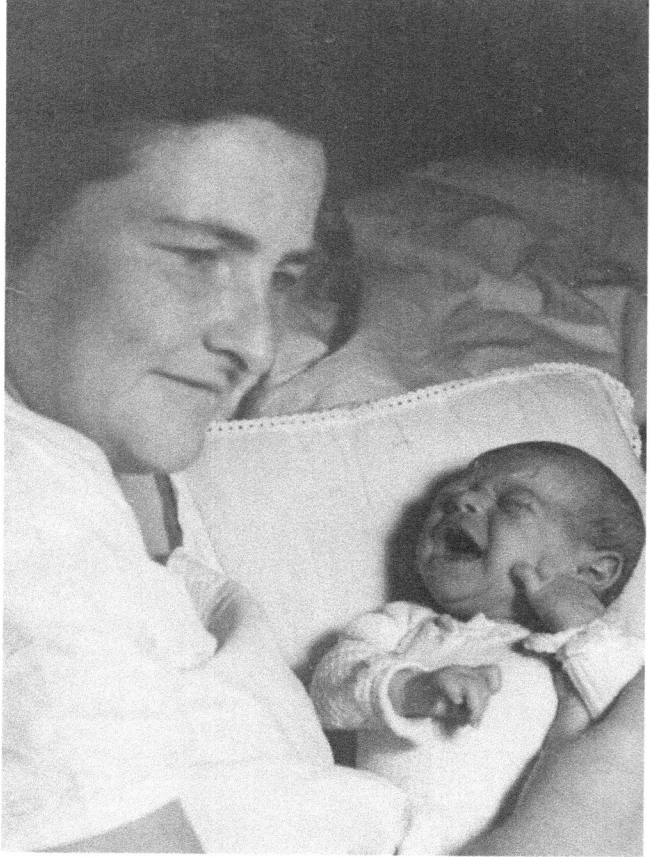

Me, 12 days old, with my mother

The following pages begin with the story my mother told Carolyn, who shared it with me at the time of the discovery of the journal. It tells of my parents, as they realized they would need to flee Germany due to the Nazis' persecution of Jews, and of their frantic efforts to do so. The story then goes on in my father's voice, through his journal, which is full of misspellings, lines struck out, penciled-in additions, inconsistencies, etc. For clarity, these have been edited, though the word choices and grammar have been largely preserved.

I have then tried to weave my parents' story into my own, reflecting not only our broad family history but also those values that have shaped our lives. I hope you will treasure this memoir as much as I treasure the memories described.

PART ONE

CHAPTER ONE

Before We Left Berlin

In the late 1930s my father had yet to fully realize he needed to get us out of Germany. The times were terrible. Jews were being persecuted; they were being sent to certain death in concentration camps. But my father was, almost fatally, a patriot. In World War I, when he was eighteen and serving in the German air force as an aerial photographer, he'd been in a crash and injured his back quite severely. He believed that since he'd sacrificed for his country, Germany would always look out for him. It took him a long time to realize what a dangerous situation he was in and that he and my mother and I needed to get out.

He had worked for Ford Motor Company after WWI, but in the late 1930s, as the Nazis escalated their persecution of Jews, he was no longer allowed to work there because he was Jewish. He was reduced to repairing typewriters in the apartment in which he and my mother, and later I, lived. I have no idea how he learned to do that—or whether there were many typewriters to repair. My mother, who had long had an important job as the executive assistant to the head of a publishing company, became the principal breadwinner during these times. After I was born, my father looked after me. He took me to play in the churchyard across the street from our apartment, but he refused to sit on the yellow bench designated for Jews. He brought a chair with him from our apartment. This was a very risky proposition; it

Charlotte's passport

could have attracted the wrong kind of attention. He had a very strong belief in doing what was right, no matter the potential consequences, a powerful character strength but extremely dangerous under the circumstances.

When they finally realized how precarious their situation had become, he and my mother knew it was urgent that our family leave Germany. They were offered an "underground railroad" trip down through Italy and then a boat trip to Israel. But my father's comment was, "Why would I want to go to Israel? I want to go to America."

My parents had obtained very hard-to-get visas, but they were due to expire on July 26, 1940. My father was nearly insane with worry, trying to assemble the necessary documentation and the American money required for our passages before the visas expired. The main problem was that, because I was not considered a Jew, he had a great deal of difficulty getting the appropriate documentation for me. My mother was not Jewish; she was Lutheran. My parents had decided not to declare a religion for me, thinking I would choose for myself at a time when I could make that decision.

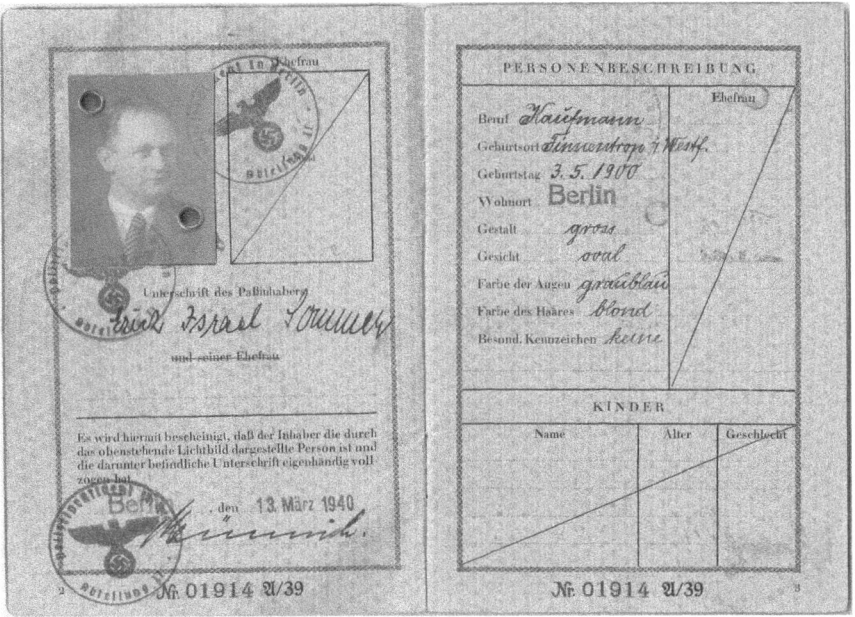

Eric's passport

As the escape plan evolved, my mother did not tell her boss about it because she was not sure she could trust him to keep the plan a secret. She was terrified that if he knew, it was possible he might inform the Gestapo and our family would be sent to the concentration camps. That could indeed have been the outcome. But she held a senior position, and her strong sense of responsibility eventually compelled her to tell him. She waited and waited, and close to the very last minute she nervously disclosed to him what our family's plan was, understanding what a great risk she was taking. He understood and wished her well. She was profoundly relieved and grateful that he was sympathetic.

As my parents prepared for the escape, they knew they would need to abide by the Nazi government's very strict rules about what we were able to bring with us on the journey. The maximum amount of money allowed for our family for the entire trip was $10.50 (equivalent to $202 in 2021). Beyond that, we were only allowed the clothes on our backs and what we were able to carry. No one was allowed to take anything of value out of the country: no gold, silver, precious stones, or jewelry of any kind. My parents decided to bring their tent

My immigration card

from their rowing club days. They had no idea if they'd be able to find a place to live in America and thought, if need be, we could live in the tent. My mother took the great life-threatening risk of hiding some silverware among our things, thinking she might be able to sell it to raise money in the US.

Finally, everything came together. Somehow my father was able to connect with a distant cousin he'd never known, Sydney Prager from Roswell, New Mexico, who agreed to sponsor our family. He provided the sponsorship documents, and we never heard from him again. My father's sister Friedl, who had a job in New York City, sent him the American money for his passage. The money for my mother's passage came from an American Lutheran group, and mine from the Quakers.

Although my father now had the American money and the appropriate documentation, he still hadn't found a way to get us out of Germany. "We had the keys to paradise," my father wrote in his journal, "but we could not enter."

Passage across the Atlantic was unsafe because of submarines, so my parents were told that the only way out of Germany was by train via Moscow and the Trans-Siberian Railroad and then on to the Pacific Ocean. This was during the short time that Hitler and Stalin had a friendship pact, so the Russians were willing to allow this. At the very last minute on July 3, 1940, just weeks before our visas were due to expire, our family was able to get a train out of Berlin. We had to move fast; there was no time to eat and only a few minutes for my parents to say goodbye to their parents, all their other relatives, and their friends.

There were eighty-two refugees in our group. The oldest was eighty-one years old, and I was the youngest, at two-and-a-half. We were about to set forth, as my father wrote, on a journey "three-quarters of the way around the world, into the unknown."

CHAPTER TWO

The Journey

Our travels took us on a seemingly endless journey through Eastern Europe, Russia—including Siberia—Manchukuo, Korea, and Japan. The train stopped nineteen times during the trip, and at fourteen of these stops soldiers and guards entered the train demanding to inspect the refugees' papers. At each stop my parents were nearly paralyzed with fear, wondering, *Is this the last time? Will we be taken off the train? Will we be sent to the concentration camps?* As we reached the German-Lithuanian border, my mother became so frightened that the Gestapo would search our bags, find the family's hidden silverware, and arrest us for smuggling valuables out of the country, that she opened the train window and threw out all the precious silverware. The risk was too great.

Our many, many train rides were dirty, hot, exhausting, and terrifying, and our boat crossing the Sea of Japan was tightly packed with passengers, many of whom were seasick. The group had no idea where we would end up, how we would end up, and whether we would arrive someplace safely.

After the seemingly endless seventeen days of arduous train travel, we had finally made it to Yokohama. There, our refugee group got on a Japanese ship, the MS *Hikawa Maru*. It wasn't terribly big, but our group thought it was beautiful: black bottom, white top, and a smokestack with red and white stripes. The trip across the Pacific took fourteen days, and as our ship approached Victoria on Vancouver Island in British Columbia, Canada, we were able to see the twinkling lights of the towns along the coast of Canada. We had only a small distance to go to reach our destination. Finally the *Hikawa Maru* docked in Seattle. At long, long last, our refugee group was in America. It was a joyous moment; my parents were enormously thankful. As my father later wrote:

> *We are glad now to live in a country which in a troubled world retains its freedom, where we can express our opinions and where we get our news through a free press and radio. We hope we will get our citizenship as soon as possible to be a part of this free, grand, wonderful country too.*

When I read my father's words long after his death, my eyes fill with tears. He'd never been one to talk about his feelings and emotions. In all the years I was growing up, he was focused on the practicalities of building a life for our family. I'd never fully appreciated the depth of

Hikawa Maru

his gratitude and his feelings of hopefulness about being in America and being truly free. I'd never thought about what this might mean to him or how his healthy defiance, and my mother's deep sense of responsibility, could well have led us to being shipped to the concentration camps. As I think about it now, it's ironic that their strong, positive qualities are exactly what could have led to the potential demise of our family.

Reading his story helps me understand much more fully why he so firmly expressed to Carolyn and me the importance of being free—to be educated, to pursue opportunities to be who we wanted to be, to do what we wanted, to live life as we wanted.

CHAPTER THREE

The Story As Told by My Father

(With Interjections by My Mother)

It was a long way from Germany to this country and it was a very difficult way too. I will try my best to tell how it was and how hard it was to get everything ready so that we could start. March 26 was the first happy news we had in 1940 and for a long, long time after too. On this day we got our American visa for which we applied two years ago. The time we applied for this visa we didn't think it would take such a long time before we would arrive in the USA. We had to wait for our quota number until March 26, 1940, the day we had to go to the American consulate. After the medical examination and after examination of all of our papers and affidavits, we got our visas. This visa was legal until July 26, 1940. On that day we found out which boat was going to the US and the day we had to be on a boat which was starting out to go to the USA . . . And we had a lot of new troubles.

So on this day now started in a hurry for us with a lot of new troubles. Telegrams were sent to my sister in New York *asking her to send us the tickets for an Italian boat because Italy was the only European country with normal traffic to the USA. We could not buy these tickets in Germany because the Italian line did not take German money. The tickets had to be paid for in American dollars. We waited and waited for an answer from New York and it took for us an awful lot of time. At last my sister wired us the money. She could only pay for the ticket for me at the Italian Line and not the rest of my family. She was a refugee too and had been in this country for one and a half years. It was a wonderful thing that she could pay the $200 dollars for my passage . . . but what happens now for Mrs. Sommer and with our little daughter, Barbara?*

We had known that the Christian churches in America and the Quaker organization had spent money to help people like us. After many visits here and there and many conversations finally our request for a ticket for Mrs. Sommer and Barbara was honored. You cannot imagine what that meant to us.

In a hurry I went to the Italian Line to book for May 5, 1940, for a ship called the Rex. The ship was leaving Italy on May 28. Visas . . . We waited from one day to the next to the twentieth. We did not get the transit visa to Italy. Today we know that Italy went into the war too and the big ship Rex never left Italy for the US. What can be done in such a case? I'll tell you that it is impossible for you to realize our feelings during these days. We had only the keys to paradise and we could not enter. At that time we didn't know anything . . . how we could start to America and knowing that our Visas would run out on July 26 and be canceled. All morning I went to the different countries consulates which worked day and night to find a way out of Germany to the US. One week followed the other without any result. One day they told us that they would try to find out a way across Finland. Another day they had us going by airplane across France and Spain to enter on a steamer in Portugal, and all that in war time. One day we got a call and we were informed that the only way for us to leave would be through Russia and Siberia. This day was June 26, and one month later our American visas would be canceled. So we had to start quickly.

We had to be ready for our trip from Berlin on July 3. There was only one week to get the passport from the government—a very difficult thing. And then we had to get all of the transit visas through Lithuania, Russia, Manchuko, China, Korea, and Japan.

I cannot tell you what that meant. I had more than a thousand things to do. I had to go to Hamburg for the Japanese visas because it was impossible to get them in Berlin at that time. In Hamburg I had to wait two days and two nights and both nights there were terrible air raids and I had to spend both nights in a basement. Lotte had to during this time, clear all these troubles with the customs officials.

We had no time to eat and only a few minutes to say goodbye to our parents, all of our friends, and all the other relatives. At twenty minutes sharp before the starting time of our train (the last train we could catch without losing our visas. Otherwise we would have had to wait for an indefinite time to get new visas). I got out our passports and we caught the train. I got very excited and when I think about it I remember it all.

It wasn't easy to think about our trip. There would be thousands and thousands of miles across three-quarters of the world and with a child only two years and seven months old and with only $10.50 in our pocket for the whole family. You know there are numerous laws for people leaving Germany. What is allowed and what we should take and what should we leave. No silver, no gold, no jewelry, no more money than three and a half dollars [each] for the family was allowed. That meant nothing of value at all.

We had known in Germany that we could get only third class tickets on the Japanese boat. But even before we had said we would go by this boat, even if there had been a fourth, sixth, or seventh class the main thing was we could go.

The train tickets which we bought in Berlin went to Moscow. And after that from Moscow to Hauchouli until Yokohama, Japan. For eight days we would be without food even though our tickets included coupons for meals in the dining car. We had with us a cake, a few cans of fruit, some fresh eggs, rye crackers, some boxes of cereal and tea. You will see that this tea (peppermint tea) was the most important thing.

In our group we were eighty-two persons. The oldest was a lady of eighty-one years of age. The youngest was our daughter Barbara who was two years and seven months old. The train in the station started with us and our daughter. After all the excitement we tried to relax, but there were so many new people and all of the people were asking "What will happen next?" The compartment was dark since the whole of wartime Germany was in full blackout. It wasn't possible to rest.

After fifteen hours of traveling we came to the German and Lithuanian border and we had our first customs examination. We had on the whole trip fourteen customs examinations. All that was very difficult, with all of the luggage as we had ten pieces and our Barbara. At one border the examination was very exact and we had to unpack all of our things while at another border it was not so exact and we could easily pass the customs inspection very quickly. Don't forget that we could not hire a porter because we were all very short of money. The young men had to help all of the elderly people from the third border on and by the third border this service was very well organized.

The people in Lithuania speak a language like Russian and we couldn't understand one word. We tried to speak to them with the German word for "greetings." Then we tried a few words of English. But no conversation would start. We had to look carefully at all of the stations to find out where we had to change trains.

Otherwise we saw the contrary too. People in rags, with incredibly dirty hands and faces, covered very often with pox.

Russian women aren't dressed nicely, but they go heavy on the cosmetics and it is depressing. The combined effect of using a lot of rouge and colored fingernails in all shades of the rainbow. The best dressed people were in the hotel.

We could see on the quay of the Volga river people resting and sleeping during the daytime. I suppose they were awfully poor people . . . it looked like that. Our driver told us that in Russia there are no unemployed people. Russia wouldn't have people enough for all the work. Maybe he told the truth . . . but I don't think so. I think only one time I could see a laughing man. People in Russia don't look contented or happy. The standard of living is low and not to be compared with the European standard of living.

And the following is about our start on the Trans-Siberian Express. We didn't see any difference with the train which we had taken to Moscow. It is all right, we got pillowcases and sheets, nearly clean, but we did not get blankets. We couldn't understand what the conductor talked to us if we asked for blankets. Later on this trip if we had known that on this trip we would never need blankets because the coach was so terribly hot. We were lucky to get a compartment in second class where four people were supposed to live and to sleep for ten long days and long nights. Men and women sleep in the same cabin. We had another refugee couple in our cabin. But some people had to share with Russian soldiers or Mongolian people, not a nice feeling. The majority of travelers have been Russian soldiers, and here I would like to tell you that Russian women also can be soldiers and officers too. When a Russian officer has to go to Mongolia or the far North East of Russia, so they go with the whole family.

The dining car is a paragraph in itself. Without regards to the dirt and to the terrible smell we never tried to take a look into the kitchen. I guess we would not feel very good for the next meal.

The worst of all was early in the morning. There were always people in rank and file outside the lavatories and frequently there was no water at all for hours and days. Shaving was a luxury and washing became more and more perfunctory. I never will forget the odor of those Russian lavatories.

Near Swertlostowsk we crossed the border from Europe to Asia and from that moment it was perilous to drink any unboiled water.

As we traveled and the wheels sang their song along the Baikal Lake, through Manchuko [Manchuria or China] through Korea and I could tell you a lot of interesting things of people we only saw in the movies until that time.

The life in Harbin, a big town with a population of 350,000 had all kinds of people. There were Russians who came to this city after the first world war. There were Europeans, Mongolians, Japanese, and so on. The people in Korea men with long beards wearing high, dark hats and long white dresses, barefoot with a big umbrella, and a long, long pipe. It would take too much time but one little scene let me tell to you. We waited for the boat to Japan . . .

There was on the train not enough water too. Sometimes we had not in the morning any possibility to wash ourselves or to brush our teeth. And in all of that terrible heat. Although when we crossed the border into Asia we found that the train stations got better. We had taken a thermos bottles with us. And now we could make at all of the stations hot tea. We were so thirsty on the whole trip but we did not like to spend one penny of our $10.50 because we didn't know what would happen on our arrival in the USA.

We crossed the Ural mountains and saw in Siberia a wonderful country with deep woods, birch trees, and for hours and hours on the ground we saw flowers and more flowers. But there were no people, no streets, no stations where the train stopped. It look awfully poor and lonely. Sometimes the station was one block house deep in the woods or mountains. If the train stopped for a short time, then all of the people and officers of the train . . . all the people jumped out of the train to have a little fresh air. The Russian soldiers picked flowers and berries for all of the women and children and I remember that the Russian soldiers were like children in moments like that. One day it happened that we lost a man at the station because he went for a second time to make tea. The train started without him. So I can tell you that on all the next stations I was afraid that Eric would not catch the train when it started. Sometimes he would get on in the last car and walk to the front where our cabin was.

The cabin which we had had four beds as I told you, two beds down and two beds higher than the others. The men had to sleep in the higher beds and the ladies slept with Barbara in the lower beds.

One night I awakened to find Eric standing before my bed. His pajamas over his chest were completely covered with blood. One night Barbara called for Lotte and she did not hear her so Eric got out of bed to take Barbara. In that very moment the train went around a curve and Eric fell into a tea glass which was standing on a little table between the beds. He got a deep cut in his chest. When I saw the broken glass I was afraid some of the glass would be in the cut. We had a medical doctor in our group of refugees but he did not have anything with him so we had to wait twenty-four hours until we arrived in Krasnojarsk, a bigger station where we hoped we would find a medical station. When we arrived there the medical doctor ran to the ambulance station. The doctor got clamps but he did not get any alcohol to clean up and sterilize the clamps. So we took whiskey from the dining car to sterilize the clamps.

The train started and we drove to Lake Baikal. The train drove nine hours around a tiny corner of the lake. We only had a little view of that gigantic lake. It was a wonderful day. The lake was surrounded with high mountains covered with snow. Do you remember that we were there in July and I told you that we had awfully hot days.

The train had to cross through twenty-one tunnels. Every tunnel was watched by soldiers. Also all the bridges we crossed were watched by soldiers and it was forbidden to look out the window when the train crossed a bridge. A few days later after we went by Lake Baikal, we crossed the Russian border to Manschukoo.

It was there where our big pieces of luggage were seen for the last time. The Russian train arrived on Manschouli and the first nice thing which we noticed was that the customs officers wore white gloves. Oh we thought if in this country the customs officers wear white gloves how clean will be our train be there. But our train was not there because the Russian train arrived too late.

We had to stay one night in Manschouli. We had no money for a hotel, only our $10.50. You know we liked to save our money for Seattle. We wanted to stay one night in the customs house. We thought that we would stay there until we could get the next train. But it was forbidden. We had to go into a hotel. But first we had to wait for our customs examination. Barbara was 'til Manschouli a very good girl and that is not only because I am a very proud father. But in the Custom's house she got tired and I put her on a table for a very short nap. Another traveler threw a suitcase on her hand and since this moment 'til today she is a spoiled girl. The trouble with Barbara on our trip began in Manschouli. While Lotte took care of Barbara, Eric at the same time went to discuss our ticket situation with the Japanese ticket office.

We heard that we could not get a sleeping car to Yokohama. That would mean that for eight days we would not have a sleeping place. In Manschuko the Japanese people got the sleeping cars. July was vacation time in Japan and Manschuko too. There were so many traveling people, that they did not give any European people any of the sleeping cars. So in Manschuko we got back the money which was paid for in Berlin. It was for a sleeping car to Yokohama and in this way we had the money to stay one night in a hotel in

Manscholi. That was our first night in a Japanese hotel. We had to sleep on the floor with a sandbag on mats and with a sandbag under our heads. I can tell you that it was not so bad and it was much better than to sit in a train for eight days and eight nights. The first thing we did in the hotel was to take a bath to clean off all the Russian dirt and dust. And we had our second wash day on our trip.

On that evening we took a little walk, first to get a little fresh air and then to have a little look around the town. It is a little town and it would have taken about thirty minutes to see the whole town. We were a small group of five people who took that walk. Right in the beginning a policeman on a bicycle came up to us and told us we had to go back to our hotel because they had to look for spies and it would be dangerous for us to continue our walk. So we went back to our hotel and slept the last night for a week.

I don't know if you remember or not that Manschuko had a war with Russia about one and a half to two years ago. But I will tell you that the people are so afraid of spies that we had to go in our train for hours and hours with window and shades closed.

But the train was clean, the restrooms were clean, we had enough water to wash, the only thing was we had no possibility to sleep.

The train drove through mountains without any woods, and marshy ground. All ten minutes a soldier with a big gun crossed the gangway in the train. We couldn't understand that at first. Later we heard that he had to look for gangsters and robbers.

The little villages we saw looked oriental. They were built flat and from loam (mud). I never would like to live in a country like that.

In the stations we saw Japanese people and in the train too. They had big bouquets of wonderful and thousands of different kinds of flowers.

After the first night with the sleeping car we arrived in Harbin. From Harbin I often read in books that it is a wonderful town. But we have been afraid to stop in Harbin because we heard that there was Typhus. I put Barbara on a line and told her again and again not to take anything. I took her always close to me. From Manchschouli we were without food. We had known that in Harbin we would find a Jewish Committee which would like to help us. It was the first help we got on our trip. The train stopped at the station we got out of the train and twenty or more people were running to our group of refugees to help us. They were mostly German or Austrian refugees and Russian people too who had built up a new life in Harbin. They took our suitcases together.

One lady took Barbara to care for her. You cannot understand what that nice help on the trip meant to us. We never could take a porter for the suitcases because we couldn't pay for them. So if we had to change trains it was very hard to carry the suitcases, take care of Barbara, and catch the train at the right time. Lotte was so very much surprised with that so very, very nice help in Harbin, in that very first moment I cried. The people all spoke German and so we could have our first conversation during the trip. They took us for lunch and dinner in a home for old people. And Barbara was able to have her nap in a real bed.

In the evening we had to start again and it was hard for us to say goodbye to all those nice people we liked so much in the short time we knew them.

The train was full of Japanese people when it arrived and it was hard to get a place to sit down. I will never forget on the train station in Harbin. It was dark and because it rained the whole day, it was very cold. One man took off his coat to wrap Barbara in it. The station was crowded and busy. The train only stopped in Harbin for five minutes and we did not know if we would catch the train because it was full of Japanese people when it arrived and it was very hard to get a place to sit down. But the boys there who caught the train put our luggage on it and got a place to sit for the three of us to sit.

The train then went on to Korea. The train climbed high into the mountains where we saw wonderful country and the first Japanese buildings. We saw people there who we had only seen in pictures. There were men there with long beards who wore high dark hats, a long white dress, had bare feet, who had a big umbrella, and were smoking a long water pipe. The women were dressed in a wide white blouse and a colored skirt. They had dark hair and brown eyes and they were carrying a basket on their heads.

It was very interesting to see all that, but it was so very hot, and the money we got back in Manschouli was gone, so we couldn't buy anything to drink. The train drove down now from the mountains, down to Fusan, a town on the Japanese Sea.

In Fusan we arrived too late. The boat with which we had to cross the Japanese Sea to go to Japan was gone. Because the train was too late on the station in Fusan, we got the back the money we paid for an express ticket. In that way we had the money to sometimes get something to drink on our trip across Japan. In Fusan we sat in the station on our suitcases. Barbara was sleeping in Lotte's arms. The men talked with the Japanese touring clerk. It was so difficult. He could not speak a good English language and the men from our group could not either. But we knew we had to stay until twelve o'clock in the night. At that time the boat would leave. With the money we got back in Fusan we went into a restaurant to have dinner, the first dinner we had since Harbin. We put the sleeping Barbara on a table in the restaurant. Then we had to sit on the station again to wait for our boat.

A lot of people came to look at Barbara because they had never seen children with blond and curly hair. Two little Japanese girls came to look at Barbara. These two went away and returned with several other Japanese girls. In a short time we had a picture like that; Barbara was sitting on a suitcase near twenty little Japanese girls with dark polished hair and were around the age of between eight and ten years old. They stood around Barbara and seemed astonished at her about her curly blond hair. They laughed at her and she laughed back at them. That was the only conservation the children had together. That would have been such a nice picture. I am sorry that I could not take it.

The children over the whole world, they haven't to have the same language, they can be white, yellow, or black, they fit together without to speak one word.

Late in the evening we entered the boat for Shimonosekie to cross the Japanese Sea. With us there were Japanese and Russian people, German and American children and grownups a colorful picture. The whole crowd had to sleep in Japanese manner in different dormitories on mats. In a short time we had a place, one of this hard sand sacks, that means pillows and a quilt. The steward offered us this terrible green tea while we had to observe what happens in different corners.

The steamer was on its way and the first victims of sea sickness retired. We were too tired to become seasick and we slept at once until Japan. We entered the train for Tokio. The trains in Japan are built for this small Japanese people. The seats are very low, and the windows too, so that it is impossible for Mr. S, [Mr. Sommer] and for all tall men to relax. It is a wonderful trip along the coast, a beautiful country, high mountains views, the one side with rocks and in between interesting tunnels.

Each small place in between the tunnels were planted with rice, the most important food in this country. This cereal plant grows only in fields overflowed with water. You can't imagine what that means. This terrible heat and all this land covered in water systems. The air is so full of humidity that it is nearly impossible for the people to breathe. But we saw thousands and thousands of men, women and children bathing in this deep blue and green ocean.

We saw many of these characteristic Japanese fisher boats with so peculiar sails. We saw big steamers and mother ships. It was too much for us in that time.

Very interesting for us was to see the Japanese having their meals. The main thing rice and then a number of things we even could not find out what that was. Served in their nice china cups on little black trays and the waitresses quick and clean and all the time smiling.

Now I can tell you the difference between the Russian and the Japanese feeling. In Russia we European people were guests. We got our meals first, and all the Russians were nice and obliging. But in Japan we had to wait patiently. Japanese first; yellow against white.

Now we were experienced travelers and it was nothing for us to travel about thirty-six hours to Tokio. Arriving in Tokio we saw big and modern factories and a very diligent population and soldiers, and soldiers, and more soldiers. This city, the third biggest city in the world, is very interesting to visit. We could see very modern buildings and temples about two thousand years old. The palace of the emperor and special residential districts. The news boys crying, and with about ten bells on a rope ringing. Nice automobiles and an old fashioned tramway, lots of rickshaws (this two wheels cars) pulled by a man with a tremendous voice, an event we will never forget.

A cousin of ours, living since two years in Tokio invited us out so we could rest from the trip and from the heat. We got iced tea and fresh linen, a light kimono to sleep in, and a bed. After two days we sought our Japanese boat, the Hikawa Maru *in Yokohama and the last part of our trip across the Pacific began.*

We got a shock when we saw our cabins, third class under a stairway. No window and on the same floor with the kitchen. A numberless population of vermin, flies, and mosquitos we had for nothing. The meals were terrible, and today if I think what this cook did with the fine food he had I am mad. But all this was of no consequence to us. First we had wonderful weather, warm but not so hot than in Japan. Second, we got acquainted with nice American families, missionary families. The children over the whole world they have to have the same language. They can be white, yellow, or black, they find together without speaking one word.

They were coming back from the Far East to have their vacation in the United States. First we had now occasion to rest in wonderful air and our sunshine. It stands to reason that our thinking went to that land we would enter soon and so it was a fine idea that the American people organized English lessons to help us learn the language and the right pronunciation. Wasn't that smart! We strolled over all decks and could inspect the whole steamer. One day we saw the rooms with the diesel engines and another day we had maneuvers with the lifeboats. Every day we had to regulate our wristwatches because on this trip across the Pacific we gained 24 hours back which we lost on the trip from Europe to Asia. We played deck games like shuffleboard and a game with rings. One day followed the other. We had the best weather. The Pacific showed its most beautiful ink-blue color to us. We saw playing and jumping dolphins and flying fishes and had a real nice time.

You will understand that we all were very much excited the time we could see far away the first Canadian mountains. We arrived in Victoria BC, the place where the immigration officers entered the boat. We have known that the immigration officers would enter the boat at three a.m. In Victoria we don't like to miss this very important moment, so we didn't go to bed this night. Like pearls on a string the lights of the coast towns glittered over the dark sea and after arriving Victoria the sun rose and gave the snow covered Canadian mountains a glorious purple shine.

During the trip to Vancouver the officials worked very hard and we had a very exact medical examination. All of us had palpitations of the heart if all our papers would be sufficient and be in order. At noon time we arrived in Vancouver. This will be the first skyscrapers we could see. You will understand that we couldn't go from the boat because we had German passports and it was wartime.

Late in the evening we left the harbor for Seattle and then we established once more how beautiful this town is, placed in all the parks, mountains and gardens and all the brightness of thousands of neon lights, we never will forget that.

You can imagine that we couldn't find much sleep in the last night on the boat. All our thinking was: What will happen in the new country? How will people be to us? Would we find a place to make our living? And I can tell you that was the most important question we always had.

We had a little nap and when we woke up, the boat was on the pier in Seattle. We had hoped that Seattle would be such a nice town like Vancouver but when we went on deck we only saw two big warehouses right and left and that was all we could see from Seattle. We had to leave the boat, and we had to go and to work to get our luggage through the customs examination, that we couldn't find any time to think what will be.

An auxiliary committee had arranged that helpful people got us a ride to Fry's hotel and we now saw what a wonderful town Seattle was. We had arrived in the new country and couldn't wait the time to get settled. Don't forget, we had nice rooms and we had plenty to eat in this nice hotel, but I couldn't feel very well, because $10.50 we saved from here, this was the only money we had in our pocket. I felt like a bluffer in this nice hotel. I can't say often enough how helpful people were to us. We found help without having to ask for any.

Let me come to the end ... we went to Chehalis, I got a job, and here again we found friends who helped us to find a home and to feel at home. I can't find words enough to say thanks to all who helped us. We are glad to live now in a country which in a troubled world retains its freedom, in a country where we can express our opinions, and where we get our news through a free press and radio. We hope we will get our citizenship as soon as possible to be a part of this free, grand, wonderful and real democratic country too.

STOPS ALONG THE WAY

The following is a list of the countries and places through which the author and her parents traveled when coming to the US from Germany, as mentioned in this chapter. Alternative spellings used in this chapter are in parentheses. See the map directly before table of contents.

- Germany: Berlin
- Lithuania
- Russia: Moscow (Moskau, Moskow); Siberia; Sverdlovsk Oblast (Swertlostowsk); Lake Baikal; Krasnoyarsk (Krasnojarsk)
- China: Manchukuo (Manchuria; Manschuko, Manchuko, Manschukoo); Manzhouli (Hanchouli, Manscholi, Manschouli, Manchschouli), in Inner Mongolia; Harbin; Shimonoseki (Shimonosekie)
- South Korea: Busan (Fusan)
- Japan: Tokyo (Tokio), Yokohama
- Canada: Victoria, in British Columbia; Vancouver, in British Columbia
- US: Seattle, in Washington State

PART TWO

CHAPTER FOUR

Becoming an American: My Early Years

On August 4, 1940, the *Seattle Times* features a photo of a young girl, a toddler, sitting on a dock surrounded by suitcases looking dazed. I am that little girl. The photo illustrates the story of our group of eighty-two refugees who have escaped from persecution in Nazi Germany, landing in Seattle after our endless and terrifying journey.

My parents have no idea what will become of us—where we'll live, how my father will find work, how we'll manage to make a new life. They were willing not just to face this uncertainty but to embrace it because it was the price of escaping the camps. They had originally planned to go to New York where my father's two sisters live. But this is not to be. There are many thousands of refugees looking for work in New York, but there are no jobs available. The Quakers initially help my parents find lodging in a small hotel in Seattle and my father find yard work for a short while.

But my family's new life in America really begins when the Quakers, who work together with a Jewish organization in Seattle, help my father find a job and settle us in tiny, isolated Chehalis, population 5,000. Our new town, Chehalis, is midway between Seattle and Portland, Oregon, on Highway 99 in the southwestern part of

Me with my parents in our early days in Chehalis

Washington State near Mount St. Helens. Because it rains so much in western Washington, the surrounding area is a beautiful, lush green. Chehalis is a very far cry from Berlin, the big, sophisticated, diverse city that my parents inhabited, where they enjoyed their lives as young adults.

Highway 99 becomes Market Street, the main street of Chehalis, as it goes through the town. The Market Street "business district" is two blocks long, with the town's one stoplight between the two blocks. Market Street is anchored at one end by the Greyhound bus depot and at the other by the St. Helens Hotel with its coffee shop and soda fountain. In between are all the stores and small shops Chehalins might ever need: Sears, J. C. Penney, Safeway, the National Bank of Washington, Doane's drugstore, Burnett's jewelry store, Schwartz's men's shop, Brunswig's shoe store, a bakery, a coffee shop, a barbershop, a beauty parlor, a tavern, and a movie theater. Families live in small, neat, nondescript houses with well-tended yards, and most attend one of the town's eight churches. A sawmill and many small farms, and beyond that evergreen forests that seem to go on forever, are just outside of town. Most families have lived in Chehalis for generations. To my parents they seemed friendly, hardworking, middle class, and happy with their lives as they are, not interested in or ambitious for anything different.

Once we get to Chehalis, we are clearly outliers—an odd little family of foreigners who speak only German. None of us knows more than a few words of English. Our family has very, very little money. We look strange. Our clothes are hand-me-downs from generous townspeople, usually awkwardly "remodeled" by my mother. And, most important of all, our family is headed by my Jewish father in a town that includes hardly any Jews.

There is no synagogue in Chehalis, so this small handful of Jewish people, together with a few from our "twin city," the neighboring town, Centralia, bring a traveling cantor to town to officiate in a rented community center at services for Yom Kippur and Rosh Hashanah, the Jewish High Holy Days. Early on in our time in Chehalis, my father is invited to join the group for the holiday services. I never knew whether he'd been observant in the years he was growing up or when he was a young adult, but he agrees to attend and he brings me along. Although I don't know anything about what these holidays represent or celebrate, I find the services exotic and mysterious—almost like a theatrical production. The cantor sings atonally in Hebrew, which I don't understand. I am fascinated that the prayers in the prayer book, also written in Hebrew, are read

Me, forever blowing bubbles

backward on the page. In the years that follow, for the most part my father does not take part in the holiday services in Centralia. Even so, I sense the holidays are important to him. I wonder now whether their importance had something to do with his wanting to honor his own parents, especially since he hadn't had the chance to say a proper goodbye to them before we escaped. And I wonder too whether the conservative tradition of the services in Centralia was something that he, as a Reform Jew, wasn't comfortable with.

My father's job is at Sears, Roebuck; he's very proud to be working for Sears, an iconic American retailer with five hundred stores around the country. Everyone in America knows Sears; everyone, or at least nearly everyone, gets the Sears catalog in the mail. My father's job is in the Sears farm store located in a separate building behind the department store on Market Street. He comes home from work and tells my mother and me about how he has to unpack and build kitchen stoves. They arrive at the store in pieces in huge cartons; he has to unload the cartons and put the pieces together. I don't think he's ever done anything like this before, and I can't imagine how he knows what he's doing. He talks about how hard he has to work, and how difficult it is not having good English. But he's grateful to have a job. He earns seventeen dollars a week. He says it's not much money, but if he and my mother are careful and live very frugally, they'll be able to manage.

We live in a small apartment at 705½ Adams Avenue, in the back of a dark brown wooden house two blocks up the hill from Market Street. My parents have a bedroom, and there are a kitchen with an old-fashioned woodstove for cooking and a sitting room on the first floor. Upstairs are a small bedroom for me and a playroom for my toys. The rent is ten dollars a month.

My favorite time of day is when I run down the hill to meet my father when he's walking home from work. Invariably I fall down and skin my knee, and as soon as one knee heals, I skin the other one. I run as fast as I can, pigtails flying, very, very happy to be meeting my father. He's around 5 feet, 11 inches and has a trim build, sandy brown hair, and, most fascinating to me, one brownish hazel eye and one blue eye. He walks in a slightly swaybacked position, usually with his hands clasped behind his back, a vestige of his plane crash in World War I. He has a big smile on his face as he waits for me. When he sees me running down the hill, he opens his arms wide. He catches me and scoops me up over his head, and when he puts me down he takes my hand. We walk up the hill hand in hand, swinging our arms in unison. I love having this special time with my father every evening.

Life is hard in tiny, out-of-the-way Chehalis with very little money, very little English, and being different from everyone else in the town. What a massive change from my parents' earlier life in Berlin! But I never, ever hear my parents complain about being in Chehalis. They always impress upon me how lucky we are to be in America and how thankful they are that we're in the land of the free.

My mother is short and round, about 5 feet, 3 inches and on the plumpish side, and has dark brown, almost black hair, blue eyes, and a very fair complexion covered with light freckles. She often has a furrowed brow and a worried look on her very open face. When she laughs, though, her face lights up and her whole body shakes. I love seeing my mother laugh, though this doesn't happen very often. My mother and her family experienced two great tragedies when she and her sisters were young. One morning her father left for work as usual, but he never returned. He'd died very suddenly during the day. My mother was forever devastated that on that particular morning, unlike every other morning, she had not kissed her father goodbye when he left for work. In our own small family, we had an unshakable ritual which my mother made sure we always performed. Every morning when my father left for work, my mother and I kissed him goodbye. Not only did my mother lose her father, but her mother experienced a great calamity when she and her sisters were girls. Her mother slipped on a banana peel in the street and fell and broke her hip. She did not recover from the broken hip; she was crippled for the rest of her life. I don't know how her mother, my grandmother, managed as a young, disabled widow with three daughters to raise. Given these tragedies, my mother's childhood had never been carefree.

Although neither she nor my father ever speaks of the persecution they experienced in Germany or of our escape, I know they worry nearly constantly about their families who are still there during these terrible wartime years. Yet they try to keep their focus on making a new life and on becoming Americans.

Learning English is a key goal early on. My parents insist we can't be real Americans if we can't speak English. My mother finds a nursery school for me at the Presbyterian Church. I quickly learn to speak English there, and I start speaking it at home, so my parents begin to learn too.

Our family also begins to participate in some very American activities. During the war years, every Saturday at noon the town comes together for a great show of public support for the war effort. They gather on the main corner of Market Street in the middle of town for a drawing of a war bond. My parents always attend the drawings and are full of pride to be part of such an important American ritual. One Saturday when I'm around four or five years old they are asked by the town leaders whether they would allow me to draw the name of the war bond winner. At the appointed hour, I'm helped up on a flatbed truck where the drawing will take place. The barrel full of names is rotated round and round, faster and faster. And, at last, I'm asked to draw out the winning name. What a thrill! Not just for the winner of the bond, but for my parents, and for me, their "American" daughter.

When I'm around four my parents take me on our first-ever vacation to Long Beach, Washington, a tiny beach village ninety-nine miles from Chehalis on the shore of the Pacific Ocean. We take the Greyhound bus. I can't wait to see the ocean, and as we get closer and closer, my mother teaches me to touch my tongue to the spot just above my upper lip. She says when I begin to taste salt, I'll know the ocean is very nearby. I keep sticking out my tongue, and at last I taste salt. We're nearly there. Seeing the magnificent ocean and the pounding waves makes me gasp with wonder.

We stay in a shack-like cabin right on the beach and spend every day digging in the sand and jumping in the waves of the freezing cold Pacific. My father strikes up a conversation with some of the local men, and they invite him to go crabbing. They give him a rake, loan him some waders, and teach him how to wade out into the ocean in his hip-high rubber boots and use the rake to catch crabs. He loves being with the group and loves being a successful crabber. Although this vacation is a very short interlude for our family, it makes me feel warm and happy and secure to be with my parents, sharing this exciting new experience.

After his success at crabbing, our neighbor, Ernie Kuehner, the Chehalis fire chief, who is a talented fisherman, invites my father to go on an annual salmon fishing trip with him and some friends. My father enthusiastically accepts the invitation. The men fish in the Pacific Ocean at Nanaimo, near Vancouver Island. Ernie brings along the tent my father had taken with us from Germany on the fishing trip, which is interestingly the only time the tent was used in America. Fishing with the guys is a big part of the American experience, and my father loves it.

On January 15, 1943, when I'm five years old, my sister, Carolyn, is born. Because she is born in America, she is the only person in our family eligible to run for president of the United States. This doesn't mean much to me, but my parents often speak of it. It gives them great pleasure. Shortly after Carolyn is born, my father says to me, "I'm so lucky to be the father of two girls. I always wanted to have girls." This makes me feel totally secure and deeply loved.

My mother has a very strong work ethic. She believes in hard work, determination, and being oriented toward goals, values she consistently imparts to me and to Carolyn. Her determination and goal orientation were vital in helping us get out of Germany. In Berlin she essentially supported our family when my father could no longer work because the Nazis prohibited Jews from doing so. Here in Chehalis, she still needs to work to help earn money for our family. Beyond that, she likes the responsibility that comes with having a job, and she likes the independence a job affords. When Carolyn, a blonde, curly-haired toddler is still in her stroller, my mother becomes an American working woman. She gets a job as an Avon lady, tramping from neighborhood to neighborhood, going door to door, and, with her broken English, selling cosmetics to the women of Chehalis. My mother pushes Carolyn, along with all her Avon samples, in her stroller, and I tag along beside them. When my mother goes into the homes of her potential customers, I stay outside and look after my sister, rocking her back and forth in her stroller, a boring job I really don't like. The best part for me of my mother's Avon-lady job is that she gets many, many tiny sample tubes of lipstick to use to demonstrate lipstick shades to her customers; as a reward for watching Carolyn, she allows me to choose one for myself to use when I play dress-up.

Two occasions of huge national importance take place in 1945. In April, I'm in my tap dancing class in a small studio next to the beauty shop, learning the waltz clog. The woman at the desk has her radio on at a very low volume. The program she's listening to is interrupted with the somber announcement that President Franklin Roosevelt has died. Our class comes to a halt; we're all told to go home to be with our parents. Our entire town is shocked and distraught. My parents loved FDR. To them, he was the personification of America. They are very saddened when he dies.

Later that year, early in September, out of the blue all the church bells in town start ringing, car horns honk, and the police and fire department sirens start screaming. The town is going crazy. I've never heard anything like this; I have no idea what's going on. We learn that World War II is over; at long last it's really over. This is such a celebratory moment in our tiny town. Everyone, including me, is dancing in the streets. My parents are simply ecstatic. America has won the war; Hitler and the Nazis have been vanquished, as have the Japanese.

But all is not well. We still have family in Germany—my father's parents and my mother's mother and two sisters, Kate and Edith. With very little communication from Germany, there's a nearly constant undercurrent of nervousness and anxiety about what's happening with them. When the war is finally over, my mother is overjoyed to get the news that her family has survived these terrible years. But the news for my father is calamitous—the worst it can possibly be. His parents, Julius and Elise Sommer, had been forcefully separated and put on trains to concentration camps, Julius to Theresienstadt and Elise to Auschwitz. There they were executed by the Nazis. My parents do not talk to me about this, but somehow I become aware of it. They go through a period of deep, crushing grief and sadness.

In Chehalis, I'm very conscious right from the beginning that I'm different, yet I want fiercely to be like everyone else, to be a normal American kid. One day when I'm in the second grade, I'm walking home from school and a group of boys start chasing me, yelling "You dirty Nazi." I don't know why they're calling me a Nazi. They must think all Germans are Nazis. I run away from the boys as fast as I can but I'm scared they'll catch me, and I don't know what they'll do to me. I see the Texaco service station and quickly, before the boys catch up to me, run into the ladies' room and lock myself in. I hear them still shouting again and again, "You dirty Nazi." I don't know what to do. I sob and sob, afraid to leave the restroom for fear they will catch me and hurt me. Finally, they seem to be gone. I don't hear them anymore. I try to unlock the restroom door so I can go home, but I've locked myself in. Now I'm nearly petrified with fear. I see a window up high on the wall, above the sink. I finally muster the courage to climb up on the sink and jump out the window, still panicked that the boys will come after me. I go home through the back streets, still sobbing and sobbing. I get home and tell my mother what happened, and she soothes me and calms me down. But she is devastated. We've had to run for our lives from Germany to escape the Nazis and my grandparents have been murdered by them. And now, for me to be called "a dirty Nazi"—this kind of taunting is not what she expected in America; it's beyond her comprehension. It only happened once, but it was deeply painful.

As I think back now to this trauma that took place when I was only seven, I realize I didn't really understand at the time why I'd been singled out. Being chased and taunted made me feel terrified and helpless. I knew I was German, but I felt like an American. It was all I knew and remembered. The boys saw me as different—a German, a refugee, an "other." Would I always be an other, always on the fringes of the real Americans?

This feeling of being different resurfaces later that same second-grade year when I become a Brownie. One of the best things about it to me is that I get a Brownie uniform, a medium brown, short-sleeved belted dress and a dark, chocolate brown beanie. I love the days of Brownie meetings because all the girls who are Brownies wear the uniform to school. On these meeting days when I'm wearing my uniform, I finally feel like I look just like everyone else, not like a little Heidi-like refugee girl with European-looking outfits and long, thick cotton stockings. My mother is very happy for me. She is an excellent knitter, and as a special surprise she knits me a pair of beige socks to wear with my Brownie uniform. At the outside of each ankle, she knits my initials, "BS," in dark brown yarn. When I get to school, all the boys start pointing at my feet and laughing. They yell at one another, "She's bullshit."

When I tell my mother what's happened, she is crushed. Speaking so little English, she has no idea about American slurs; until now she hasn't heard the expression, "bullshit," and she certainly doesn't know the BS abbreviation. The socks have once again reminded me and everyone else that I don't really belong. My mother and I agree that I should never wear them again. It's sad, though. She lovingly knitted these socks for me and I loved how special it was that she did. Somehow for them to become a source of shame is heartbreaking for us both.

My parents continue to budget their limited funds very carefully. My mother is an incredibly talented and effective manager. Starting life in America with a paltry $10.50 and not even a spoon to her name, she manages our household and our lives very skillfully. She is extremely parsimonious, spending wisely and always trying to save as well. She keeps her ledger in her writing desk and meticulously records every penny the family spends. She has wonderful taste and always wants the best of everything she can manage for the family. But money is very tight, and she has to be very careful. One of her prize possessions and indulgences, collected piece by piece over a period of many years as she scrimped and saved, is her set of elegant Rosenthal china in a pattern she loves, called Moss Rose Pompadour. Each piece has beautiful red rosebuds with soft green stems and leaves on a cream background.

My father is paid every two weeks, and by the end of the pay period we are no longer able to have meat for our family dinners. My mother prepares a couple of favorites for us during those days. One is spinach, which she grinds in a food mill and serves with fried eggs on top. Another is a German recipe she calls "milk rice," white rice cooked in milk until it's soft. My mother serves it with melted, browned butter and sugar and cinnamon. I have no idea that she makes these dinners because money is especially scarce. I think both dishes are delicious. We hardly ever have money for ice cream. On those rare occasions when we do, we buy quart bricks of Neapolitan—stripes of chocolate, strawberry, and vanilla. My mother slices us each a portion. This is a great treat for all of us; we savor it.

My parents' first priority is buying a house. They've been carefully saving their money bit by bit for about five years and are very excited when they've saved enough to make that goal a reality. They buy a small white house at 692 Adams Avenue, two blocks up the hill from Market Street and across the street from our apartment. It has three small bedrooms, one for my parents and one each for Carolyn and me, a combination living room-dining room, a tiny kitchen, and a tiny bath. There's a long unfinished enclosed back porch where my mother has her washing machine, and my father will build long wooden shelves. The property has several fruit trees: cherries, apples, pears, crab apples,

Our house in Chehalis

quince, and walnuts. In the springtime our yard is under a gorgeous cloud of beautiful pink and white blossoms. To me, this is what heaven must look like. During the early years when we have very little money, my mother learns to can the fruit from the trees. My father is in charge of picking it all, and my mother sets up an entire complicated canning operation in our tiny kitchen. She peels the fruit, puts it in jars, and puts the jars into a scary-looking pressure cooker which makes clicking sounds and whistles and steams; this is where the operation is completed. Our whole house gets steamy and smells wonderful. My mother is sweating and her face gets very red. She cans jars and jars of our different fruits, and my father lines them all up on his shelves on the back porch. We eat the fruit seemingly forever.

We also have homegrown vegetables. My father plants a victory garden in the 1940s, something being done by Americans all across the country to support the war effort. He tends to his vegetables in the early evenings, after his workday at Sears. He is mindful that cultivating his victory garden is a very American thing to do, and is gratified by the success of his efforts. But it is not so gratifying for me. His most bountiful crop is kohlrabi, which I dislike. We eat it for what seems like every meal.

On April 18, 1946, we become naturalized citizens of the United States—real, authentic Americans. I am eight years old. My parents have been yearning for this day since arriving in the US; they've prepared by studying and passing exams on American history and civics. We go to the Lewis County Courthouse in Chehalis; Judge John Murray, a kindly but stern older gentleman wearing a black robe is presiding. It is a very formal, sober ceremony. My parents raise their right hands and swear their allegiance to the United States of America. As a minor, I become a citizen by virtue of their naturalization. We each receive a formal document, a notarized Certificate of Naturalization, certifying that we are now legitimate citizens of the United States. My parents are in tears.

Because we have so little money and live so frugally, we have never gone out to dinner at a restaurant in all the years we've lived in Chehalis. My father says that on this momentous, special day, the day we've become citizens, he's going to take our family out to dinner to celebrate. We go to the coffee shop at the St. Helens Hotel on Market Street and squeeze into a booth for our celebratory dinner. I have no idea what I'm actually eating, but I am thrilled to be out to dinner in a restaurant. My parents are so excited and so happy, laughing and talking about our being Americans at long last.

After the war, in 1947, my parents bring my mother's mother to America from Germany. Though her name is Elizabeth, my parents called her the German diminutive, *Lieschen*. Carolyn and I call her *Omchen*, the German diminutive for Grandma. She lives with us in our tiny house in Chehalis for several years. She takes over Carolyn's bedroom and Carolyn moves in with me. With her broken hip, it's difficult for my grandmother to get around; she requires a lot of attention. She has to wear an ugly, complicated iron brace on her leg and hip. To me, it looks like a torture device. It's attached to her waist, under her dress, by a wide leather corset-like belt and extends from her waist to her foot. One of my most detested jobs is helping her put on her brace. It makes me very uncomfortable to be in such close quarters with my grandmother and to be doing such a personal task for her. Although my mother usually does this for her, I dread the days when she's not able to and I have to do it.

My mother is devoted to my grandmother and relieved she's out of war-torn Germany and with us in America. And my father is very generous to her. He does everything he can to make her feel welcome and happy. But, maybe because she's had such a hard life, she's very mean-spirited and does not treat my father kindly. She behaves in an imperious way, as if she is in charge of the family, and sometimes her words to my father are nasty and denigrating. He stays calm, but the situation creates a great deal of tension in our family. My grandmother's harshness to my father seems very wrong to me, and because of this I never develop a very close relationship with her. I try to steer clear of her as much as possible in our close quarters. Carolyn, on the other hand, is thrilled to have a grandmother like all her friends do. When my grandmother arrives in Chehalis, Carolyn greets her with the only words she knows in German, *"schlürfe nicht,"* "don't slurp," with which our father admonished us whenever we slurped our soup. Our grandmother was taken aback, and my parents had to laugh. Carolyn develops a strong relationship with our grandmother; she gets along with her much better than I do. A few years after my grandmother's arrival, in 1949, my parents bring my mother's sisters, Kate and Edith, to America. They move to Seattle where they're able to find work, and sometime later my grandmother goes to Seattle as well, to live with Kate. This is a good solution for our family; we're able to breathe more easily again.

Earning money is very important to me, as our family has so little. I start working when I'm ten, picking strawberries at Norstad's, one of the strawberry farms outside of town. I leave the center of town with the other kids and a few adults who pick; we huddle together in the predawn chill on an open flatbed truck. We arrive at the fields just as the sun is rising and work hard all day long, crawling in the dirt along the rows of strawberry plants and picking as fast as we can. One summer, I earn one hundred dollars, which seems amazing. I open a savings account which becomes the beginning of my college account. My parents have impressed upon me and my sister again and again the vital importance of education's power to open doors to opportunity, and now that I have a college account they believe I'm beginning to understand.

My father has been doing well at Sears. He works hard at his job; his coworkers and customers like him very much. Sears gets a new manager, Walter Holts, who recognizes that my father has potential to grow and to take on more responsibility. He mentors my father and eventually promotes him to work in the shoe department, and later in the men's department of the main store on Market Street, significant achievements. Some years later, my father is named manager of the men's department, with several colleagues reporting to him.

My father likes the companionship of other men. Once he's working in the main store, he gets together for coffee every afternoon at the local café with Norman Brunswig, who owns the shoe store, and with several other men who work on Market Street. They sit lined up at the counter on swivel stools, laughing and joking and catching up on the latest local gossip.

My father noticed early on that having a car is a key part of the American way of life. He writes in his letters to Germany that in America, "even the shop girls and waitresses have cars." He wants passionately to have a car, and finally, in 1948, he is able to buy a black Studebaker Champion, which becomes his pride and joy and which he fondly refers to as "the Studie." To my parents, buying the Studie is a major milestone. It's both a symbol conveying that they are authentic Americans just like everyone else, and it's a physical means to real freedom. They can go *wherever* they want *whenever* they want.

We soon begin taking road trips, first throughout the Northwest and eventually to California, which to me is like the magical Land of Oz. My father drives, and my mother sits in the front seat next to him with her maps in hand, navigating and recording our starting and ending mileage each day and our gas and food expenditures in her notebook. We always stay in rustic-looking cabin courts where my mother can cook our meals. Our food is packed in a cooler chest which rests on the floor of the back seat between Carolyn and me. The cooler holds our lunch fixings so we can make sandwiches when we stop along the road at midday. The butter is always packed in a special wide-mouth red thermos, and my mother has usually prepared a fried chicken we eat cold the first night. After that we shop for dinner ingredients every

My sister, Carolyn, with me on the Oregon Coast

day at local markets. Carolyn's and my job is to drag the cooler into the cabin when we arrive and back into the Studie when it's time to leave.

My parents are ecstatic that we're seeing and experiencing America beyond the bounds of Chehalis. We also go to British Columbia and Alberta, in Canada, where we stay at Banff and later at Jasper. We go to Victoria, the lovely old English town on Vancouver Island we'd first seen from the *Hikawa Maru*, though I was too young at the time to appreciate the pearly lights of the towns along the shore or the snow-capped mountains in the distance that had so enchanted my father. My mother has heard about the very English, very traditional Empress Hotel and Butchart Gardens in Victoria, which she can hardly wait to see and to show us. She plans for us to go to the hotel for afternoon tea. She makes sure we have our dress-up clothes, so we can all dress properly as we go off for tea. Tea is served in a large, impressive room; a pianist is playing lovely background music on an enormous grand piano. It is a very imposing formal occasion. I've never done anything like this; it's beautiful and elegant and awes me. I realize in later years that giving me this experience was all part of my mother's plan to help me understand that there was a world that extended far beyond life in Chehalis.

We go to California, and it's dazzling. All along the highway we see huge structures that look like giant oranges; in fact, they're orange juice stands, selling freshly squeezed California orange juice. It's more delicious than any orange juice we've ever tasted. We spend time at Mount Shasta, Mount Lassen, Lake Tahoe, Yosemite, and, most glorious of all, San Francisco. San Francisco is like a fantasy—a beautiful, bustling city with steep curvy hills, Chinatown with ducks hanging feet first in the small grocery shops, cable cars with people jumping on and off, Alcatraz, Fisherman's Wharf, the sparkling San Francisco Bay with the Golden Gate and Bay bridges; it all seems like a magnificent dream. My mother has seen a movie in which the stars have drinks in the Top of the Mark cocktail lounge at the Mark Hopkins Hotel, and she wants us all to see it. Once again, we put on our dress-up clothes and go to this magical rooftop space where we can see all of glorious San Francisco spread out before us.

Since I was very young I've understood that my mother was not healthy. In the early days after our arrival in America, she develops a goiter, a condition resulting from problems with her thyroid, which leads to a surgery. She is always very stressed and nervous in the aftermath of trying to get out of Germany and the terror of the escape journey itself. After that she, of course, constantly worries about her family and my father's family in Germany during the war, and is devastated when she learns of my father's parents' executions in the concentration camps. She has migraines from the time I can remember. She calls them "sick headaches." Whenever she feels a sick headache coming on, she lies down in her quiet, darkened bedroom, sometimes for two days, until she feels better. We all have to be very still so as not to bother her during these times.

But all of these health issues are a prelude to the one that overwhelms our family and becomes our central focus. When I am eleven years old and my sister, Carolyn, is six, my mother is diagnosed with terminal breast cancer and told she has only a year to live. I am stunned, and devastated. My parents have gone through so much and are finally in America where they are making a good new life for our family. And now, this. And it is completely out of our control. There is nothing we can do to make things better. My parents take me with them to the office of Grant Armstrong, a prominent lawyer in Chehalis whom my parents admire. They need guidance from the lawyer to think through how they should prepare themselves for what is to come. I know they must be terrified. My father must wonder, *How am I going to manage? How will I take care of these two young girls? What am I going to do?* And my mother must be thinking to herself, *I can't die. I have two young girls I need to raise. I need to teach them the many life lessons I want them to have as they grow into adulthood.* This is a scary time for my parents, and I am in shock. I can't imagine my mother dying. This is too overwhelming a thought for me even to contemplate.

My mother has a mastectomy, though it turns out the cancer has spread, undetected, by the time she has the surgery. When my mother returns home from her long stay in the hospital, she shows me her scar. To me she looks horribly disfigured. I am repulsed and have to turn away. I feel very guilty that I can't look at my mother's body at this very vulnerable moment for her.

The rhythm and dynamics of our household change. I take over many of the household duties my mother is too weak to handle. I am responsible for doing the grocery shopping, the cleaning, hanging all the laundry on the outdoor clothesline and taking it down when it's dry, and doing all the ironing. My mother is very particular about how she wants things done. She teaches me how she wants me to iron my father's handkerchiefs, hems on the inside, and how to iron a man's shirt. I don't object to taking over these household chores. I simply need to become a caregiver of sorts. This is the way our circumstances have developed. Although I don't realize it at the time, this experience prepares me to some extent for what's to transpire later in my life.

My mother is a force of nature and a driving force in my life. She has a fierce will to live and, looking back, it's no surprise to me that she lives many years beyond her original death sentence, ultimately passing away not when I'm twelve but when I'm twenty-five years old. Living with my mother's illness is for her and for me and for our family like living on a roller coaster—moving from remission to crisis and back again. We live in a constant state of underlying anxiety, never knowing what will come next or when it will come. Despite the ravages of her illness and the terrible state of uncertainty and even dread it creates among all of us, my mother does not complain. She tries always to stay optimistic and also tries, very successfully, to lead us all in living as normal a life as possible. And this life, as it evolves, becomes my sense of what is normal.

My mother believes experiencing traditions together is very important to building deep family ties, and no matter her health problems she establishes and maintains these traditions for our family. Birthdays are very important. My mother tells each of us that on our birthday she will cook the dinner we request. I always ask for spaghetti and meat sauce, and my mother's response always is, "No, this is not elegant enough for a birthday dinner. I will make *Wiener schnitzel* [her signature dish] for your birthday!" She does this, and, of course, we all love it.

Every Sunday afternoon, my mother arranges a very special and elegant coffee hour for our family. We have a big Sunday dinner at around twelve thirty or one, after which my father goes into the bedroom for his afternoon nap. While he is napping, my mother, who is a very talented baker, bakes one of her special recipes for our coffee hour—a fruit pie, apple dumplings (which are my favorite), or cream puffs that she serves with freshly whipped cream. While the house begins to fill with the delicious aromas of the baking treats, my mother and I set the table for our coffee hour with fresh linens, her treasured Rosenthal china, and the silver-plated coffee pot that must have been sent to her from Germany. By the time my father awakens and emerges from his nap, we are all set to sit down for coffee. Carolyn and I are not allowed to drink coffee, but my mother prepares tea for us. And on very cold afternoons in the winter my father pours a bit of rum into each of our cups. We feel very grown up drinking our tea with rum.

My mother has many special recipes for cookies that she bakes only at Christmastime, and the whole family participates for many days in cookie baking. The house smells delicious as batch after batch bakes in the oven. My father's job is to frost the cookies that Carolyn and I have cut into shapes: stars, bells, Christmas trees, and Santas. He has a special brush he uses to paint the cookies with the colored frostings he mixes.

Every year we all go as a family to the Brunswig farm just outside of town to chop down our Christmas tree. My father carries it into the house, puts it into its stand, and supervises us all as we decorate it. Our excitement builds to a high pitch in the days before Christmas. Carolyn and I are waiting and wondering and hoping and praying that we'll get the gifts we've wished for. At last our celebration takes place after dinner on Christmas Eve. First we open our Christmas stockings and then we all open our gifts. Carolyn and I each usually get at least one very special gift we'd been pining for.

My mother knows my father likes the piano. Although money continues to be tight in our family, she finds a small secondhand spinet she's able to afford with the savings she's been salting away and buys it for my father. This is her best gift ever for him. The piano gets squeezed against the wall alongside the front door. Now when my father comes home from work, while he's waiting for dinner, he sits down and plays the piano. He smiles and relaxes during his musical interlude; I sense he's very happy. I'm amazed at how beautifully he plays; I never had any idea he could play until we got the piano—one more aspect of his creativity.

It's now April 13, 1949. I'm in the sixth grade, the tallest person in my class at Cascade Grade School. I have brown hair and wear glasses and always stand in the middle of the back row when we have class pictures taken. We have just returned from the washroom after gym class when there's a huge roaring noise. I think the boys are making the noise as they run back to our classroom. But this is not what's happening. We are actually in the midst of a massive earthquake, 7.1 on the Richter scale. Our substitute teacher, Jean Wall, isn't sure what she's supposed to do. She rushes us all outside and orders us to lie down in the field that separates our school from the junior high. I've been to San Francisco, and I remember learning that in the San Francisco earthquake of 1906, hundreds of people died as enormous cracks in the earth opened and closed. I know that we should not be lying down in an open field. I want to run away, but I'm afraid to move because Miss Wall is adamant that we stay still where we are. I am paralyzed with fear that I might die in a crack in the earth. The actual earthquake is over in less than a minute, and we are safe. There are lots of aftershocks and lots of damage in Chehalis. Many chimneys have fallen down, but the worst damage is to the high school. It hasn't completely fallen down, but it is so badly damaged it cannot be used and will ultimately need to be torn down.

Chehalis needs to build a new high school—fast. The land needs to be assembled, the design developed, and the construction completed in record time. Chehalis hires a new school superintendent, Chester Rhodes, to take charge of this job, and he moves to town with his family.

One Sunday evening when I'm thirteen, my friend, Patty Hotsko, calls and invites me to go with her that evening to the Methodist Church Youth Fellowship. I tell her, "But I'm not a Methodist." She says, "Don't worry. That's not a problem." She tells me that Youth Fellowship is a gathering for teenagers to socialize, play games, sing, have snacks, and generally get to know one another. This sounds like fun, and I agree to come. I meet Patty that evening in the basement of the Methodist Church, which is crowded with other teenagers. And this is where I meet Don, Chester Rhodes's son. He's in the ninth grade and I'm in the eighth grade. I've admired him from afar at school, but he's never acknowledged me, and we've never spoken. I think he's very nice looking—he's around 5 feet, 10 inches and has a slim build, light brown hair that he wears in a closely cropped crew cut, blue eyes, and a great smile. He sits next to me as we have our snacks and starts chatting. I think he's flirting with me, and I try to flirt back, but I've never had a boyfriend before and I'm not really sure how to flirt. As we come to the close of the evening, Don asks if he can walk me home. I'm thrilled; I say, "Sure!"

Don becomes my first real boyfriend; I am totally smitten. I love being with him, talking with him, going places with him, and I think he feels the same way about me. He's smart and funny, and he's a great basketball player. I'm mesmerized as I watch him play. He plays the baritone horn in the band, and one day calls me on the phone and plays "My Funny Valentine" for me. This is just about the most romantic thing I can imagine. He takes me to the movies, and Carolyn tags along—not my idea of the perfect date, but my mother insists. Carolyn sits behind us; Don offers her a quarter to go and sit someplace else in the theater. She's torn, but she finally takes the quarter and moves away.

One evening after Don walks me home from a date we're standing at the foot of the steps leading up to our house. Don has his arm around me and we're whispering our good nights. All of a sudden, on this quiet night, I hear a loud, sharp banging on the living room picture window that overlooks our yard and the steps. Startled, Don and I jump away from one another. I look up at the window and there is my father in his long, flapping European nightshirt. He has a fiercely angry look on his face and waves his arm at me to come into the house immediately. I'm deeply embarrassed. I leave Don and run up the stairs and into the house as fast as I can. I brush past my irate father and run directly into my room and close the door. I now share the room with Carolyn, who is eight at the time. Carolyn whispers to me in the dark, "Barbara, don't say good night to Don in front of the house. Stop up at the corner where no one will see you." And that's what we do from then on.

After a few months of our going out together, I happen to be looking out the window in junior high one day as I'm waiting for class to start, and I'm startled to see Don walking another girl to band practice, carrying her trombone. Don just drifts away. He never says anything to me about breaking up. He is just gone. I'm crushed, deeply. He breaks my thirteen-year-old heart into a million pieces, and I never forget it.

CHAPTER FIVE

Becoming an American: My High School Years

It's September 1951, the beginning of freshman year at the brand-new high school. I'm excited and happy to be in high school. I love it. My high school years seem like a magical movie to me. I'm in a small town I now know and love and feel a part of; I'm beginning, after my childhood experiences of difference and otherness, to feel like I belong. My parents continue to emphasize how important it is to be in America because America offers freedom to *be* what you want, to *do* what you want, to *strive* for what you want to achieve. They remind me of the importance of education, telling me again and again that education is the key that opens the door to opportunity. They encourage me always to aim to be the best I can be, and this means working especially hard at academics now that I'm in high school. I do work hard, and I do well academically. But what I mainly care about is being part of a group of friends doing what high school kids do.

I have a group of good friends. My best friend is Dixie Gillingham. Dixie is short, has curly brown hair, and wears glasses. She's very lively—bouncy, fun loving, and always laughing. Her parents and uncle and aunt own Skinny and Fatty's Two Yard Birds Surplus Store, a very successful operation on the outskirts of town selling all kinds of surplus items from World War II—everything from boots to guns to Jeeps and more. They get their surplus mainly from Fort Lewis, near Tacoma. Dixie is one of the first kids in my high school to have a car, an Army surplus '49 Ford, khaki green in color. She loves to drive and picks me up for school in her car every morning. In Washington State, girls have to pass two years of home economics—cooking and sewing—to be eligible to graduate. Neither Dixie nor I can sew well; actually, we're terrible. We develop a routine. Every evening we drive to the high school when no one is around, sneak into the home ec room, take our sewing out of our cubbies, and bring it home to my mother. She helps us by sewing for us the items we're having such trouble with. We then drive back out to the school and put our sewing back into our cubbies. Although my mother has great integrity and has raised me never to cheat, she doesn't feel sewing matters that much in the scheme of life. I'm sure she must have thought there were more important things for girls to focus on in school than ensuring they were trained to become good housewives. She's happy to help us on to graduation.

Dixie often comes to my house and stays for sleepovers, gossiping and laughing with me, whispering until the wee hours. I have German-style feather beds in my room, *"Federbetten,"* as my mother calls them in German. Dixie loves sinking into her soft, fluffy feather bed when she stays over. She likes spending time with my family and especially staying for dinner. She adores my mother's cooking and can't wait every year for her famous delicious Christmas cookies. Having a group of good friends, especially my best friend, Dixie, at long last makes me feel I belong.

I'm involved in loads of activities, and my classes are challenging and interesting. I continue to work hard and eventually graduate third in my class of 101. One of the teachers who becomes very important in my life is my English teacher, Thelma Brooks, who sparks my love of literature. Miss Brooks is a single woman who lives in an apartment not too far from our house. She is thin, has an angular face, and very tight springy gray curls. Miss Brooks has a very authoritative manner and has extremely high standards. I want her to think well of me and of my work. One day, she says to me, "Please stay after class; I need to speak with you about something important." I am intimidated. I can't imagine what she wants to talk about. After class I go to her desk.

BARBARA SOMMER
"Always a friendly smile."
Chehalin 2, 3, 4; Crimson and Gray 1, 2, 3, 4, Assistant Editor 4; Chsota 2, 3, 4; Honor Society 2, 3, 4; G.A.A. 3, Secretary 3; Girls' League 1, 2, 3, 4 Cabinet 1, 3; All-School Play 2, 3, 4; Student Council 4; A.S.B Secretary 4; Nurse's Aid 3, 4 Usher 3.

My high school yearbook photo from senior year

She says, "You mustn't wear so much rouge on your cheeks." I say, "I don't wear rouge. I don't wear any makeup—just a little lipstick." Miss Brooks does not believe me. She pinches my cheek and looks at her fingers. No rouge. She says, "Oh!" Miss Brooks's approach to me was stern, but even with her brusque manner, she gives me the sense that she cares for me and wants me to present my best self to the world. So in a strange way her pinch of my cheek and her realization that I was telling the truth became a bonding moment for us both.

For me, belonging means much more than getting good grades. It means being involved in the key activities that keep Chehalis High humming. I run for election as student body secretary, mounting a very active campaign with lots of my friends supporting me by helping me create campaign buttons and posters. And I win! This is thrilling; I can hardly believe it. My other important post is assistant editor of the *Crimson and Gray*, our high school paper. I like to write and am pretty good at it; my main job is to write a gossip column that appears in every edition. I talk about all the latest goings-on at Chehalis High —who's dancing with whom at our after-game dances; what the entertainment is at our annual bonfire pep rally before our big Thanksgiving game with our archrival, the Centralia Tigers; what the plans are for the mother-daughter tea being planned by the Girls' Club; and on and on. Everyone looks forward to learning the latest, hottest news in my column, and it becomes the talk of the school. I work on CHSOTA (Chehalis High School on the Air), our high school radio program, work on the yearbook, and am in a number of plays, including *The Great Big Doorstep* in which my long-ago boyfriend, Don, is the lead.

Football games are a very big deal in Chehalis. On cold fall nights I walk to the football field to see the Bearcats play. From a distance I hear the band playing Bearcat fight songs and see steam rising from the field. There's excitement in the air. The whole town, even my parents, show up for the game. This is all part of being a *real* American. Chehalis High's colors are crimson and gray, and on game days we all try to wear some piece of red clothing. I have a bright red Jantzen sweater set, a short-sleeved pullover and a long-sleeved cardigan that I wear on these days with a gray and red pleated skirt my mother has made for me. All the popular girls collect Jantzen sweaters, but they are very expensive, so my collection is very small. I've saved my money a long time to be able to buy my red sweaters. When I wear them, I feel like, finally, I look like one of the popular girls at CHS, not like a refugee girl. I also wear Armishaw's saddle shoes from Nordstrom's in Seattle. Armishaw's shoes are special: cream with camel-colored saddles. I'm very happy to own and to wear them. To me, they are the hallmark of all-American girls.

During my high school years, my mother has a period of protracted remission. She begins working for the local newspaper, the *Chehalis Advocate*, which is published once a week. She starts as a proofreader and eventually becomes the "society reporter," writing about all the local social activities—weddings, engagements, teas, out-of-town visitors, and the like. As I think back on it, I realize that she and I are reporting on gossipy social activities during the same period—she for our town and I for CHS. What a surprising achievement for two recent immigrants: to have our ears to the ground and to capture the local buzz in the local vernacular. My mother loves working at the paper. She admires the owner, Ron Ingraham, who likes her very much and appreciates her dedication and hard work. She feels she's in the midst of all the activities of our small town, and she's making an important difference helping to support our family. It always strikes me as amusing, and amazing, that a German refugee who learned English as a second language in midlife becomes very successful as a newspaper reporter. Only in America!

Over these same years, I babysit, clean people's houses, work at the *Chehalis Advocate* folding and addressing newspapers for delivery, and take inventory twice a year at Sears, counting everything from shoes to fishhooks. I do anything and everything I can to earn money. During these high school years, my after-school job at the National Bank of Washington is by far the best one I've ever had. I earn much more money than I ever have, and I like the people with whom I work. Every afternoon I go around to each of the desks to pick up letters the secretaries have typed that day and then I march all the mail to the post office. The officers of the bank, all of whom are men, slap their knees and laugh when I come around, saying I'm "the only female mail girl" they know. They think this is very funny. Little do I know that this would be the first of many times that I'd be the only female in the various business situations in which I'd find myself.

When I'm sixteen I get my learner's permit, and my father takes me to an isolated country road near the Chehalis airport to teach me to drive. We are in his prized possession, his Studebaker. He calls out instructions, explaining the "H" positions of the stick shift. I'm conscious that I need to be very careful. I don't want to have any problems with the Studebaker. I'm soon able to get my license, and my father allows me to take the Studebaker to the local tennis courts to watch my friends play a match. As I'm pulling away from the curb to leave when the match is over, I catch the door of the Studebaker on the bumper of the next car and bend the door back so far I'm unable to close it. I'm terrified to tell my father. I'm shaking as I tell him, as I know how important his car is to him. I think my father will lose his temper and punish me severely. I tell my father I'll take the car to the body shop, have it repaired, and pay for everything myself with my babysitting money and my savings. My father is very calm. He says I'm doing the right thing—taking responsibility for the car repair. I'm profoundly relieved and grateful that he treats me in such an adult way.

But my father does not always keep his temper in check; occasionally, but very rarely, he gets angry. Carolyn and I are raised to treat our parents with great respect. I know not to talk back or sass my father. Once during my high school years I have an incident with him over a bottle of water my mother keeps in the refrigerator so the family can have cold glasses of water to drink at dinner time. We sit down at the table and my father lifts the bottle to his lips and drinks directly from it. I tell him I think this is disgusting. He's furious that I have the temerity to criticize him. He gets very red in the face and shouts at me, *"Ich bin der Meister,"* "I am the master," or the boss. He makes it very clear to me that he is in charge of our family and, like a good German child, I am not to question him.

There are two groups of kids at Chehalis High, the smaller group who plan to go to college and the rest. I'm definitely going to college, and I want to go to a top-notch one. I've understood and wanted this from the beginning. Whenever our family takes a road trip, my mother plans a route that takes us to college towns. We visit the University of Oregon in Eugene, Oregon State in Corvallis, Reed in Portland, and Stanford in Palo Alto. Reed is a small, private liberal arts college with an outstanding reputation. It is known to be highly intellectual and somewhat left-leaning politically. My mother would love for me to go to Reed, but it doesn't appeal to me at all. When we go to Stanford, I think, *This is it; this is where I want to go.* Stanford seems to me like the perfect college. I like everything about it. But I know, sadly, Stanford is not in the cards. Even with my college savings, my family simply does not have the money for me to attend.

In the winter of 1955, my senior year at Chehalis High, a visitor comes to talk with those of us planning to go to college. Douglas McClane, the director of admissions at Whitman College, tells us about this small, private liberal arts college in Walla Walla, in the southeastern corner of Washington State. My family and I have never seen Whitman; we've never been to that part of the state. Whitman sounds very interesting to me. Mr. McClane talks about its outstanding academic reputation and its most famous alumnus, Supreme Court Justice William O. Douglas. All very impressive. Mr. McClane has a bristly moustache and dark horn-rimmed glasses; he's very serious and earnest as we talk. He tells me he thinks I'm the kind of person who would do very well at Whitman. I say, "I'd love to think about Whitman, but it's impossible. My family does not have enough money to send me to Whitman." He tells me, "I think Whitman can help with a scholarship and a work grant that will go far toward paying your way." My parents and I are overjoyed. This is a dream come true. I make plans to go to Whitman in the fall.

First, though, I have to take the SATs, which are not given in Chehalis. Very few people from Chehalis High apply to colleges that require the SATs, so to take them I have to go to the University of Washington in Seattle, one hundred miles north. My English teacher, Miss Brooks, offers to drive me there and to wait for me while I take the test. The UW campus is huge, and we go to an enormous lecture hall filled with test takers. I don't know a soul, and I'm so frightened my teeth are chattering and my knees are knocking. I have no recollection of the tests, but Miss Brooks waits for me outside the lecture hall until I finish. She then drives me back home, but first we stop near Tacoma at the Poodle Dog restaurant for dinner. I'm thankful that Miss Brooks has taken me under her wing when I was so intimidated, so scared. I have the feeling that she believes in me, and this means the world to me.

My mother is concerned that I've been too happy with too little in Chehalis. Of course, Chehalis is all I know. I don't have a broad worldview. I've just wanted to be part of the American scene in this American town, with these American kids who seem to be having all kinds of American fun. When my mother tries to make clear she wants more for me, I think she's being snobbish, and I try not to pay too much attention to her.

Whitman will be my transition; my time there will begin to open my world beyond Chehalis.

CHAPTER SIX

The Whitman Years

It's May of 2009. I'm in Walla Walla at my fiftieth reunion at Whitman. It's a sunny, crystal clear day. I'm having lunch outdoors with a few of my classmates. One in particular begins to monopolize me. She seems very impressed to have learned I've had some success in life. In the midst of our conversation, she leans into me and confides in a whisper, "We really wish we could have pledged you [to a sorority], but you know, it was the Jewish thing." No one else at our table hears this exchange. The lunch continues; everyone continues to chat; the sun continues to shine. But I nearly fall off my chair. I'm shocked.

It takes me back to September 1955, the beginning of my freshman year at Whitman. Everything starts out well. As my father drives into the parking lot of Anderson Hall, the freshman women's dorm, my parents and I are greeted by Maggie Iversen, a sophomore with short blonde hair wearing the white skirt and sweater uniform of the Spurs, a sophomore women's honorary society. Maggie smiles widely as she welcomes us to Whitman. She immediately begins to help us unpack the Studie and carry my things into my room. I'm already beginning to feel comfortable. I feel I've made my first friend at Whitman.

In the mid-'50s Whitman is very "Greek." Most students belong to fraternities and sororities. Rush takes place during the opening weeks of freshman year. It's an exciting time with many parties, teas, and

Arriving at Whitman, September 1955

other events as the sororities get to know and evaluate the freshman girls and decide whom to invite to join them. The moment arrives when invitations to join are delivered to the freshman girls. I do not receive a single bid—not one, from any of the five sororities on campus. I cannot believe this is happening; I'm wondering if it could possibly be a mistake. It's not a mistake. I'm humiliated—mortified, to be so publicly rejected. I've wanted so much all my life to be a typical American girl, to belong, and at Whitman this means being a sorority girl. From the start of my college years, I'm once again an outlier. I try and try to figure out what's wrong with me—why I'm failing to be accepted. I'm crushed and heartbroken. I don't really know how to handle this excruciating public shame. I try to stand tall, to focus on my classes, to make some friends, and to work at my three jobs that help to pay my way through college. I go out on a few dates with a fellow freshman, Gordon Draper. Gordon is tall and gangly, has dark hair, and wears horn-rimmed glasses. He's very studious and very nice, but we have absolutely no chemistry, so our relationship is short-lived. It's a very, very difficult time for me. I'm deflated and lose all my fragile confidence. Although my American dream is not shattered during these early days at Whitman, there are definitely some cracks in it.

Some months later, I do get invited to pledge Delta Delta Delta. It's never clear to me why I was not pledged during the time everyone else was. I am so thrilled to be a Tri Delt that I never ask, and no one ever talks about it. Some of my Tri Delt sorority sisters become very dear friends who have remained my friends to this day. My first Whitman friend, Maggie, is a Tri Delt, and I also feel especially close to Judy McClane, the daughter of Whitman's admissions director who'd been so helpful to me, and to Judy Garwood and Laurell Boniface. We all study together, play bridge, gossip, tell each other our innermost secrets, and laugh a lot. Forever afterward, though, I have the niggling thought in the back of my head that I'm not a desirable first choice; I'm an afterthought.

When I entered Whitman I'd felt that at long last I'd become an authentic American girl, completely assimilated and just like everyone else. At my reunion lunch I was shocked to learn that this was not the case at all. I was still an "other" in 1955 at Whitman. Anti-Semitism was the barrier for me. This had never, ever entered my mind; I had been totally naïve—oblivious from the beginning. I was appalled to realize the reason we escaped from Nazi Germany for the land of the free is the same reason I was initially shunned by Whitman's sororities.

During my early years at Whitman my mother's health continues to decline. She begins seeing a doctor in Seattle, Dr. Ahearn, at what's now the Fred Hutchinson Cancer Research Center. Periodically she has to travel the hundred miles from Chehalis to Seattle for checkups and treatments with Dr. Ahearn, whom she trusts completely. She takes part in various experimental treatments. One is the first ever cobalt treatment series which leaves burn scars down the length of her back. My family moves to Seattle during my sophomore year at Whitman so my mother can be closer to Dr. Ahearn and the facilities for her treatments. My father transfers to Seattle's huge, main Sears store on Airport Way where he is given a major promotion: he's named the head of the men's department, a giant step forward for him. My parents buy a small gray house in the Montlake district of Seattle, near the University of Washington, Lake Washington, and Seattle's gorgeous arboretum.

I'm very excited to become a big city girl; I have lots of friends from Whitman who live in Seattle. But the move is hard for Carolyn. She is torn from her friends and the happy life she's known in Chehalis just as she's entering high school. She has to leave her small school where everyone knows everyone else and enter Garfield, one of Seattle's largest and most diverse high schools. It takes her some time to make friends and find her way, but when she does she appreciates some of the opportunities Garfield offers that she'd never had in Chehalis. One thing she especially likes is Garfield's ski trips. Garfield organizes buses to take students into the mountains for a day of skiing. Carolyn learns to ski and makes good friends on these trips.

I've always found Seattle beautiful—green and sparkling, surrounded by mountains, the Olympics on one side and the Cascades on the other—and nestled between Puget Sound and Lake Washington. And the city is vibrant, pulsing with energy. Boeing is Seattle's major employer, and I am lucky to get a summer job in Boeing's personnel department the first summer we're in Seattle, and every summer thereafter.

During my summers in Seattle, I have dates with a number of different men, some from Whitman, some I've met at Boeing, and even one from Chehalis. They come to my house to pick me up and try to make conversation with my parents. My mother makes it very clear to me she doesn't think any of these "Northwest boys," as she calls them, is worthy. For the most part she finds them immature, shallow, not polished or worldly, and not ambitious. She's concerned that I don't understand this and once again might be too easily satisfied with too little. I don't like her constantly pointing this out to me, but in my secret heart of hearts I think she may be right.

My Whitman graduation portrait, May 1959

While I'm away at college my mother learns that the German government is providing restitution moneys to qualified Jewish refugees who had escaped from Nazi oppression. She works diligently on the arduous and comprehensive task of completing the application documents. Collecting and assembling all the required information takes her many weeks. Carolyn tells me my mother is often in tears as she sits at her typewriter preparing the required documents. She believes ardently that our family deserves restitution, given the terror and devastation we've gone through. She understands the application needs to be ironclad and very persuasive.

She completes and submits the application and the waiting game begins. She and my father have no idea what the odds are that their application will be approved. They hope for the best. And at long last, word comes that restitution moneys will be forthcoming.

Receiving restitution makes a major difference in the lives and mindsets of my parents. My mother has always had to be extremely careful managing money because there never has been quite enough. Restitution moneys give my parents financial breathing space. Though I am away from home at this time, I am very aware of their much greater sense of financial freedom. My mother writes me how happy she is that she and my father can go to the symphony when they want to, go out to dinner at a restaurant from time to time, and occasionally stop for a drink after the theater at their favorite cocktail lounge, Trader Vic's in the Benjamin Franklin Hotel. They are, at long last, able to indulge themselves a bit.

In the summer between my junior and senior years at Whitman, in 1958, I'm working at my summer job at Boeing's huge manufacturing Plant 2. I take emergency calls at the switchboard for workers on the assembly line. My job is to listen to the caller's emergency and, if I judge that it's truly an emergency, pass the call on to the worker being called. I love this job. It's fun to work on a switchboard, and it's interesting though often disturbing to listen to the stories of the callers. A few other college girls also work on the switchboard, and we become friendly as we get to know one another.

One afternoon when I'm on duty at the switchboard, I take a call and am alarmed to hear my mother's voice. I can't imagine why she'd be calling, and am panicked that she might be having a health crisis or that we're having a family emergency. My mother says, "I have terrible news." I asked her, uneasily, "What's that?" She says, "There's been a very serious car crash." My mother goes on to tell me that five of my friends from Whitman who were driving cross-country together from New York have been in a devastating crash in Idaho. Three were killed and two, including my very good friend, Laurell Boniface, are very, very badly injured.

One of those killed is Gordon Draper, the first man I dated as a freshman at Whitman. I can't believe it. Laurell is so severely injured, her body is completely broken. She spends many months in the hospital and stays out of school for a semester. When she returns, we see that she's recuperated well physically but is deeply wounded psychologically. We have a very difficult time communicating our feelings of sadness and despair to her. They're impossible to put into words. Whitman is a small community; everyone knows everyone else. The accident and the deaths and injuries of our classmates and friends are an overwhelming shock not just to me, but to our entire campus.

I never forget my intense feeling of tragedy and loss. This is the first time in my life that something so unbelievably harrowing has happened to people who are friends of mine. One minute life is good and everyone is happily contemplating a return to school, and the next minute life is over for three of my friends and changed forever for the other two. And there's nothing I, or anyone else, could have done to change things or make them better. I'd always been aware of tragedy and death in Germany, most excruciatingly brought home to me with the murder of my grandparents. But this is different. This is the USA, and these were bright and vibrant young people who were my contemporaries and my friends. This tragedy marks a turning point for me, a sad loss of innocence.

CHAPTER SEVEN

Program Girl

It's September 1959. I'm about to embark on the most profound experience of my life—one that will completely transform my sense of the world and my mindset.

In the winter of early 1959, my years at Whitman are coming to a close. I have no idea what I'll do next. Young women in the late '50s don't really have many options. We can become nurses, teachers, or typists or get married. None of these options interests me at all. So what am I going to do? What's the next move?

From the older sister of a friend, I hear of a graduate program run jointly by the Harvard Business School and Radcliffe Graduate School. Women are not admitted directly to the Harvard Business School; it's for men only. So this program, for women, called the Harvard-Radcliffe Program in Business Administration (H-RPBA, or "the Program"), is said to be "separate but equal." H-RPBA is modeled after the first year of the Harvard Business School's MBA program—the same courses taught by the same professors but in a different place, across the Charles River in Cambridge at Radcliffe. It's a one-year program, with graduates receiving a Certificate in Business Administration, not a two-year program resulting in an MBA like the one for the men at HBS.

I'm intrigued by the possibility of going to a Harvard-sponsored graduate program that will prepare me for a business career, something that sounds much more exciting and fulfilling than the teacher, nurse, typist, and wife options traditionally available to women of the '50s. I decide to apply to the Program and am overjoyed to learn I've been accepted. Once again, though, money is a problem. My family and I don't have enough money for me to go. I write to the Program admissions office to let them know how disappointed I am that I won't be able to come and why, and am astounded to hear from them that they'll grant me a scholarship enabling me to attend. I am excited, intimidated, and more than a little scared. My parents are elated. They're thrilled I'll be going to Harvard, in their minds the best of the best.

I work all summer at Boeing to earn money for the year ahead, and finally the big day arrives—the day I leave Seattle, my family, and everything I know and am comfortable with and set off for the great unknown. I'm to fly from Seattle to Chicago, change planes, and then go on to Boston. The planes are jets, quite a new thing in 1959. My mother, who confuses the pronunciation of *j* and *y* with her German accent, calls them "yets."

Air travel, on jets, is a very elegant, formal affair. Travelers wear their dressy clothes and are served very luxurious meals preceded by a cocktail hour. I wear my best black and white checked short-sleeved dress, black pumps, and white gloves and carry a black handbag. My parents surprise me with a beautiful corsage for this momentous occasion. Once we say our goodbyes and I board the plane and settle into my seat, I decide to celebrate with a martini—or two. The flight attendants bring starched white table linens to each seat and serve warmed mixed nuts with our drinks. Then they bring their rolling cart and carve roast beef for the travelers. Wine is served with our roast beef dinner. All of this alcohol is a bit much for an inexperienced drinker. But by the time I've eaten, changed planes, had a nap, and arrived at Logan Airport in Boston, all is well.

I get into a taxi at Logan and give the driver my address in Cambridge: 46 Concord Avenue. I ask him to please call out the views. He pulls over to the side of the road, stops the cab, turns around and looks at me and says, "What are you talking about?" He has a very heavy Boston accent, and I can hardly understand him. I explain that I've just arrived from Seattle, have never been in Boston before, and am eager to see the sights and learn the history. Once he understands, he is very friendly and points out the key landmarks and their significance. I've never seen a roundabout before, and on our trip to Cambridge we pass through several. I ask my driver to explain what their function is. By this time, he's laughing. I'm sure he thinks I'm a real hick, but he takes his time and answers my many questions. We pass MIT, the Harvard Business School, Storrow Drive, Boston Harbor, Harvard College and Harvard Square, and, as we turn onto Concord Avenue in Cambridge, Radcliffe and Radcliffe Yard, where I'll be going to school. Boston is like no other place I've ever known—a huge city, full of history, buzzing with activity, electric with excitement. Even during this introductory cab ride from the airport, I'm tingling with anticipation. I sense I'm going to love my time here. I feel like I'm living an incredible dream. I can't wait to jump in and start this major new life chapter.

My taxi pulls up to 46 Concord in Cambridge, the cooperative house in which I've been assigned to live for the year with twelve other "Program girls." Forty-six Concord is an old, shabby, slightly rickety-looking wooden house with gray shingles, tall and narrow, with a small enclosed front porch. When I open the door and walk in, I'm greeted by Miss Gibson, the owner, an elderly, short, round, gruff, gray-haired woman who wears a dress that reaches the floor and has a cigarette hanging out of her mouth. She lives with her cats in a couple of rooms to the left of the front door. She directs me to my room on the second floor, up a steep staircase, and that's the last I see of her.

My Program housemates at 46 Concord come mainly from the Northeast and Midwest; one comes all the way from India. There's no one like me, who grew up in a small, isolated farming and logging town. My housemates have graduated from Ivy League colleges, state universities, and small, private liberal arts colleges. They are all smart, and all have ambitions that go far beyond being nurses, teachers, or typists. I've never before been a part of such a high energy, go-getter group of women with such a variety of backgrounds. Although we're all friendly with one another, we don't form deep friendships. All my housemates are heads down, full speed ahead, focused on devoting the year to getting a Harvard-related business education.

I begin to meet some of the men of HBS, and I find them very impressive. Most are veterans, many from occupation forces in Europe; they seem very worldly and confident. They are well dressed, in business clothes, and seem ready to conquer the business world. Their conversations and stories of their experiences are fascinating to me. They are different from anyone I've known before.

Each day, all of us Program girls hike down Concord Avenue to Radcliffe Yard to attend our classes at the Radcliffe Graduate School. I realize right away how little I know about the principles of running a successful business. Although I've always worked, and earning money has always been important to me, I don't fully know or understand all the functions involved in making a business prosper. That soon begins to change, as we take on a full complement of mind-opening courses in the basics of business. The courses are identical to those the first-year MBA students at HBS take: marketing, finance, production, administrative practices, human relations, and written analysis of cases (WAC). The cases are based on real-life situations researched and written by the HBS faculty. A case, with the company's name disguised, details the company's problem, or the issue it needs to address, presents relevant facts or data that might bear on the problem, and then poses the question, "What should the company do? What analysis leads you to this answer?" There is no one magic answer; the magic is in the power of the argument we present. We are called on at random to lead the case discussion; we always have to be prepared, because we might be called on at any time. The case study approach with oral presentation is completely new to me, and at first I find it very intimidating—very scary. Each day when I go into our classroom, my hands are sweating and I can hardly breathe as I wait and wonder to see if I'll be the one called on to present the case. As the year goes on, I get more comfortable, more confident participating, and I can actually exhale. Although I don't appreciate it at the time, the HBS case method process of diagnosing business problems, considering alternative solutions, and developing an analytical framework with supportive data and fact-based argumentation for my solution is an ideal learning experience for my later career. Our oral presentations prepare me for a lifetime of such presentations in my jobs over the years to come, and the tight written presentations we learn to make in our WAC class is perfect training for the reports I'll be writing in all my future positions.

Before I come to Boston, my mother tells me about the Boston Symphony Orchestra, the distinguished orchestra that's one of

America's most valued treasures. Charles Munch is its world-famous conductor, known for his electrifying performances. I'm not well-educated in classical music, but when I get to Boston I'm eager to learn, and one of the first things I do is buy tickets to the Boston Symphony Orchestra rehearsals. Going regularly to listen to the glorious music of the Boston Symphony Orchestra is only one of the experiences that's helping me to grasp what the wider world is all about.

I meet Dick Anderson at an HBS party early in the fall. I'm very taken with him. He's a good-looking former Navy officer and a Yale graduate. He invites me out for an afternoon and evening and takes me to the Isabella Stewart Gardner Museum. This is another one of Boston's wonderful cultural treasures. I've never been there, or to any museum, with a date, and I think the whole experience is wonderful. We go to dinner at a tiny restaurant in Boston's North End, the Italian neighborhood, and Dick asks me if I'd like to order veal parmigiana, which I've never heard of. I try it and love it. We then go dancing at the Navy Officers' Club. This entire day and evening is different from any date I've ever had at Whitman or in Seattle.

Although the Program is modeled after the first year of Harvard Business School's MBA program, its one-year duration, which awards a Certificate in Business Administration, rather than the two-year HBS program resulting in an MBA, is separate but not at all equal. Although I never thought much about this when I was applying to the Program, it now strikes me as somewhat ridiculous and unfair to women. The implicit message of the entire plan is that women aren't likely to be able to achieve as much as men or to work as long, and maybe they're not as intellectually capable, so it probably isn't worth investing in educating them for the second year required to achieve an MBA. It doesn't escape me that HBS students are called "men," whereas we in the Program are referred to as "girls." This is the first time I'm aware of encountering tacit discrimination. Although my parents had always impressed upon me that education opened the doors to opportunity, I am beginning to think maybe opportunity for me, as a woman, might be limited, even with a Harvard Business School–related education. I wonder, *Will I find limitations once I enter the working world?*

HBS regularly invites very distinguished, well-known, and successful senior executives, nearly universally men, to come to HBS to

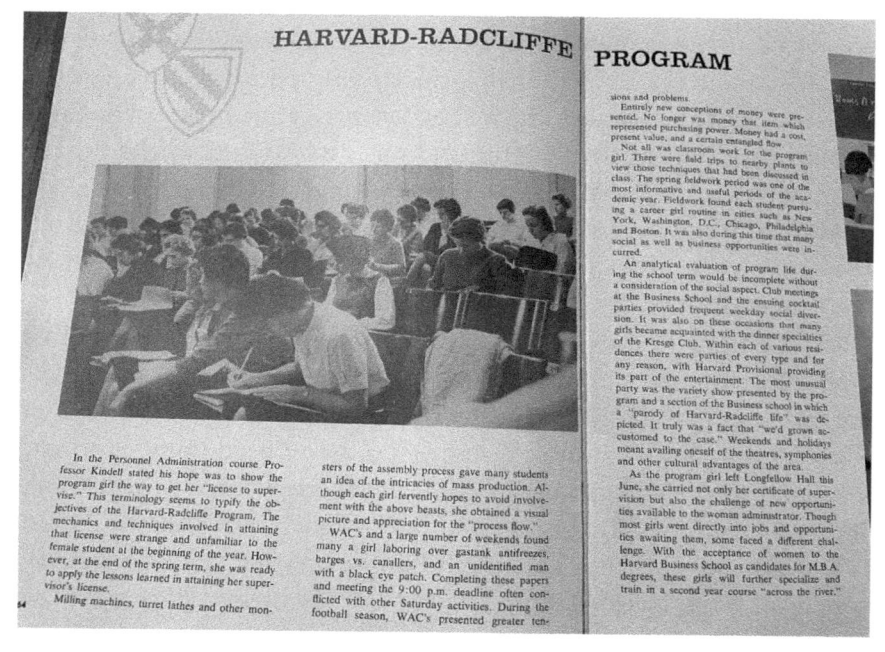

Me, Program Girl (in the first row on the right)

speak about their real-life experiences. And after the speeches, they host cocktail parties so students can meet and socialize with these powerful business leaders. HBS does not allow women to attend their classes, but we Program girls are invited to the speeches and to the cocktail parties that follow. Attending these events is eye-opening for me. I'm awed by seeing and hearing the business leaders of America and the world tell their stories. I never dreamed I'd be in a position to do this.

After the cocktail parties, HBS holds small dinners to honor the speakers. A handful of MBA students is invited, and one of the Program girls is usually included, the only woman among the dinner guests. I am excited to be invited to one of the dinners. The dinner is at the Harvard Club in Boston. The host is a highly regarded member of the HBS faculty, Professor Malcolm McNair, a big, burly man with a walrus-like moustache, who is a pioneering giant of retailing. He is known around campus, and beyond, as The Walrus.

On my appointed evening, I go to the Harvard Club and walk up to the front door. The doorman says, "No, no, no. You can't come in this door. This entrance is for men only. Go around to the alley and enter through the kitchen door." I'm very conscious that it's not right that women can't enter the front door, as men do. This is another clear inequity, but I try not to think too much about it. I'm focused on the honor of being included in this special dinner group, the only woman at a table full of men: HBS students, our host, and our honored guest. The conversation is lively, but I'm so rattled by the experience I can't remember any of the details by the time I return to 46 Concord Avenue.

After Christmas each of the Program girls starts a six-week internship geared toward applying our learning in a real-life business situation. I'm assigned to work in the research department of the New England Mutual Life Insurance Company in downtown Boston. I find my time at New England Life disappointingly dull. The work is very slow-paced and doesn't seem to be critical to the fundamental operations of the company. Nothing much seems to happen. Having been surrounded by such bright, confident, ambitious people at the Program and HBS, I'm struck by how low-energy and plodding most of my coworkers at New England Life seem to be.

The best thing about my internship is that I meet and become fast friends with Pat Siskind. Pat is a Wellesley grad a couple of years older than I. She'd moved to Boston after her recent marriage and joined the department just before I arrived for my internship. She'd worked for several years before this in economic research at First National City Bank in New York. Pat grew up in Indianapolis. Her mother is from Tacoma, so Pat can relate to my Washington roots. She and her husband, Bernie, are intrigued by my Chehalis background and my move to Boston and the Harvard-Radcliffe Program. Pat is warm and open and very friendly. She and Bernie are very generous to me. They invite me to their home and include me in trips to Crane Beach north of the city when the weather turns warm. I'm very taken with how sophisticated and worldly Pat and Bernie are. Pat and I talk about everything; I can ask her about anything and get her advice. I watch Pat very carefully; she becomes my role model as I evolve from my small-town roots. We become dear friends during my days in Boston. Although I don't know it at the time, our friendship is destined to last the rest of our lives.

* * *

During spring vacation my classmate Lynette Beall and I decide to take a trip to visit Washington, DC. We've never been there before and are eager to see the sights and learn about what goes on in the capital. I'd been a political science major at Whitman, and always followed the work of and admired Washington State's Senator Henry "Scoop" Jackson. I tell my friend that when we get to Washington, I'm going to march into Senator Jackson's office, tell him I'm his constituent, a graduate of Whitman and about to graduate from H-RPBA, and that I want to work for him. I have my polished HBS-style résumé in hand as we enter the office. There are several women at typewriters and I tell the one who greets me what I want. She says dismissively, "Thank you, dear. We'll keep your résumé on file. If anything comes up, we'll be sure to call you." I hadn't expected much, so I'm not overly disappointed.

Early in the year as my housemates and I prepared to attend our very first HBS cocktail party we were a bit uneasy. We were making our first foray to HBS and most of us didn't know a soul among the five hundred HBS men who'd be there. But my housemate, Suzanne Rollins, said, "Don't worry. I'll introduce you all to Jimmy Feigin who grew up in the same apartment building I did in Brooklyn. Jimmy will introduce us to his friends, and we'll all be fine." She did, and that's how I first met Jim Feigin, very briefly. I didn't see him again until a couple of weeks before graduation.

Just before Mother's Day, Jim and I are both at the Harvard Coop, at opposite ends of the greeting card counter, each looking for a Mother's Day card. Jim is around 5 feet, 10 inches or so, has dark, nearly black hair and brown eyes. He's solidly built, and to me he looks very, very strong. We lock eyes and slowly begin to inch toward one another. To me, this feels like a movie, unspooling in slow motion. Soon we begin to talk. Since my teenage years, I've had a fantasy that when I meet "The Person," fireworks will explode, sirens will blast, and bells will ring; it will be a magical moment, very clear and obvious. This doesn't happen when I re-meet Jim. We really don't know one another and until now have never had a real conversation, but I feel so comfortable, so at ease with him I sense we're destined to know one another better. I think this could turn out to be a really important relationship.

As we're chatting, Jim tells me his business school friends are having a pre-graduation, end-of-year, end-of-HBS party in a couple of days, and he asks if I'd like to go with him. I already like him very much; I say, "Oh, yes. That would be terrific." Before the party, Jim and I go to Jane Buehler's apartment. She's engaged to Jim's roommate, Don Yates. Jane and Don are from San Francisco; they plan to be married in June, shortly after graduation. They prepare a wonderful, California-style dinner of grilled chicken and guacamole, another dish I've never heard of. Dinner is great; we all like one another and have fun; and we're off to the party. After the party, at which I meet many of Jim's friends, Jim invites me to the Boston Red Sox baseball game at Fenway Park the next day. I'm thrilled to be invited and very excited to go. I've never been to a big league sports event. My education continues.

My whole relationship with Jim from very early on is easy and natural. We have a great time together. I love talking with him and hearing about his life, and he always makes me laugh. Jim was born and grew up in Brooklyn. After graduation from Cornell and time in the Army, Jim went into Macy's very well-known and well-regarded retail training program. This experience convinced him he didn't want to go into retail. Jim Hilborne, his boss at Macy's, an HBS MBA graduate, urged him to go to Harvard Business School. And now, he's about to graduate from HBS; he's accepted a job in the executive training program at Seagram's in New York City. Jim tells me he's Jewish but his family, like mine, is not observant.

Jim says that in high school, his friends, who knew he was strong, called him "Young Bull," which he loved. He also mentions that his astrological sign is Leo, the lion, another symbol of strength and power. Clearly he likes not only being strong, but being perceived as strong. Jim has smallish hands and feet and slim, attractive legs. He has a wonderful smile that lights up his whole face and makes his dark brown eyes twinkle and shine. He has a big, booming infectious laugh that makes everyone who hears it laugh along with him. When he gets excited, he makes a funny noise, almost like purring, his eyes light up, and he has a huge smile on his face. He rubs his knees and stamps his feet, almost a baby gesture, a gesture of pure happiness. Jim knows so many things about so many things—literature, art, politics, sports, music, and history—especially Russian history, which he knows in great depth. All of this never ceases to surprise me. He's very witty in a really sly, intelligent way. He's also boisterously funny.

As all of this is percolating at year's end, my phone rings and, to my great surprise, it's Senator Jackson's office saying that Senator Jackson does, indeed, have a spot for me. I know immediately that I'm at a major life crossroads. Whatever decision I make—Washington, DC, or not, will affect the trajectory of the rest of my life. *Should I go to Washington or shouldn't I? What will I do if I don't go to Washington?* I haven't figured that out. But I make what turns out to be the most important decision of my life. I decide I'm not going to go to Washington. I like Jim very much, and I like the way our relationship is developing.

And then graduation is upon us. My parents come from Seattle and are very excited to be a part of the big event—a Harvard graduation. The whole experience is really beyond their wildest dreams, and it makes me happy to see them so happy. Jim skips the HBS graduation ceremony and leaves for New York to start his job at Seagram's. The plan for our family is to go to New York after graduation to visit with my father's two sisters. Jim and I talk about this and agree that we'll meet in New York, and he'll be able to meet my parents then.

My parents like Jim right away. My mother, who calls Jim "Yim," again confusing her *j*s and *y*s, tells me she feels he's definitely an interesting, mature person of value and strength—a real man. She admires the fact that he's traveled, he's been an officer in the US Army, and he has an Ivy League education and now an MBA from HBS. She recognizes his intelligence, likes his personality and sense of humor, and sees that he's ambitious and on his way to a promising future. She's also struck by his interest in her and in my father. She is relieved that finally there's a man of real substance in my life—a long shot from those Northwest boys she never had much use for.

My parents go back to Seattle, and I go back to Boston where I've taken a job once again at New England Mutual Life Insurance Company. I really hate this job, but I need something to tide me over while I figure out what to do next. Pat Siskind is still at New England Life and we talk a lot about the possibility of my going to New York. She knows New York well, having lived there for years, and encourages

Harvard-Radcliffe Program graduation, June 1960

me to go. I finally screw up my courage and decide to leave Boston and look for a marketing job in New York. New York is the center of the marketing world, and New York is where Jim is.

I want to look professional and well put together when I go job hunting in New York and later for work. I'm on a limited budget so I shop carefully. I think "Jackie Kennedy" in terms of the look I aspire to. I find two dresses I think will work, one a black slubbed silk and the other a beige waffle weave. I take them to the dressing room and try on the black one first. I'm nervous about the unknown I'm about to face, but when I look in the mirror the nervousness doesn't show. Instead I see a young, confident professional. I square my shoulders and inhale deeply. I know I can do this. *Get ready, New York, here I come!* I pack up my belongings in one of the old steamer trunks from Berlin; I quit the job I hate; and I take the train to New York.

My year in Boston has been truly transformational. My world is bigger, broader, deeper, more interesting and stimulating than I could ever have imagined. I've learned from the best how to tackle business problems and issues and find solutions. I've met and become friends with fascinating people with intellectual energy and curiosity. I've been introduced to cultural and historical wonders and experiences I've never known. Most importantly, I've developed the confidence and enthusiasm to embrace whatever I might choose next. And I feel I'm at the cusp of another bigger, better adventure than even Boston was. At last I'm beginning to understand and appreciate my mother's always wanting more for me than what Chehalis could offer.

CHAPTER EIGHT

New York, New York

It's September 1960, and I arrive at Grand Central Station in New York City on the train from Boston. I have no money, no place to live, and no idea what will come next, but I can hardly wait to find out. As I stand at the stoplight outside Grand Central wearing my black silk dress and my Jackie-like pillbox hat, waiting to cross the street, I feel a throbbing under my feet. I love the energy, the vibrancy of New York. It's a thrilling moment. Much later I learn that the subway runs under the street and that's what causes the street to vibrate.

My father's sister Friedl and her husband, Fritz, who live in Forest Hills, let me stay in their basement when I first arrive. They have no children and live with their Schnauzer dog. They are very set in their ways and are not used to having their routine disrupted. It's clear to me that I shouldn't take advantage of their hospitality. I need to make my stay brief. My key priorities are to find a place to live and a job—fast. Pat introduces me to a friend of hers, Bonny Blumberg, who's looking for a roommate. Bonny and I meet and hit it off, and I move into Bonny's apartment at 315 East Sixty-Eighth Street in Manhattan.

I'm very eager to start a marketing career, but in the early '60s women are not hired for line marketing jobs, the ones that really matter, with profit and loss responsibility. My only way into marketing is through the back door, into marketing research. I know nothing about marketing research, but I think I can learn if I'm in the right place. I buy the *New York Times* and scour the help wanted ads, which in these times is the way to find a job in New York. I circle one for a marketing research trainee at the Vick Chemical Company (now part of Procter & Gamble), the parent of such famous brands as Vicks VapoRub, Formula 44 cough syrup, Lavoris mouthwash, and Clearasil acne medication. I'm very excited to be invited to interview at Vick, a company I'd originally learned about as a case history in a bestselling book of the time, *The Organization Man*.

I make my way to Vick's offices located in the old and somewhat worn Chanin Building, on Forty-Second Street across the street from Grand Central Station. Vick's offices are very spare and functional, not at all modern or fancy. My interview is with Tom Dunkerton, who runs the Marketing Research Department. Tom is in his forties, lanky and loose-limbed, and very friendly, with an open face and an easy laugh. I sit down across from him and wait nervously as he reads through my résumé. He questions me a bit about the Harvard-Radcliffe Program, tells me a little about the Marketing Research Department, and to my great surprise, offers me a job on the spot as a marketing research trainee. I feel extremely lucky to find this job so quickly. I get started right away and learn that each year Tom hires six or seven very smart, capable women—recent graduates of the highly prestigious Seven Sisters colleges, and two or three men who are recent MBAs. It doesn't escape my notice that the men are assigned individual offices and have telephones and secretaries, while we women sit in a big, open bullpen, share a phone, and most certainly do not have a secretary, even to share among ourselves.

I dig in and begin to learn a lot about marketing and about the role market research plays in the decision-making process of the company. I am trained to conceptualize and implement the market research studies that will inform important marketing decisions. One of my first assignments is a project to help determine which would be a more financially efficient and effective technique for introducing Vicks Formula 44 cough syrup, national advertising or an in-home sampling program in which actual product samples are delivered to people's homes. Sampling turns out to be more effective, and the implementation of a national sampling program leads to a highly successful introduction of Formula 44, which soon becomes a megabrand. I'm full of pride to be a part, albeit small, of such a major success.

Before long, I'm assigned to go on my first-ever business trip, to Greenville, Mississippi. There I'm responsible for checking the supermarkets and drugstores where Vick's brands are sold, and for hiring and training local women to track the movement of those brands into and out of the stores. Learning about store audits and tracking sales is another important part of my marketing and research education. I'm on my own in Greenville and take my responsibilities very seriously. I want to do a good job. I've never before been in the Deep South, and I want to soak up as much of the experience of being there as possible. I learn that Greenville's economy is based on cotton, so I make a trip around the area to see huge cotton plantations with cotton planted as far as the eye can see. What a long, long way from the farms I used to know outside of Chehalis.

During the course of the year, it's announced that our department, a repository for reams of data kept in paper form and for library materials, is going to have a cleanup day. We're told to wear our old clothes so we can all pitch in to help clean. The day arrives, and it's immediately clear that the women are to be the cleanup workers, whereas the men in the department, wearing their business suits, stay in their offices doing the "real work" of market research. I'm handed a big broom and directed to sweep out the library. As I go about my assignment, I wonder: *What's wrong with this picture? I've completed a graduate program run by the Harvard Business School, and now I'm sweeping the floor.* It doesn't occur to me to object, though. I'm grateful to have a job in a blue-chip company and to be learning so much. I keep on sweeping.

When I moved to New York, Jim and I began to see one another regularly. We often met in Greenwich Village at Washington Square Park where we'd walk and talk, getting to know one another, and then sometimes we went out to dinner nearby. Now the Jewish holidays are approaching, and Jim, who's working at Seagram's (which is owned by a prominent Jewish family, the Bronfmans), asks me, "Are you taking off the Jewish holidays?" I've never learned much about the holidays and about the traditions surrounding them. "Do you think I should?" I ask him. He says, "Yes," and explains that, in New York, it's considered respectful for people with Jewish backgrounds, even those who aren't especially observant, to take off the holidays. I go to my supervisor at Vick to tell her my plans. She asks, "Are these the happy holidays or the sad ones?" I'm mortified. I have no idea. I tell her, "I'll have to get back to you."

I've been at Vick for nearly a year. I've learned an enormous amount and have had very favorable feedback about my job performance. I think it's time for me to have a conversation about a career path plan and a compensation increase. I screw up my courage and make an appointment with Tom Dunkerton, who'd hired me. I tell him how much I've enjoyed and appreciated my time so far at Vick, and say to him that I'd like to plan with him the next steps in my career path here. He takes a hard look at me then leans back in his chair and starts roaring with laughter. I'm puzzled; I don't know why he'd react this way. He sits up and says, "There is no career path." I'm stunned; I can't imagine what he's saying could be true. He then goes on to say, "They never stay." I ask what he means: "Who never stays?" He says, "Women. They get married; they have babies; they leave." Clearly the implicit message is that Vick does not want to invest in the development of careers for women.

"I do plan to get married," I say, "and I do plan to have babies, but I plan also to have a career. I went to graduate school in business, and that's always been my plan."

Tom, in his friendly and nice way says, "Barbara, I'm sorry, but I can't help you. If you want a career path, you'll have to leave." I've loved my time at Vick, but it's clear I need to move on. There's no future for me there. And so I do, and eventually find my way into the advertising business.

CHAPTER NINE

Jim

It's September 17, 1961, a little more than a year after the day we locked eyes at the Harvard Coop. This is the day Jim and I get married.

Here's how it all comes about.

As Jim and I begin to spend more time together, I learn more about him—his family, his background, how he thinks. Jim tells me about one of the great tragedies of his life. The summer Jim finished his sophomore year at Cornell his father, Harold, who was only in his midfifties at the time, had died of a heart attack on the street in midtown Manhattan. Jim had had to go to the morgue to identify his body. What a crushing trauma. Harold had been one of five brothers; the family had emigrated from Russia when he was a young boy and had settled in Brooklyn. He had been a lawyer. His office had been on Forty-Second Street in Manhattan, across from Bryant Park. He had been involved in a very famous case connected with a huge Boston nightclub fire in 1942 in which nearly five hundred people had died.

Jim adored his father. His father, like Jim, had been an avid sports fan and had taken Jim to baseball games, hockey games, and boxing matches. Jim tells me his father had been a quiet, reserved man who fiercely loved his boys, Jim and his younger brother, Billy. He had been about fifteen years older than Jim's mother.

Jim is now living at home in Brooklyn with his mother and Billy. He knows he'll need to be out of town for several months during his time in Seagram's training program; he doesn't think it makes sense for him to rent an apartment until he's finished with the program. Jim invites me to his home on Eastern Parkway, a beautiful boulevard in Brooklyn across from the Brooklyn Museum. As we're taking a walk down the parkway, Jim asks me, "Do you like good humor?" I think this is an odd question, but I say, "Sure, I like a good joke." Jim bursts out laughing. He points to a Good Humor ice cream truck; he was asking whether I'd like an ice cream bar. We didn't have Good Humor ice cream in Chehalis.

I meet Jim's mother, Natalie, a primary school teacher. My sense is that she's probably a very good one. She's much younger than my parents, probably in her mid- to late forties. She's around 5 feet, 3 or 4 inches and a bit on the stocky side. She colors her hair strawberry blonde and religiously goes to the beauty shop on her block every Saturday to have her hair done and her nails manicured. She has longish, oval-shaped nails that she polishes with coral-colored nail enamel. Natalie smokes a lot. As I get to know Natalie a bit better, I come to realize that she always seems to have a battle royal going on with someone—one of her siblings, one of their spouses, or one of her close friends. As soon as one of these battles gets resolved, she starts another fight with someone else. She seems to be a quite self-centered person who needs and thrives on conflict. This is very different from my own family experiences.

As we get to know one another better, I ask Jim, "How did your parents manage? Your father sounds like he was such a soft-spoken, steady person, and your mother is so volatile and so self-centered and difficult—even a little hysterical. How did they get along?" Jim really isn't able to answer.

Billy is my age. He too is a Cornell graduate, and he's preparing to go into the Army. Billy has a very funny sense of humor, loves to laugh, and makes me laugh a lot too. Jim loves his brother dearly and feels very responsible for him, particularly since the death of their father. Although Jim has told me his family is not observant, they do have a Seder each year for the Passover holiday. Jim invites me to join his extended family at his home for their Seder. I've never been to one

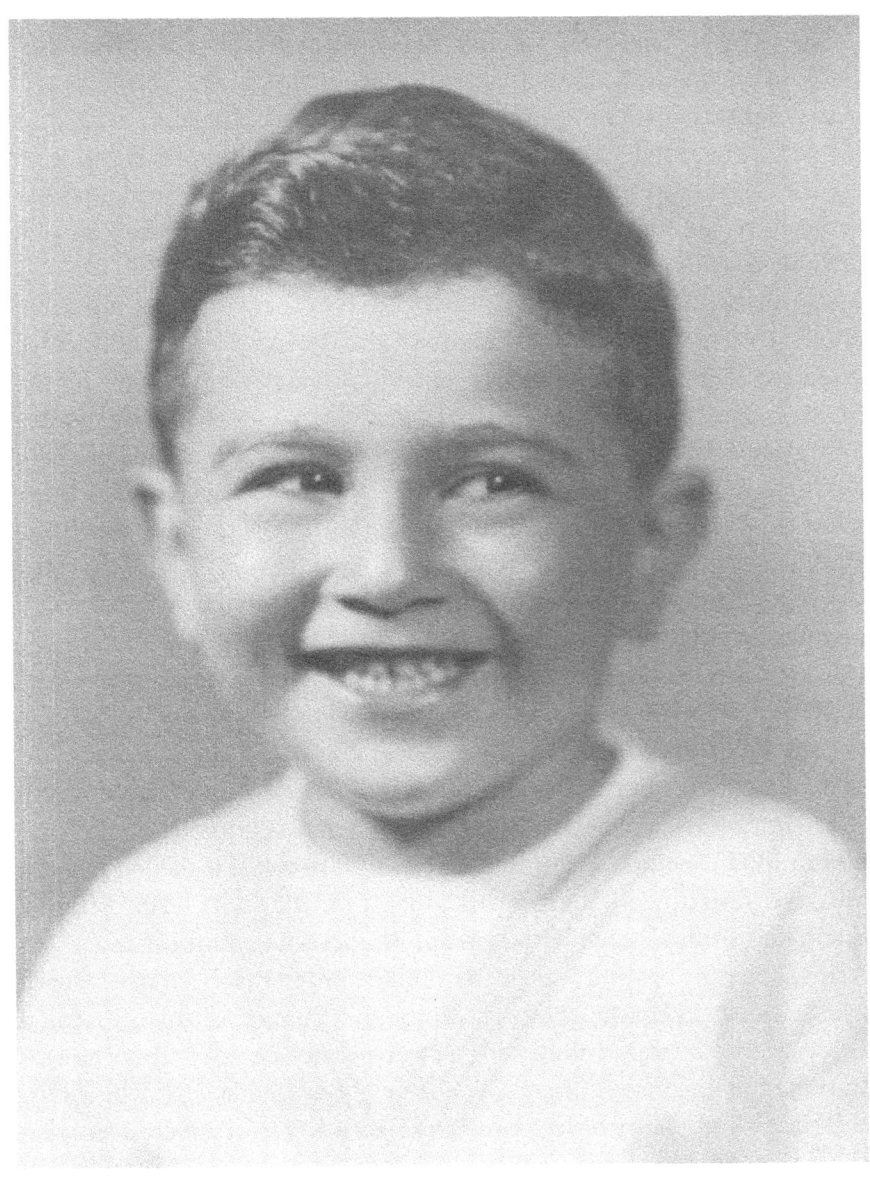

Jim

before and have no idea what to expect. I vaguely know there are special rituals and special foods, but I don't know what they are. Several days before the Seder, Billy pulls me aside and tells me the newest person at the Seder has to wear a special long, white robe and has to get down on his or her knees and kiss the hem of each person at the table. He goes on at length about all the other rituals I'll have to perform. He is very serious when he speaks, and I believe him completely. It all puts me into panic mode. I ask Jim where I'll get the white robe I'm to wear for the Seder, and he's puzzled. I tell him what Billy had said, and Jim roars with laughter. At this point, I realize it's all an elaborate joke, and I'm able to exhale.

Over these first months of our time together, Jim tells me more about his early life, filling in many of the details. He and Billy both attended Froebel Academy, a small, private elementary school in Brooklyn. One of the best things about Froebel is that Walter O'Malley's children went there as well. O'Malley owned the Brooklyn Dodgers and often invited the Froebel kids to Dodger games. Like most Brooklynites, Jim loved the Dodgers. He was crushed when the Dodgers moved to Los Angeles.

After Froebel, Jim went to Midwood High School in Brooklyn, a magnet for bright high school kids. Jim liked his time at Midwood. He was identified by the faculty adviser of Midwood's newspaper as a very good writer and was named sports editor, a job he'd loved.

Jim had wanted very much to go to Lafayette, a small, private liberal arts college, but it was not to be. Jim got a major scholarship to Cornell, so this is where he went. He was an economics major and was in ROTC, which was important to him because it helped pay the bills and gave him a path forward, at least for the short term. After he graduated from Cornell with honors, Jim became an officer in the US Army. His first posting was at the Philadelphia Quartermaster Depot where he was in charge of buying all the toilet paper for the US Armed Forces, quite a responsibility for a twenty-one-year-old! Then he was stationed in Germany, where he became good friends with fellow officers. They had plenty of free time and had wonderful adventures traveling all over Europe together.

Jim liked the Army. He liked the responsibility that came with being an officer. He liked the companionship of his fellow officers. Since his father had died when Jim was still young, I think the Army was a maturing experience for him. Being in the Army meant he was on his own, doing his own thing. Jim was proud to have been promoted to First Lieutenant before his time in the Army came to an end.

Billy and Jim

And now, after a year in the Macy's training program and an MBA from HBS, Jim's work in the first-ever executive training program at Seagram's entails his spending three months in each of the various sectors of the company, including the distillery in Louisville, Kentucky. He's in Louisville at Kentucky Derby time, and he invites me to come for Derby weekend, which is a very major event for Louisville and for Seagram's. His inviting me for the weekend is also a very big event for me. I know Jim really likes apricot prune pie, which I've never heard of before, but I find a recipe and bake him one, complete with a fancy lattice top. I put it in a box and carry it on my lap on the airplane to Louisville and present it to Jim. He's floored—totally touched and amazed. I send my parents a photo I took of Jim when I was in Louisville. Carolyn tells me she's overheard my mother exclaim to my father, "Look at how well pressed his pants are, and how his shoes are shined." These are signs to her of a man who's aware and who cares.

In the late spring of 1961, Jim is back in New York on the next leg of his training program. I'm eagerly hoping, now that he's back, he'll ask me to marry him, but he says nothing. To make matters more fraught, my mother has been bombarding me with letters saying that maybe Jim is not serious, and maybe I shouldn't be wasting my time waiting for something that might never happen. Fortunately, she is in Seattle and I'm in New York, so we don't have to have these conversations directly. I'm extremely irritated, though, that my mother does not let up on her continual rat-a-tat-tat of warnings. I'm very comfortable with Jim and I feel deeply that we're right for one another, so I decide to ignore my mother's advice and let things evolve. I do begin to wonder though: *Is there anything going on in his mind besides going out to dinner and ball games and movies?*

One evening Jim takes me to dinner at a small, cozy restaurant we both like, the Minetta Tavern, in the Village. As we're having our drinks, in the course of our conversation I think I hear him say, "When we're married . . ." I'm not sure I've heard him correctly, so I ask him to repeat what he said. He then says, "I thought we'd get married in September." I'm thrilled and totally stunned, so much so that I spill my entire drink, ice cubes and all, over the fully set table. And that is my proposal!

We begin to talk right away about an engagement ring. Jim tells me he wants me to have a ring I love, so rather than surprise me with a ring he picked out, he wants us to go together to choose one. We select a gorgeous round diamond in a four-prong Tiffany setting. I adore it and put it on my finger immediately. I'm walking on air.

My parents are overjoyed. They both think Jim is a mature person of real depth, a good man, and although they've spent only limited

Jim with his parents, Natalie and Harold

time with him, they're beginning to love him. Jim and I decide we'll be married in New York. My parents are in Seattle, and my mother has serious health issues, so it's essentially up to us to plan the wedding. I take the lead, and though I've had no experience in wedding planning, I figure it out as we go.

I notice that Natalie seems to feel disappointed in Jim's decision to marry me. I believe she feels Jim is "marrying down." She actually says to my face shortly after we're engaged that "no one will ever come between a mother and her firstborn son." I am bowled over that she would make such a harsh comment to Jim's new fiancée. She clearly thinks that as an unpolished girl from a tiny hick town in Washington State, I don't know the proper way to organize a New York wedding. She inserts herself into our planning activities to the extent she can.

Jim and I decide to get married at Garfield Temple, a Reform Jewish temple in Brooklyn, where Jim had briefly gone to Sunday school when he was a boy. Since I've never practiced any religion and I've never been to a Jewish wedding, I have no real idea what to expect. Jim and I meet with Garfield's rabbi, Eugene Sachs, whom I like very much. Rabbi Sachs is warm and welcoming. He tries to get to know us a bit and explains what will take place. We plan a simple wedding with around 125 guests. Carolyn will be my maid of honor, and Billy is to be Jim's best man.

Although I do all the New York wedding planning activities, my parents are the hosts of the festivities. I am relieved and delighted that my mother, despite her very fragile health, feels she'll be able to come and be part of our wedding. My parents arrive in New York about a week in advance of the wedding so they can spend time with Jim and me, get acquainted with Natalie and Jim's extended family, and participate in some of the pre-wedding social activities, including a shower given by Bonny, my roommate, and Pat, who has moved back to New York with Bernie. She continues to be my go-to person, now for wedding planning advice. I've told my mother about Pat, and about how she's been able to guide me and answer my questions about anything and everything. Whenever I tell my mother I'm not sure about some aspect of organizing the wedding, she says, in her German accent, "Ask Mrs. Ziskind." Excitement builds among all of us as we get closer and closer to the big day.

My mother has never had an explicit conversation with me about sex or about the sexual aspects of married life. When she gets to New York she tells me she wants a few minutes alone with me. She has brought me an exquisite white nightie for my wedding night. She gives me this very special gift and tells me how much she wishes for true and complete happiness for Jim and me. I get the implicit message from her that she's talking about all aspects of our lives together, including our intimate life. I'm nervous and excited contemplating it.

On the morning of September 17, 1961, my wedding day, I'm in the West Side apartment hotel where my parents are staying so we can all get ready for the wedding together. I am taking a bath when my mother knocks on the door and asks whether she can come in to speak with me about something very important. She has a very serious look on her face. Her sober tone and demeanor make me very uneasy. My mother closes the door and then says, in a very quiet voice, "I want you to know that Kate [her sister and my aunt who has never been married] had a baby some years ago in Germany." She tells me nothing more. My mother then stands up and leaves the bathroom to dress for the wedding. I finish my bath, thinking to myself: *That was so strange.* I wonder, *Did Kate have a secret lover? Did she get raped by a Nazi during the war? What happened to the baby? Why in the world does my mother feel she has to tell me this on my wedding day? Maybe she thinks that as an about-to-be married woman, I'm now worthy of being told this deeply buried family secret.* I'll never really know. The subject is never discussed again—by anyone.

I wear a beautiful white silk and lace knee-length wedding dress and veil, and my father, looking very handsome in his morning suit, walks me down the aisle to meet Jim, who is beaming as he awaits me at the altar. I'm on cloud nine, bursting with joy and conscious of the enormous importance of the moment. We go through the brief ceremony, and, at the end, Rabbi Sachs asks first Jim and then me to repeat a Hebrew phrase. We do this, and afterward Jim does the ceremonial stamping of the glass, symbolizing the finality of our marriage. After the ceremony, we walk back down the aisle together ... and *we're married!* Jim whispers to me, "Do you know what you said in Hebrew?" I say, "No," and he tells me, "You said you are going to take out the garbage for the rest of our lives!" I burst out laughing and laugh all the rest of the way back up the aisle.

Natalie has friends who are members of the Unity Club, a lovely social club in Brooklyn very near Garfield Temple, and they graciously invite us to use the club for our reception. Natalie has said to me, "Your parents don't really know anyone here, so I think I should stand at the head of the receiving line and greet everyone. Then the guests can go on and later meet your parents." Her *chutzpah* takes my breath away. I say, "We're not going to be doing it that way. My parents are the hosts of this party. They will be at the head of the line, then Jim and me, and then you." This is what happens. But clearly, Natalie has really wanted to take over.

We have a wonderful, festive afternoon of dining and dancing. I'm nearly moved to tears to see my parents dancing together, both with broad, happy smiles on their faces. I don't think I've ever seen them dance before. This is a capstone moment for them; they are deeply joyful about our marriage and about being able to host our celebration.

Our wedding, September 17, 1961

Soon it's time for Jim and me to change our clothes and leave for the airport and our honeymoon. I have bought a beautiful red knit suit for my going-away outfit, a big splurge for me with my fifty-five-dollar-a-week salary at Vick Chemical Company. I had written my parents about the suit and how much I loved it. My father wrote back to me immediately and said, "Your mother and I would like to give you your suit as a gift for your wedding." This was very poignant, very touching. Once Jim and I are changed, I pin the orchid from my bouquet to my

Young marrieds

suit as is the custom for new brides, and Jim and I grab hands and run through a gauntlet of our guests, all of whom throw rice at us.

I don't know what Jim has planned for our honeymoon. He has told me for some time that we're going to go on a leaf tour of New

England, which I can't imagine is true. As we near Idlewild Airport (now known as JFK) I'm very curious and very eager to know our destination. Jim says, "We're going to Bermuda." I'm awed; I've never been to the Caribbean or any of the islands and can't wait to go on this romantic honeymoon.

Bermuda is beautiful. We stay at the Castle Harbour Hotel, a lovely, elegant, traditionally British hotel. Jim and I start our married life blissfully happy. My initial nervousness about our intimate life vanishes. Jim and I are totally comfortable with one another. We love the closeness of our romantic breakfasts outdoors, our time together on the beach, and the intimacy of our delectable dinners for two. There's music and dancing every night. We feel like we're the only two people on earth, totally loving one another, in our own private version of paradise.

After a fantasy-like week, we go back home to our new apartment at 245 East Eightieth Street in New York City. The apartment is nearly empty; we have very little money to buy furniture and have agreed we'll go slowly and buy one piece at a time. We have a borrowed bridge table, four borrowed bridge chairs, our bed, and a TV set my parents have given us as a wedding gift. We have no dresser; we keep our clothes on shelves in a closet. My parents stay in New York until we return, so we're able to spend a bit of time together before they go back home to Seattle.

Every Sunday morning in the early days of our marriage Natalie rings our doorbell, uninvited. When we stumble out of bed to answer the door, she boldly announces that she's come from Brooklyn with the bagels she knows "Jimmy likes." Clearly, having come all the way from Brooklyn, she expects to join us for breakfast. We don't like her intrusion on our privacy. We invite her to our first Thanksgiving as a married couple; we have a few other guests as well. When we're all gathered at the table she announces to everyone, "Oh, Barbara's OK. I really wouldn't have cared if Jimmy had married someone purple." Our guests are shocked.

This intrusive behavior goes on for some time. Natalie intimidates me, but I feel it would be disrespectful to confront her. She is, after all, Jim's mother and my mother-in-law. Finally Jim decides he is going to sever the relationship with his mother and focus on his nuclear family.

When he tells me what he's going to do, I think back to how my parents had made family such a fundamental priority, and how my father had lost his own parents so tragically. I say, "Jim, you can't do that. She's your mother." But he says, "I'm doing it. I'm not going to live like this." I think Jim feels he needs to take definitive action because Natalie is disrupting our lives in a very negative, hostile way. I sit on our bed crying as he tells me his plan. I feel bad about it. I say to Jim, "This is your mother. Are you sure you want to separate yourself from her?" He says, "Yes. I want to have a happy family life. I'm not going to let her intrude like this." As much as it seems inconceivable to me, I can see his decision and action lift a huge weight from his shoulders.

CHAPTER TEN

More about My Mother

October 6, 1963, a little more than two years after Jim and I were married, is the day my mother dies. Her health, always fragile, had become precarious in the months that preceded her death. Jim and I go to Seattle to spend time with her and my family during what will likely be her last summer. We've been saving our money so we can make the trip, and finally, in August, we go. As we come down the Jetway from the plane at the Seattle airport, I spy my mother, who has come with my father and Kate, one of her sisters, to meet us. I'm horrified at how terrible she looks. She is gaunt, nearly skeletal. I try not to cry. I can see she is dying, and although I've known this time was coming for many years, it breaks my heart to see her looking so weak and vulnerable and to know what's about to happen. At the same time, she is overjoyed to see us. The first thing she does is hug and kiss each of us. I can feel how thin and bony she is. Then she asks me to show Kate my engagement ring. My mother has always loved beautiful things—her elegant Rosenthal china and the handsome Biedermeier dresser that she'd bought secondhand, to name just a couple of her prize possessions. She thinks my ring is exquisite. She revels in my having it.

Jim and I spend a week in Seattle and then need to return to New York. We're both acutely aware this is the last time we'll be with my mother. It's a devastatingly sad goodbye for all of us. During September my mother goes back into the hospital for the last time. Her cancer has invaded her entire body and has entered her brain. I know that every day could be the day I get the call telling me she has died.

My father calls to tell me the news on October 6. I'm not surprised, but I'm deeply, deeply saddened. My mother had fought so hard for so long to live, first to survive Nazi Germany, our terrifying escape, and the difficult and stressful times of starting a new life in a foreign land, and then to survive cancer. Finally she just couldn't fight anymore. I immediately call Jim to let him know. Although Jim and I work across the street from one another, we never see each other during the work week. We have slightly different schedules, and we like keeping our business and personal lives separate. We don't commute together, have lunch together, or visit one another's offices. But on this day, Jim knows how crushed I am and says, "Let me take you out to lunch." At lunch, we plan our trip to Seattle. We buy our tickets after lunch and leave early the next morning.

My mother is cremated. She had not wanted a funeral; she wanted a graveside service which my father arranges. It's at a very serene, very green and leafy cemetery in Seattle. Jim and I walk with my father to her gravesite under a big, beautiful tree. While I'm grieving my mother, I begin to think about my father, and later I talk with Jim about him. I'm concerned about how he'll manage—how he'll cope. He's spent many years focused on my mother and her health issues and concerns and constantly worrying about what will happen next. My mother and father were equal partners in their marriage. She was not my father's subordinate; the two complemented one another in every way. Now, she is gone, and with me in New York and Carolyn in college at George Washington University in Washington, DC, he'll be alone. This will be a huge change for him, as it is for anyone who loses a spouse after so many years. He and my mother had endured so much hardship, in many ways alone together, which I think will make her loss especially wrenching for him. I wonder how he'll deal with it. I feel inadequate; I don't know how I can possibly be supportive or helpful to him.

In the days and weeks after her death, I think a lot about my mother. There are so many questions I wish I'd asked her, so many things I wish I knew ... *What was her childhood like? What kind of education did she have? What was her courtship with my father like? How did she feel about escaping Germany? About making a new life? What were her hopes and dreams? Her worries and concerns? What terrified her? What elated her? What did she feel about having children?*

Based on what I do know, and on my life experience with my mother, I wish I could tell her how deeply I admire her bravery and courage through the escape and its aftermath and through her many years of devastatingly ill health. Through it all, she showed us every day her fierce will to live and her devotion to her family. Throughout her life she consistently tried to impart to me some key life lessons. Over the years I've come to appreciate how important they are as principles to live by.

Dream big; work hard; never quit.

Always understand and appreciate the power of education to open doors to opportunity.

Be honest; tell the truth.

Walk tall; be proud.

Be (yourself); don't act.

Have high standards; don't settle for second best.

Do your best; always strive to be the best you can be.

Be nice; be generous-spirited; always think the best of people.

Understand and be careful with money.

When you come up on bumps in the road, and you will, pick yourself up and move on.

CHAPTER ELEVEN

Welcome to the World of Advertising

I get my first job in the advertising business at a prominent agency, Benton & Bowles (B&B), whose clients include such blue-chip companies as Procter & Gamble, General Foods (now part of Kraft), and Bristol Myers, among others. I'm interviewed for the job by Val Appel, a short, trim, intense man whose shoulders are always hunched and whose jaw is always clenched. Val, who works in his shirtsleeves, has short, dark hair, and wears dark horn-rimmed glasses. Val made it clear to me in my initial interview with him that he's very serious about his work—very committed to doing the right things the right way. I liked him and respected him the moment I met him. He wanted to be sure he was hiring the best possible person for the job for which I was applying, so he gave me a test as part of the hiring process: a set of research data to analyze, and then a report to write about my findings and conclusions. I take the test home and work carefully on it, trying to apply everything I learned in my WAC class in the Harvard-Radcliffe Program. I want the job at Benton & Bowles very badly and know I have to do very well on the test to satisfy what I instinctively understand are Val's high standards. I take my work to Val, and I wait and wonder what will happen. He finally calls and offers me a job in the advertising research group, studying alternative ads or TV commercials to learn which is more memorable, more likable, more persuasive, and which communicates more effectively. And so I start my life in advertising—to me a wonderful world of creativity combined with business strategy. Perfect.

As I plunge into my work at B&B, I learn more and more about the advertising business and about how advertising is made and how it works. It's a collaborative business with teams of strategists, writers, artists, filmmakers, and media specialists working together, each bringing their particular expertise to the task at hand. I love working this way. I get good feedback about my job performance, and I'm very happy with my progress.

On Friday, November 22, 1963, I'm returning from lunch to my office at Benton & Bowles. As I near Rockefeller Plaza I see a crowd gathered at the window of a building in Rockefeller Center. They're watching a teletype machine that clacks out the news in real time. I'm horrified to read that President John F. Kennedy has been shot by a sniper as he was riding in a motorcade in Dallas. He's now being rushed to Parkland Hospital. This is surreal. None of us in the crowd can believe it. We're stunned into silence. I finally tear myself away from the teletype window and dash back to my office. By the time I get there my colleagues have heard the latest: JFK has died from his gunshot wounds. I call Jim, and we agree we'll both leave our offices and meet at home. We turn on the TV and stay glued to it for the entire weekend, hardly able to speak as the story unfolds and then is retold again and again. The entire nation, and the world, are in shock. We watch aghast as the assassin, Lee Harvey Oswald, is shot and killed on live TV by a man named Jack Ruby, a local nightclub owner, as he enters the Dallas Police Headquarters. We continue to stay riveted to our TV for JFK's funeral, brought to tears by seeing his two young children standing with their mother, Jackie, as their father's coffin is carried to the Capitol to lie in state. We find it hard to believe that this terrible nightmare is actually happening. How could this young, vital, optimistic leader have been gunned down in cold blood in America? How is this possible? The worst has happened, and it's been totally out of the control of anyone. No one can undo it or make it better.

During these early years of our marriage, I had a very unsettling experience with Jim. He had an impacted wisdom tooth that got badly infected. I got very nervous, thinking, *The tooth is close to the brain; if the infection travels there, what's going to happen?* Somehow, I convinced Jim to go to the emergency room where they took his blood pressure. The doctors were alarmed because it was so high. Jim ran out of the emergency room to the street the minute he heard this. He wanted nothing to do with any emergency room or doctor. The infection died down in time, but over the years, Jim's doctor phobia created an undercurrent of worry and concern for me, having experienced all the years of my mother's ill health. No matter how much I begged and pleaded, though, I could never persuade Jim to see a doctor. He would get angry with me and not even discuss it.

Jim and I have been married for nearly five years when at long last we learn that I'm pregnant. We've been wanting to have a baby for quite some time, and we're overjoyed. We can't wait to become parents. I feel very well during my pregnancy and continue my regular work routine. Jim and I plan that I'll continue to work until the baby is born, take a few weeks off, and then return to Benton & Bowles.

The time comes for me to discuss my pregnancy and my plan with Val. I make an appointment to see him, go into his office, sit down, and tell him my plan. He's completely nonplussed as he listens to my story. His face turns red, and he says, "We don't do that." I ask, "Do what?" He explains, "We don't give women maternity leaves. That's not B&B's policy." As my mother had taught me, I don't give up or give in. My mother had continued working in Germany as she and my father planned our escape, and then she finally had to go to her boss and tell him the plan, not knowing what his response would be. Like my mother, I'm very firm as I tell Val that the plan I've outlined to him is what I want, and I ask him how he can help me. After a long discussion, which I can see is very difficult for him, he says, "Well, I'm going to have to talk with the higher-ups about this."

I'm in a very nervous state of limbo, wondering how Val's conversations will go. Several days later, he calls me into his office and says, "You have it; you have a maternity leave. Of course you won't get paid during the time you're out, and we can't guarantee you'll get exactly the same job when you return, but you will have a job." And that's how, with Val's help, I pioneered Benton & Bowles's maternity leave policy, getting the agency's first one ever and paving the way for other women who came after me. I know my mother would have been very pleased.

Our baby is due to be born on the Fourth of July, so on that day Jim and I stay home and wait. I'd been interviewed for a television program some months earlier about some innovative research with children I'd been doing at Benton & Bowles. The interview is aired on July 4. Jim and I watch, and wait and wait, and no baby. I go back to work after the Fourth of July weekend, and my colleagues are petrified. They're afraid I'll have the baby in the ladies' room or the elevator.

I go into the office every day until July 9, when I wake up and tell Jim I think I may be feeling little twinges. We call the doctor who says, "Come on up to the hospital." We bring a small black and white TV set with us to Columbia-Presbyterian, and we watch the bullfights while we wait throughout the very, very hot afternoon and evening. A nurse comes into my room and I ask her, "How will I know if I'm really in labor?" She lets out a big belly laugh and says, "Honey, you're gonna know!"

I finally go into the delivery room during the night, and the labor goes on and on. At around eight o'clock in the morning, I hear my doctor, Susan Williamson, say to her nurse, "OK . . . now!" And the nurse takes a flying leap onto my stomach and out pops our beautiful baby boy whom we name Michael. I've never before heard of this approach to birthing babies, but it's very effective. Michael is born at 8:01 a.m. on July 10, 1966. He looks like he's ready for the first grade. He weighs over eight pounds, is fully formed, and has a full head of dark brown hair and big brown eyes. He looks fantastic, and Jim and

I fall in love with him instantly. Jim comes into the delivery room in his scrubs, and Michael grabs his finger and doesn't let go. Jim is in heaven.

I'm in the hospital for several days, holding Michael and feeding him when he's brought into my room. I quickly realize, though, that I have no idea how to be a mother. Although I babysat for years when I was in high school, I've never been responsible for caring for a newborn. I'm intimidated by the thought of going home with Michael and being in charge of this tiny, helpless infant.

We hire a very brusque and bossy baby nurse, Tanaka, for the first week or so to teach me the ropes of infant care. She has a very aggressive attitude, and Jim wants to fire her. I persuade him to let her stay long enough to teach me the basic routines of caring for Michael. There are endless rounds of feedings, baths, diaper changes, formula preparation, laundry, and walks to the park. As soon as one round ends, the next begins. It seems relentless, and I'm in a perpetual state of exhaustion. During these early days of my maternity leave, it's a constant challenge for me to get out of my nightgown and showered and dressed by the time Jim gets home from work. I finally feel confident enough that I can bathe Michael in the kitchen sink without dropping him. Jim and I agree we can let Tanaka go and take over on our own.

The first night we're alone with Michael and in charge, Michael cries and cries the entire night. Jim and I take turns walking him up and down the halls of our apartment, trying to soothe and calm him down, but to no avail. He wails and wails. Magically, though, from the next night forward, Michael sleeps through the night.

We love being parents. We're enchanted with Michael and mesmerized with his every development. Every one of his "firsts" seems magical to us—his first smile, the first time he rolls over, his first efforts to crawl, and on and on. To us, each of these "firsts" is a magnificent achievement. Michael is a big boy. He's a hearty eater and he grows quickly. We can sense early on that he likes music. As soon as he begins to toddle, we put a small phonograph in his room so he can dance to Herb Alpert and the Tijuana Brass. Jim and I love watching his laughing face and his bouncing body—his pure joy as he dances.

* * *

Meanwhile, my father, about whom I've been so concerned since my mother died, tells me he plans to marry Kate, my mother's younger sister. I hadn't been aware my father had been contemplating this, but when I hear his plans, I'm very happy for him. I've never been especially close to Kate. When I was growing up, she lived in Seattle, and I lived a hundred miles away, in Chehalis, so we didn't see one another often. And when we did, she never seemed to have much feeling for Carolyn or me. Though Kate and my mother were not very much alike—my mother's children and her family were the center of her life—the two were very close. When my family moved to Seattle and I was away at college and later in Boston and New York, Kate was very helpful and supportive to my mother as her illness progressed. Since I wasn't there to help with caregiving during this period, I was especially grateful to Kate for all she did. And now, she and my father will be married. When I tell my friends about this, many of them ask me, "Aren't you upset? Doesn't it bother you that your father is marrying your mother's sister?" But no, it doesn't. I'm delighted for them. They've known one another since they were young people in Berlin. And although Kate had stayed in Germany during the war years, my parents had brought her to America after the war, in 1949. With Carolyn in Washington, DC, and me in New York, I've worried about my father being alone. I think he deserves to have companionship and to relax and enjoy life after so many years of stress and worry, throughout my mother's illness and before.

When Michael is born, my father is "tickled pink," as he says, to become a grandfather. I write him and Kate that "Michael is the sunshine in our lives." They come to New York to visit us and to meet Michael. My father is as captivated as we are. He loves giving Michael his bath and taking him to the park in his baby carriage. Kate, who still does not seem to have much feeling for children, keeps her distance. (It occurs to me that maybe Kate's attitude is related to the secret my mother told me on my wedding day: that Kate had had a baby when she was in Germany.)

By the time Michael is a few months old, I feel like I'm ready to go back to work at Benton & Bowles. We hire a nanny, Sarah Bradshaw, to

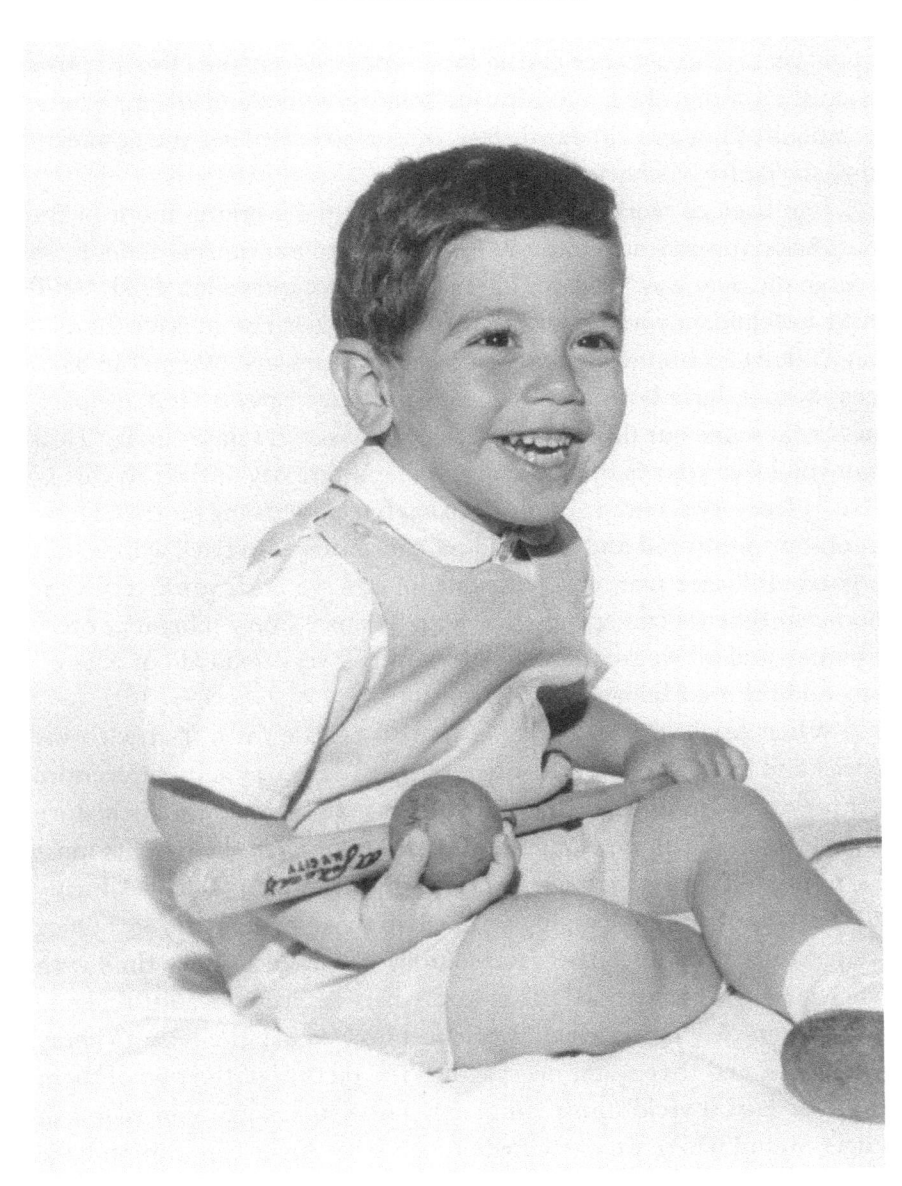

Michael

care for Michael. Sarah comes every weekday from 8 a.m. until either Jim or I gets home, and Jim and I are in charge in the evenings and on weekends. Sarah, an African American woman who grew up in Virginia near Fort Lee where Jim went to Army boot camp, has had many years of experience caring for young children and clearly knows what she's doing. She has a calm and steady manner and an empathetic personality. Jim and I instantly feel comfortable with her and confident that she'll give Michael excellent care.

I go back to work and become the original working mom in the professional ranks at Benton & Bowles. There are no role models, so I forge my own way forward. I get two kinds of questions. First, "Will your husband let you work?" I explain that this is not an issue for us. I say, "I don't *let* him work, and he doesn't *let* me work. We met in business school, have both always planned to have careers, and are partners who make our decisions together." The second question is, "How can you leave your baby? Don't you feel guilty?" My answer to this is, "No." I feel very secure with my decision to be a working mother. I have a totally committed and involved partner in Jim, we have worked out a good childcare plan and partnership, and we both work very near home so that we can spend time with Michael every morning, every evening, and all weekend long. All told I feel very good about where I am, and I think Michael will thrive.

When Michael is two, I take him to Seattle for a visit with my father and Kate. Michael cries on our flight all the way across the entire country, and I'm unable to soothe him or calm him down. As history repeats itself, I gain newfound appreciation for what my parents must have endured caring for me when I was the same age as Michael during all the days of our challenging escape trip those many years ago. Once we get to Seattle, my father is absolutely delighted to have time with Michael. He takes Michael to his yard where he grows beautiful plants and flowers. My father teaches Michael how to use the hose to spray the plants, and they water everything. The picture of the two of them together is still vivid in my mind. My father takes us to an island in Puget Sound where we participate in a Native American salmon bake and watch Native American dancing. Michael is mesmerized, and my father is bursting with happiness to be giving Michael this fascinating experience.

As I watch Michael with my father, I think back on all the changes that my family and I have gone through since Jim and I were married: our having Michael, my mother's death, our estrangement from Natalie, my father's marriage to Kate, and my becoming Benton &

Michael with Grandpa, Seattle

Bowles's first working mom. A lot has happened and a lot has changed, much of it good but some sad. I've had to be resilient to adjust to all these new circumstances, something I'd learned from my parents through observation and osmosis as I was growing up.

CHAPTER TWELVE

This Is the Year That Was

During my time at Benton & Bowles, I've become aware of the great new business success of another agency, Grey Advertising. Grey seems to be reeling in one new account after another. I try to learn a little about what's driving Grey forward.

    I go to several conferences where I hear Alvin Achenbaum, one of Grey's most senior executives, talk about Grey's innovative approach and how it came about. In the late 1950s and early '60s, the advertising business was dominated by very WASPy, country-clubby agencies who built their businesses based largely on longtime school ties and club relationships. In contrast, Grey had been founded in 1917 by two young Jewish men who built a small clientele among local fashion and retail businesses. By the 1950s, when television was coming into its own, packaged goods companies like Procter & Gamble and General Foods began devoting huge budgets to TV advertising. Grey's management was determined to compete successfully for these big budgets in this new television advertising world. They realized early on though that, since they were not WASPs with long-standing school ties or club relationships, they'd have to figure out another way to prevail.

    As they analyzed the possibilities, they said, "Let's start by thinking about the way advertising is created." They dug in and studied themselves as well as their competitors. They came to recognize that in the entire business, all agencies, including Grey, were creating advertising based on gut instinct, occasionally informed by conversations its creators, nearly all men, had with their wives. To the extent any research was done, it was the type I'd done at Benton & Bowles—research *after* advertising had been developed to determine how the ads, or commercials, performed relative to their objectives.

Grey's management said, "We're going to turn this on its head. We're going to work on the up-front strategic end of the equation, *before* the advertising is created. We're going to figure out what the advertising should be about. Who should it be for? What are the motivating promises that relate to what our clients' brands can deliver relative to what people are looking for and what competitors can offer? Let's disrupt the paradigm and go a totally different way. Let's base our strategies not on instinct, but on facts, knowing and understanding consumers' wants and needs, their hopes and dreams, their worries and concerns, and how our clients' brands measure up relative to the competition." Grey's belief was that such fact-based knowledge of the consumer could form the foundation for building strong marketing, communications, and brand-building strategies. It was clear to Grey that to implement its plan for success, the agency needed to develop a powerful and highly differentiated market research capability, with innovative tools and techniques that did not exist at the time. If Grey could do this successfully, it would represent a major breakthrough in the advertising business.

Under the pioneering leadership of Al Achenbaum, Grey developed a set of proprietary quantitative research tools and techniques for collecting and analyzing consumer data: as Grey calls it, consumers' ABCs—their attitudes, their behavior, and their demographic and psychographic characteristics. Grey then uses its deep data-based understanding of consumers to create cutting-edge marketing and communications strategies. This focus on quantitative consumer attitude research as the spark for strategic planning is unique in the marketing world at this time, although over the years it will become the model followed nearly universally by marketers the world over. Grey, led by Alvin, markets this approach aggressively to both clients and prospects. And this is what is driving Grey's great success.

As I listen to Alvin tell Grey's story at various conferences, I think to myself: *This is where I want to work.* At Grey, consumer research is at the heart of what makes the agency tick. It's what the agency uses to compete for its business and what helps Grey's clients compete effectively for their businesses. I want to be a part of this. This is where market research is the catalyst for making things happen.

I land an interview for a job in Grey's Marketing and Research Department, but am devastated to be turned down for it. The woman who interviews me, Betty Coumbe, tells me she thinks that eventually I could do very well at Grey, but at the moment I simply don't have the right experience. I've only done small-scale advertising research at Benton & Bowles, and I need experience doing larger-scale market research. She tells me that if I find someplace where I can do that for a year and come back to see her then, she will hire me. I'm very fortunate that one of my colleagues at Benton & Bowles is leaving to start a strategic consumer research department at Marplan, the research arm of the Interpublic group of advertising agencies, and he asks me to come with him as his associate. I decide immediately to do this, as it's my stepping-stone to Grey.

Exactly one year later, I go back to Betty Coumbe and tell her about my experience of the past year. She hires me on the spot as an assistant research director in what I view as the Harvard Business School of market research departments. I'm ecstatic, thrilled to know I'm on my way to what I feel instinctively will be an exciting and fulfilling career.

March 1, 1969, is the day that at long last I start a new job at Grey Advertising, which is becoming one of the largest and most successful advertising and marketing communications agencies in the world. I arrive at Grey and am shown to my tiny office, which is at the end of a long hallway next to a broom closet. I'm assigned to work on the Revlon account, one of Grey's most important and prestigious pieces of business. Revlon has a number of different brands of cosmetics sold at different price points and in different channels of distribution. Under the aegis of Al Achenbaum, Grey has conducted a major consumer research study to help guide Revlon in organizing its portfolio of brands. The questions the study helps to address are: Which brands should be directed toward which sets of consumers? What should be the motivating appeals for each one? In which channel of distribution should each be sold, and how should each be priced? Across from my little office is a much larger office, filled from wall to wall and floor to ceiling with huge data charts from the presentation Al and his team have given to Revlon management. I am told that I need to learn everything in this entire room. I am scared to death. I have no idea how I'm ever going to do this. I'm not sure what the Grey people are even talking about. There are huge books of computer data from the study which I take home every night and pore over until the wee hours, trying to understand what the data are telling me.

There is a big problem, though. Revlon does not like, or believe in, the thrust of Grey's original analysis, so Grey has to revamp its entire analytical approach, a huge and very expensive undertaking. Essentially, from a marketing decision-making point of view, this second analysis comes out in the same place as the first. This helps me understand that there's more than one way to skin the cat. But what an unnerving introduction to my new life.

Meanwhile, Jim and I have been eager to have another baby. We love our life with Michael and we want him to have a sibling. Very shortly after I start my new job at Grey, I learn that I'm pregnant. I'm worried that I might get fired, since I said nothing to Grey about wanting to get pregnant when I interviewed for the job, a subject that often comes up in job interviews with young married women in the '60s. I begin to show my baby bump much earlier in the pregnancy than I did with Michael. Since I'm beginning to look pregnant, I decide I need to go to Al Achenbaum and tell him my news. Having gone through the stressful experience of needing to invent a maternity leave at Benton & Bowles, I'm very uneasy about what Alvin will say when I tell him my plan: work until the baby is born and then come back a few weeks later. I don't know what Grey's policies are and have no idea what Al's reaction will be. I steel myself to talk with him and am surprised and delighted when he says, "Wonderful news. Of course—do what you need to do and come back when you can. We want good people, and we do what we need to do to keep them. Your job is going to be here for you." I think to myself: *I really have landed in heaven.*

* * *

When Jim, Michael, and I go to the beach on vacation in the late summer, Jim looks at me and says, "I think you're having twins." I tell him second children are always different; I can't imagine I'm pregnant with twins. My doctor, Dr. Williamson, also scoffs at the notion. I continue working and going for regular checkups with Dr. Williamson. I do seem to be getting much bigger than I was with Michael, but I tell myself this is because it's my second pregnancy. In the fall, I leave a meeting at Grey to go for my checkup at Dr. Williamson's office at Columbia-Presbyterian hospital. She goes through her routine exam and then says, "I think maybe we should take an X-ray." (This was before ultrasounds came into use.) I'm very startled and ask her, "Why would you do this?" She answers, "Well, maybe you're just a little bit big for this stage of your pregnancy." I go to the X-ray room, everyone leaves, and I lie there alone in the dark nervously contemplating what the X-ray might show. All I hear is the buzzing and clicking of the X-ray machine. After what seems like a very long time, the door opens and Dr. Williamson comes in followed by several other people: her nurse, the X-ray technician, various assistants. I can't imagine why all these people are there. Dr. Williamson and I make eye contact and I hold up two fingers in question to her. She shakes her head "No," and holds up three fingers. I am speechless—incredulous, and I start sobbing and sobbing. She says, "Let me show you," and helps me off the table to the X-ray screen. And there are three tiny bodies, head to foot in triangle shape. Triplets!! What an amazing surprise. I cannot believe it. I can't stop crying, not because I'm upset but because I'm so shocked. Everyone except Dr. Williamson leaves the X-ray room. She stays with me for a while and finally says, "Do you think we should call your husband?" I immediately tell her, "No! I don't think this is something Jim should hear about on the phone."

I finally gather myself, get dressed, and take a cab to Jim's office at Chesebrough-Ponds, where he's begun working in the cosmetics business. I tell the receptionist that I'm Jim Feigin's wife and I'd like to see him. She calls him and he comes bounding out. Since I never go to Jim's office, he senses I have something important to tell him. He asks me, "Twins?" I tell him, "No, there are three babies." He can't stop laughing. He is so happy; he feels like he's hit a grand slam home run. He is thrilled. Dr. Williamson has made a point to tell me that multiple births are high risk, and the more babies, the higher the risk. But even with this admonition, I allow myself to be thrilled and excited along with Jim. This is so totally unexpected and so totally amazing.

I continue working at Grey and plan to do so until the babies are born. It turns out that my immediate supervisor, with whom I've just begun to work, Shirley Young, is also pregnant. It is extremely unusual in the business world of the late 1960s for women to work actively throughout pregnancy. One day Shirley and I have a meeting with the CEO of our client, Playtex, in his office in the Empire State Building. He is quite taken aback to see two women executives waddle into his office, both clearly well along in pregnancy. He says, "Well, I see we have four visitors here today," and Shirley says, "No, there are six of us." She explains that I'm expecting triplets, the two of us laugh, the CEO is abashed, and we go on with our meeting.

Early in the holiday season, Jim is inaugurated as the president of Cosmetics Industry Buyers and Suppliers (CIBS), an important trade association in the cosmetics and toiletries industry. The inauguration takes place at the CIBS annual holiday dinner dance with hundreds of guests dressed in formal attire celebrating in the ballroom of the New York Hilton Hotel. Jim is called to the stage to take the gavel, and then the MC asks Jim's wife (me), "the little woman," to please to come to the stage. I am quite far along in my pregnancy now and I totter up to the stage, belly first, followed by the rest of my body. The band plays "A Pretty Girl Is Like a Melody," and I'm given a bouquet of long-stemmed red roses. Jim is shaking as he tries to conceal his laughter. He never, ever thinks of me as "the little woman" or the "pretty girl [who's] like a melody," and I certainly don't look like either, given my immense shape.

The babies are not due until March. I continue to work as planned as year-end approaches. I have a huge belly, but I'm getting skinnier and skinnier. I can't eat anything. Every time I try to eat, I get sick. The problem is there's no space left in my stomach for food. Right after Christmas I leave a meeting at Grey to go to Dr. Williamson's office for my checkup. She says, "I think you need to come into the hospital now." I say, "Really? Why? I just left a meeting in my office and I need to get back." "No," she says. "You need to come in now. You need to be able to eat. We need to give you mini-meals throughout the day and night because these babies need to get some nutrition. The fact that you're getting sick every time you eat is a major problem." So I check into Columbia-Presbyterian, eating my mini-meals all alone while Jim is at home caring for Michael. On New Year's Eve I look out the window into the dark night wondering how 1970 will unfold.

The babies are not born in March but on January 15, 1970. Relative to my experience having Michael, who was a big boy, it's an easy birth because they are so tiny. When I'm rolled into the delivery room, I see it's jam-packed with what seems like a massive crowd of people: Dr. Williamson and her nurses and assistants, a team of doctors and nurses for each of the three babies, and our pediatrician, Dr. Leo Wilking, who cares for Michael. Dr. Wilking is a tall, slim, patrician-looking man, perfectly cast for his role in the delivery room. To me, he looks just like a stork. Fathers are not yet allowed in delivery rooms, so Jim is just outside the door, peeking in and eagerly awaiting news.

As the babies are born, we learn the three are identical boys, a very rare occurrence. Peter is born first, at 10:20 p.m. He weighs 5½ pounds. Daniel is born five minutes later, arriving rear end first and weighing 4½ pounds. He is very jaundiced, so he is whisked away immediately to the neonatal unit to be treated. Jim comes in, and we are told that our third baby is not viable. He is not fully developed, and we're told he did not have a chance. Jim and I have very mixed emotions in this highly charged situation. We are ecstatic to have two new baby boys, although they are born prematurely and are still very tiny and not fully developed. We need to concentrate on making sure everything possible is being done to bring them along and help them mature. We are very anxious and stressed about their well-being; we can't really focus on the loss of our third baby. Michael was such a big, robust, fully formed baby, I'm shocked at how different Peter and Daniel are from that. Being premature, born a couple of months early, they are as scrawny as two chickens. Their eyes are a vacant-looking plum color. I feel very guilty that I find it hard even to look at them.

Because Peter and Daniel are so tiny and underdeveloped, they need to stay in the neonatal unit for a few weeks after they're born. I have much less time with them during the early weeks of their lives than I had with Michael when he was a newborn. I worry nervously that this may affect my ability to bond with them. I go home after about a week, while the babies are still in the hospital. I'm very eager to be with Michael. By this time, I've been in the hospital for several weeks and I'm concerned that he feels I've abandoned him. I'm still very weak and very, very thin—nearly twenty pounds lighter than my normal, nonpregnant weight. As a person who's always felt chubby, I'm delighted to be thin, but Jim can't look at me. He tells me I look like I just got out of a concentration camp.

When I get home Michael and I spend time together, and then I go to bed early. In the middle of the night, I wake up abruptly. I'm lying in a fast-growing pool of blood; blood is gushing out of me. This is terrifying. I've never experienced anything like it. I know this is an acutely dangerous situation. I need to get to the hospital fast. Jim pounds on our neighbors' door and asks them to come and look after Michael. Finally, wrapped in bath towels to soak up the torrent of blood, Jim and I get into a cab and we careen as fast as the driver can go to the ER at Columbia-Presbyterian. Dr. Williamson is called, and she takes me into the OR immediately for procedures to staunch the bleeding. As I'm wheeled in, I feel myself losing consciousness. I can't talk—can't form words, but I think to myself, *I can't die. I have two new babies and Michael. I can't leave Jim alone with them. I can't die.* I lose consciousness while the doctors are giving me many blood transfusions. As fast as the blood pours in, it pours out. Finally, Dr. Williamson and her team are able to stabilize me. As I regain consciousness, I think to myself, *I'm alive. I'm so grateful.*

I spend a nearly a week in the hospital recuperating. It's lunchtime and Jim has come to visit and spend the lunch hour with me. I'm happily enjoying a spaghetti and meat sauce lunch when all of a sudden I feel the bleeding begin again, even more furiously than before. I'm losing so much blood, so fast, I'm nearly paralyzed with fear that I'll die. Dr. Williamson is summoned immediately and rushes into my room. She asks Jim and me, "Do you want to have more children?" We look at one another, and I say, "We're very happy to have our three boys." Dr. Williamson says, "We need to get you to the OR immediately and do a hysterectomy to stop this bleeding." I tell her, "Please, please go as fast as you can." Once again, I feel myself losing consciousness—fading away and frozen with fear. When I awaken from the surgery I'm still in a fog from the anesthesia and mistakenly believe I've had cancer surgery, like my mother. I'm grateful to be alive, but ask Dr. Williamson whether the cancer had spread. She explains what's actually taken place and tells me immediately the surgery was a success. She goes on to say that I'd had a very rare condition that had caused all the bleeding. My placenta had fused with my uterus, and my uterus had been unable to shed it after the babies were born, as is the norm. The condition is called *placenta accreta*. This experience has been traumatic for me—physically debilitating and psychologically devastating. I still can't believe I nearly died, twice, and am actually now on the road to recovery. Dr. Williamson, who is a professor at the Columbia University College of Physicians and Surgeons, has a completely different take on the situation. She's intrigued and says, "Barbara, you are going to be one of my most interesting teaching cases."

Finally, I'm able to go home with our two new baby boys, ready to launch the next phase of our family life. I'm still in a fairly weakened state, very thin and recovering from major abdominal surgery and from a challenging pregnancy. I'm very focused on spending time with Michael, from whom I've been away for forty-five days altogether during these tumultuous times. I know he's confused and probably angry at my having left him for such a long time. I get a call one day from Miss Garver, his teacher at nursery school. She asks me, "Mrs. Feigin, is everything all right with Michael?" I ask why she is asking me this. She says, "Well, Michael has been climbing on the tables and jumping from one to the other and yelling a lot. We're wondering whether there's anything going on at home we should know about." I explain to her that Michael, and our family, have gone through a turbulent time during the past couple of months, with my being in the hospital for such a long time, our new babies being born, and my complications and surgery afterward. I say, "I should have called and told you about all this, but I was consumed with just getting through what was happening." Miss Garver thanks me for telling her, and after this conversation is especially caring and attentive to Michael.

Peter and Daniel

There is more disruption for Michael, as we need to rearrange our entire apartment. His world is being turned upside down. At first we turn our small dining area into a makeshift nursery for the babies. After a short time, we move them and all their paraphernalia—cribs, changing table, playpen, and all the rest, squeezing everything into Michael's fairly small bedroom. Michael feels invaded. I'm worried he'll lash out at the babies in some way. Jim and I buy him a huge, life-size plastic clown that rocks back and forth on its base. Jim teaches Michael to punch the clown and try to knock it down when he feels himself getting angry. This helps for a while.

Jim and I work together to develop a routine for caring for the babies and bringing steadiness and stability to our new family dynamic. Things are very hectic. Jim is working hard at his job at Chesebrough-Ponds and I'm trying to recuperate and to give Michael the attention he needs. The babies are so tiny they need to be fed frequently. Jim and I stagger out of bed a few times during the night when we hear them cry, make our way to the kitchen, and each of us takes one and gives him a bottle. Often during these feedings I feel Jim poking me with his toe; I'm nodding off to sleep and he's trying to keep me awake.

Even in my half-asleep state, I love holding the baby I'm feeding. He has that wonderful new-baby smell and is relaxed and snuggly—just the best. Jim goes through exactly the same thing I do, and I poke him from time to time to keep him from falling asleep. He loves holding his baby, but he has to go to work in the morning and to be coherent. All of the feeding commotion usually wakes Michael, so we then need to go to his room and comfort him and rock him back to sleep. This is all exhausting, but we try, together, to keep going and to stay sane.

During these early days, I'm becoming increasingly unnerved because I can't tell Peter and Daniel apart. Others think this is very funny, but to me, it's not funny at all. The seriousness of my problem is brought home to me when I take the babies for their first checkup with Dr. Wilking, their stork-like pediatrician. I undress the boys for their exam and am propping their two tiny naked bodies on the examining table when Dr. Wilking walks in. He asks, "Which one should I take first, Mrs. Feigin, Peter or Daniel?" I give him a blank, nervous stare, not sure how to respond. I tell him I'm having a hard time telling them apart and say, "Maybe you can help me."

Dr. Wilking says, "Mrs. Feigin, I've never had a mother like you." This shakes my confidence even further. Peter and Daniel look exactly alike, though thankfully Peter is still just a bit heavier than Daniel. With slow and careful observation and with Dr. Wilking's help, I think I can tell who's who. But I know this difference in weight won't last long; I'm stumped as to what to do going forward. I decide to have bracelets made with beads spelling out each of their names, and for a while this works well. But one morning, I go into their room where both are in their playpen and I see one of the bracelets has come off and is on the floor. I have a major sinking spell; I realize my plan is not going to work. I need another solution—fast. I think and think about what to do and finally have a brainstorm. I decide that when the babies have their smallpox vaccinations, I'll have them vaccinated on opposite arms, Peter on the right arm (PR) and Dan on the left (DL). They will be scarred, but correctly identifiable, for life. I've been determined to be able to refer to them correctly by name. Now I can be confident (at least most of the time) about doing that.

It's now springtime, 1970. Peter and Daniel are three months old and are sleeping through the night. I'm eager to get back to work. I've regained my strength; we're developing a new routine for our family life. Our longtime nanny, Sarah Bradshaw, is ready to take on the challenge of caring for all three children, Michael and the new babies, Peter and Daniel. Jim and I agree; it's time to move forward. We are about to embark on the most delicate and challenging balancing act of our lives.

CHAPTER THIRTEEN

Mad Woman

In the spring of 1970, I'm a "Mad woman," back at Grey on "Madison Avenue," as the advertising business is known, although Grey is actually three blocks east of Madison, at 777 Third Avenue. I jump back in, taking on as much responsibility as I'm able to handle during this early time of my return. So much of life is about luck and timing, and the timing of my return to work is very lucky. One of my assignments and one of Grey's most important accounts is Kool-Aid, General Foods' powdered soft drink mix which is sold during the summer months for moms to prepare for kids. Kool-Aid management is struggling to determine how to build the Kool-Aid business, which is enormously profitable. Grey's team proposes a piece of strategic consumer research, and because my supervisor is on leave with a broken leg I take the lead in conceptualizing and designing the research, conducting the analysis, and developing action implications.

    I make the presentation of our work to a roomful of senior Kool-Aid executives, all men. This is my first major presentation for Grey. I'm very nervous but try not to show it. My hands are sweating, and I make several trips to the ladies' room before we get started. I've rehearsed carefully; I know the data backward and forward. I take a deep breath and launch into my presentation. The Kool-Aid group is rapt. They lean forward as they follow along with me. I walk through the data, showing them, to their great surprise, that although moms ostensibly buy and prepare Kool-Aid for their kids, who clamor for it, once it's in the fridge the lion's share is consumed by adults. I go on, showing them that both kids and adults would like to be able to drink Kool-Aid year-round, not just in the summer when it is currently on grocers' shelves. And finally, and very importantly, I show them that moms know their kids (and the adults in their families) love Kool-Aid, but they feel guilty whenever they prepare it because they know it has no nutritional value. I then walk the group through Grey's recommendations for building the Kool-Aid business: sell Kool-Aid year-round; and focus one advertising campaign featuring the cartoon character, the Kool-Aid Pitcher Man, to trigger kids' craving for Kool-Aid, which leads to its being purchased and prepared. Finally, add vitamin C to the product and advertise this in a separate, complementary campaign to moms, reassuring them and giving them permission to serve it to their kids because in fact, with the addition of vitamin C, it does have nutritional value. When I've gone through the last slide, the room erupts into applause. Kool-Aid management immediately begins to implement Grey's recommendations. This paves the way for a massive, extremely successful business-building effort for Kool-Aid, which becomes the number three soft drink in America, behind Coke and Pepsi. Kool-Aid's expansion becomes one of Grey's important success stories, and Grey's management credits me with the pivotal role I've played. I'm very proud of what I've accomplished and confident about taking on more.

Revlon continues to be one of my assigned accounts. Charles Revson, who owns the company, is well known for his brilliant creative mind. But he's also thought to be rather mean-spirited, and this is the tone he sets for his company. Revlon's relationship with Grey is driven largely by fear. Revlon's executives thrive on humiliating the agency's team and making us grovel. Mr. Revson is known to call the agency team to the Revlon offices in the General Motors building for meetings at 5:00 p.m. on hot Friday evenings in the summer. We have no choice but to show up. Revlon is one of Grey's premier accounts, for whom we do compelling advertising of which we're very proud; we have to go when Revlon calls. The meetings never start on time. We're asked to wait in a tiny interior room with no windows and with the air conditioning turned off for the weekend. After we've waited an inordinately long time, all of us sweating mightily, we peek out of a crack in the door to see what's happening, only to learn the lights are off and the entire Revlon staff has gone home for the weekend. Occasionally, we also learn that Mr. Revson is not even in town. He's off on his yacht, the *Ultima II*—named after his prestige, most expensive cosmetics line—on one of the seven seas. So, our angry and humiliated team, all of us dripping wet, leave the darkened offices of Revlon and go off for our own diminished summer weekend.

One day I get a call from one of Mr. Revson's most senior aides. He is very ominous looking, always dressed completely in black—suit, shirt, tie, shoes—has slicked back black hair, and an angry, nearly sinister look on his face. I've never heard him speak. I'm unnerved to get a call from him, and can't imagine what he wants from me. Once he's sure he's speaking to me, he says quietly in his gravelly voice, "I've got to swear you to secrecy. You cannot tell anyone about this call." I uneasily agree, and he goes on. "Mr. Revson is considering introducing a line of cosmetics with Elizabeth Taylor, and he wants to know the extent to which this represents a consumer opportunity." I ask him to continue. He says, "We want you, Barbara, to do a piece of research to help us understand this and to come over and talk to Mr. Revson about it. But you are not to tell a soul—no one in Grey, and no one outside of Grey." I think to myself: *This is Revlon; this is one of Grey's most important accounts. How can I not tell a soul?* So I tell my supervisor, and her boss, and eventually Ed Meyer, chairman and CEO of the agency who oversees the account. I'm just a tiny peanut on the Grey team, but I tell them all, "You can't say anything. I will be the front person on this 'secret' assignment, but please all help me on this." We do the research and learn that there is no consumer appetite for an Elizabeth Taylor brand of cosmetics. This is the era of the movie *Love Story*, and Ali McGraw, with her wonderful natural look, is today's aspirational role model for women. Elizabeth Taylor, with her larger-than-life glamour, is not what women are looking for right now.

I make an appointment to go to Revlon to present the results of the research to Mr. Revson and his team. The meeting is to be over lunch in his very grand, very rococo dining room. I'm greeted at the elevator by Mr. Revson's butler, in full butler regalia. He escorts me to the dining room, where Mr. Revson's executive team, all men, are seated around the table, all looking very upset. Mr. Revson is not yet in the room. An article about him is about to be published in *Vogue* magazine, and the Revlon people, including Mr. Revson, have just seen an advance copy. Mr. Revson is having health issues, and his photo is quite unflattering. The butler sets a gold chair at the head of the table, rolls a gold side table next to the chair, and places a gold telephone on the table. Mr. Revson strides into the room, visibly furious. He laces into Revlon's senior advertising executive: "How could you allow this to happen?"

I sit at the table, quietly shaking inside, thinking, *Now I have to present to him; he's burning with anger and I'm about to tell him a story he doesn't want to hear.* This is very scary. As directed, I'm the only one in the room from Grey. None of my teammates, who officially don't even know about this research, are there with me to offer support. I stand up and go through my presentation in as professional a way as I can muster. As I conclude, I say, "Based on the data we've collected from consumers, Elizabeth Taylor—her look, her feel, her attitude, her aura, are really not what women are aspiring to today. So it would be a very tough row to hoe, introducing a new line with her imprimatur." Mr. Revson immediately lashes back, "We do not *ask* women what they want; we *tell* them what they want." I say, "I'm simply reporting what we learned from consumers." In times past I've heard Alvin Achenbaum say, "We (Grey) *propose*; you (our client) *dispose*." This is one of those moments. I pack up my materials and leave the dining room. I wonder to myself what Mr. Revson will do. As time goes on, I realize that even though he has disparaged the research, he decides not to go forward with an Elizabeth Taylor line. Once again I'm convinced that our research has played a significant role in influencing a major business decision.

In 1972, I'm named a vice president of Grey. I'm euphoric. I understand that above all else, Grey is a meritocracy, and I'm very gratified to have earned this promotion. I continue to work hard and to have some important successes in helping to drive Grey's business forward.

One of my perks as a Grey VP is that the company pays for an annual physical for me. As I tell Jim about this, I realize he hasn't had a physical since we've been married. I ask him when he's planning to get one, and he tells me he's always been very healthy, and therefore there's no need for him to see a doctor. I say to him that as a father of three young children, he owes it to his family to take good care of himself, but he won't discuss it and won't go for a physical. I think Jim is phobic because his father died at a young age, and he's afraid of what he might learn if he goes to the doctor. The situation makes me very upset, even angry, but nothing I say makes him change his mind.

In 1975, I'm named one of the youngest ever and the only woman senior vice president of Grey. I'm amazed and slightly, but only slightly, amused to receive a brass plaque from the *Wall Street Journal* inscribed with their announcement of my promotion. Across the top of the plaque, adjacent to the announcement, the *WSJ*'s slogan is engraved: "Everywhere the men who keep getting ahead in business read the *Wall Street Journal*." Not a word from the *Wall Street Journal* about the women, or even the people, who keep getting ahead. I wonder when this will begin to change.

My promotion to senior vice president, December 16, 1975

I'm now the number two person in our department, working for the brilliant Shirley Young, who's taken over for Al Achenbaum. During the years we work together, Shirley becomes my mentor, teaching me much about how to approach my work and consistently giving me opportunities that I feel are just a bit beyond what I'm capable of handling. She pushes me, encourages me, gives me counsel and guidance, and ensures that my successes are known and appreciated by the rest of Grey management. I admire Shirley immensely. She teaches me to focus and concentrate on the big things that matter. I've learned from Shirley that the most important part of solving any business or marketing issue happens up front: digging in to define and articulate the problem and its various dimensions and puzzling out what we need to know to address the problem in the most creative way possible. Once this strategic framework is developed, Shirley and I say to one another, "The rest is just work." We're a strong team and work well together to make things happen.

We also become good friends. We have much in common. Like me, Shirley is an immigrant. She's Chinese and came to America as a child with her mother and two sisters after her father, a diplomat, had been executed in the Philippines by the Japanese. She is a Wellesley Phi Beta Kappa a couple of years older than I, and she actually worked at Benton & Bowles a few years before I did. She's married, and, also like me, is the mother of three young boys. Our friendship deepens over the years; it will last throughout our lives.

In the 1980s, during the years she and I work together, Grey takes on a new client, the trendsetting retailer, Bloomingdale's, whose flagship store is on New York's Upper East Side. Marvin Traub, the creative genius who transformed this formerly stodgy family department store into a glittering, cutting-edge international showcase, is an impresario extraordinaire. Bloomingdale's becomes a go-to destination not just for New Yorkers and tourists but for movie stars, business titans, icons such as presidents' wives Jackie Kennedy and Lady Bird Johnson, and even Queen Elizabeth and Prince Philip when they visit New York. Marvin Traub pioneered the concept of retail as theater;

he creates exciting events highlighting the drama and the products of faraway exotic places like India, China, Italy, and Portugal. Bloomingdale's becomes *the* place to see and be seen. Grey partners with Bloomingdale's for its first venture into television advertising, a very big move for the store. As part of its original campaign, Grey develops the unforgettable and perfect tagline to capture the essence of the store, a line being used to this day: "Bloomingdale's. It's like no other store in the world."

As Marvin Traub works with Grey and begins to learn about our process of using strategic consumer research to catalyze business and traffic-building strategies, he decides to hire a Grey alum to bring some of this "modern marketing" thinking into Bloomingdale's. Our former colleague is put in charge of the Men's Store at Bloomingdale's. On his first day at work, he calls me and says he wants Grey to do a piece of major strategic consumer research that will provide a road map for building the business of the Men's Store. Knowing Marvin Traub's highly effective creative, instinctive approach to marketing the store, I cannot imagine this would be what he wanted. I ask our colleague if he's sure that doing a strategic study at this early stage of his tenure at Bloomingdale's makes sense. He is insistent.

We go to work and prepare a powerful proposal. Shirley and I pack up our charts and go off to the Bloomingdale's boardroom for our presentation. We set up, and the "Bloomies" management troops in: Marvin Traub, together with the chairman of the board and a number of women, all wearing hats. They remind me of 1930s movie stars. Our colleague sits in the second row, behind all the management people. He does not introduce us or set up the meeting. So Shirley and I launch in, introducing ourselves and explaining why we're there. We take out our first chart, and Mr. Traub asks, "Is this why we're here?" We say, "Yes," and plan to move to the next chart, whereupon Mr. Traub stands up and says, "Thank you very much, but I don't think we should waste your time." He, the chairman, and the women in hats all march out, followed by our colleague, who does not say a word. When they are all out of the room, Shirley and I burst out laughing. We've always felt that, during our time in the trenches, we've seen and experienced just about everything. And we've certainly learned to roll with the punches.

* * *

Although Grey is known primarily for its work with packaged goods clients, we actually work with many Fortune 500 companies in every other type of business as well: financial services, technology, health care, travel and leisure, automotive, entertainment, retail (as with Bloomingdale's), restaurants, corporate reputation—you name it. We also work with the US government, doing recruitment advertising for the US Navy and various projects for the National Highway Traffic Safety Administration (NHTSA).

One of my most important accomplishments is helping to spearhead the development of a program for NHTSA designed to combat drunk driving among teenagers, which is responsible for a massive number of traffic fatalities and has become a significant societal problem. NHTSA has historically done advertising focused on the fear of death associated with drunk driving accidents, but none of these efforts work. Fatalities continue to rise. Not knowing where to turn or what to do next, NHTSA comes to Grey for help. We dive into this problem, starting with a major piece of strategic research among teens. We study the who, what, where, when, and why of drinking and driving, but we also go well beyond that. We do a deep exploration of the attitudes and emotions teenagers associate with drinking and driving, something NHTSA has never considered before.

Our work leads to a complete change in approach. We develop a comprehensive communications program, led by advertising, focused on *preventing* drunk driving rather than the fear associated with its *aftermath*. The program we create is driven by the motivations of friendship and empathy, not of fear and terror. Our advertising features friends and peers in potential drunk driving situations, spelling out specific actions they should take when they find themselves in similar positions: taking a friend's keys, having a friend stay over, calling a cab, naming a designated driver. The entire campaign is highlighted and summarized by a tagline that becomes very famous: "Friends don't let friends drive drunk."

The program is a magnificent success. Teen drunk driving fatalities begin to drop almost immediately. I'm full of pride that our agency, catalyzed by the work I helped to spearhead, is making a difference that matters deeply to our country—a life and death difference.

I get more and more involved with Grey's new business activities, working to help build our portfolio of accounts. I begin to work much more closely with Ed Meyer, Grey's chairman and CEO. Ed is brilliant, powerful, and known to be the most successful businessman in the advertising business. He's built Grey into a worldwide powerhouse. He's tall, trim, has dark brown hair, and is beautifully (and very expensively) dressed in clothes mainly from Paul Stuart. He exudes an aura of confidence and authority. He teaches us all in no uncertain terms that the focal point of our work needs to be our clients: how can we help them solve problems, build their brands, and build their businesses? He is a complicated man, very, very smart and very intense. He motivates his people sometimes with charm and sometimes with fear and intimidation to get what he wants from them. He has an uncanny ability to understand which approach to use at what point with each of us.

One of my very first new business pitches is for the giant Pizza Hut account. I've been with another client and arrive in Wichita where the pitch is being held much later than the rest of our team so have not been able to rehearse with them. I've not been aware of how closely Ed directs our presentations, coaching each person on our team on exactly what he or she should say. When I join the group at dinner, Ed begins to question me very closely. He wants to know what I'm planning to say. I tell him I'm going to tell the Kool-Aid story, with which he knows I've been very involved. He looks at me and says, "Yes, but what exactly are you going to say?" He makes me very uneasy and shakes my confidence. I wonder if he is really asking me to tell him literally what I'm going to say. He says again, very sharply this time, "Do you understand me? I do want to know exactly what you're going to say." I'm shaking in my boots and stammer out the story I plan to tell, totally intimidated by Ed. He responds, "No, no, no . . . Here's the way you need to frame the story." I'm embarrassed to be grilled, even bullied, by Ed in the presence of my colleagues. I don't realize this is Ed's MO; he always does this, and everyone's used to it. The joke is that someone in the group is always "in the barrel." This is my first time in. Ed is very manipulative, very controlling—always making crystal clear what he's looking for and that he expects us to follow his direction. I tell the story as Ed has instructed, and I realize he's absolutely right. It's a much more compelling approach. Unfortunately for all of us, we do not win this business.

This defeat brings home an important lesson to me, though: selling Grey in our new business pitches starts with a deep understanding of our prospects. And that starts with listening carefully and empathetically as they describe their situation, their goals and ambitions, and their worries and concerns and then presenting ourselves—our capabilities and experiences—in a way that addresses those needs. I learn to listen to Ed, who's exquisitely tuned in to drawing prospects out and listening to them carefully, and to be open to his coaching. In retrospect this seems obvious, as it's an exact parallel to the way we try to understand consumers. My consciousness has been raised to a high level, and I'm learning about important nuances to consider when we're selling Grey.

In our new business activities I'm usually the only woman in the room and generally play a leadership role. Our teams work very hard for days and nights and weekends, killing ourselves to do a terrific job. During all these times, Jim is in charge at home, looking after the boys and making sure things there continue to hum. We're building a great record at Grey, winning many new business competitions, but we lose some too. And when we lose, I worry and stew that I must have done something wrong to cause us to lose. I experience a mini-crisis of confidence and self-doubt. After a time, I notice the men on our teams never think this way. They calmly debrief, talking about what we, as a team, have done right, where we might have misfired, and how we can learn from the experience and do a better job next time. During these years, my three sons play basketball, and I notice they deal with their losses the same way. They never stew. They review, analyze, plan how to do better next time, and pull up their socks and move on. I've never played competitive sports; none of the girls in my generation have, so we've never learned this approach. This is an epiphany for me. I learn enormously from my boys' basketball experience about how to succeed in business.

* * *

In 1983, Shirley Young steps away from her role at Grey to work in an executive marketing position at General Motors. I am promoted to executive vice president of Grey and head of our newly named department: Strategic Services Worldwide, which more clearly communicates our focus. We don't believe in or do research as an end in itself, but rather as a springboard to strategic marketing and advertising decision-making. I'm responsible for building on the formidable legacy of Alvin Achenbaum and Shirley Young. This is quite humbling and a bit intimidating for me. I'm very proud, but I have to pinch myself to believe I'm actually stepping into the shoes of these giants whom I heard speak years ago and who inspired me to want to work at Grey.

I'll be leading a department of seventy-five people and working with our agencies around the world. Grey has built a massive network of offices worldwide, and many of our clients, including Revlon, Procter & Gamble, 3M, and Mars, to name a few, want to build their brands to achieve worldwide dominance. The special research and analytical tools and techniques our Strategic Services operation can bring to bear are catalytic in helping us help them achieve their goals. And my job is to take the lead in making this happen. All of this is a very tall order, and I'm determined to give it everything I have. My parents, from the day we embarked on our arduous escape, had always dreamed big and had urged me to do so too. But I'm sure they could never have imagined this level of achievement. I can hardly imagine it myself.

Ed names me to the Agency Policy Council (APC), consisting of the six most senior executives at Grey, all men except me, who work with him to block out Grey's strategic priorities and the agency's path forward. Grey has more than 2,500 employees in our New York headquarters and many more around the world, so being named to the APC as one of the agency's top six executives is an amazing accomplishment for me, one I could never have envisioned. I continue to pinch myself. The APC meets each week for breakfast in Ed's personal dining room, across the hall from his office. We all take our accustomed seats; mine is on Ed's left. We're a very congenial group. We all know each other well, having worked and been in foxholes together for many years. As we tuck into our bagels and bacon and eggs, I hear occasional cursing

WORLDWIDE MANAGEMENT

AGENCY POLICY COUNCIL

Photographed in New York (l. to r.)

Alec Gerster, Executive Vice President (EVP), Media & Programming Services; Steve Felsher, EVP, Finance/Worldwide; Steve Novick, EVP, Creative Services; Barbara Feigin, EVP, Strategic Services; and Bob Berenson, President, Grey New York.

Me with Grey Agency Policy Council. I am the only woman in the room.

and off-color comments or jokes, but nothing that I find especially offensive. Generally Ed is very businesslike and focused as he leads us through our conversations. Occasionally, though, when he's irritated about something, he loses his temper, raising his voice and lashing out. When that happens, we all freeze and go silent, and, more often than not, breakfast comes to a quick conclusion and we all slink out.

* * *

It's been very important to my success to have had others who believed in me and helped me along the way: Val Appel, Betty Coumbe, Al Achenbaum, and Shirley Young, to name just a few. I'm now in a position where I can mentor others, especially women, and help them to find their own way forward. I'm very conscious of wanting to do so. Just one of those is Doreen Massin. Doreen comes to my office one day to interview for a job as an associate director of Strategic Services. She tells me she's been wanting to work at Grey, for me, for years, having heard me speak at many conferences. She says that for all those years I've been her role model. Doreen is very knowledgeable about Grey's approach and my role and that of Strategic Services in Grey's success. This reminds me of how I felt, years ago, about wanting to work for Al Achenbaum at Grey. Doreen is smart, she's a creative thinker, she writes well, and she's upbeat and full of energy—raring to go. I offer Doreen a job, and she's thrilled to join our department. Just as Shirley Young had done for me, I try to give Doreen plenty of opportunities, some of which she finds daunting. I push her, guide and counsel her, and make sure that Grey management is aware and appreciative of her achievements.

One memorable example is an assignment Grey is given by our client Mars. The company, whose key confectionary brands are chocolate, is trying to decide whether to mount a major global business-building effort in the sugar candy market. Grey is asked to help Mars assess the size and nature of the consumer opportunity worldwide. This is an assignment with major business implications. If Mars decides to go forward, they will need to build several new plants in various areas of the world. So the pressure is on for Grey Strategic Services to perform. We have to design a piece of strategic research which can be translated and implemented in many different countries—a very challenging job. I ask Doreen to take the lead on the project. She is flattered and excited, knowing how important it is both to Mars and to Grey, but at the same time she's a little overwhelmed. She works hard on getting the questionnaire designed so that it can be executed all over the world and finally comes in to talk to me about it. She talks and talks, pouring out all her thoughts and ideas, not yet quite clear on how to focus and streamline her approach. After listening to her and seeing her many notes, I try to help her by writing down for her four key questions I think will give us the answers we need. She listens carefully and then she tells me, "All of a sudden a light bulb went off in my head. I saw the organizing framework for the study." She's so excited to have seen the light, she jumps up, runs around my desk, and gives me a big hug. Doreen leads the study. When all the data from around the world have been collected and analyzed, she prepares a sharp, focused presentation that confirms the vast opportunity the sugar candy market represents for Mars. Soon after, the company sets up factories in Europe so they can begin to capitalize on it. This is a great success story for Grey, for Grey Strategic Services, and for Doreen. As time goes on, Doreen is wildly successful in her career, highly respected and valued at Grey and beyond. And I feel gratified to have helped pave the way, at least a little bit, for her success as well as that of others over the years.

When I become an executive vice president I'm assigned a huge, stunning office in the southeast corner of the thirty-sixth floor. It has floor-to-ceiling windows, is flooded with sunlight, and has fantastic views for many miles to the east and south over the New York City skyline, all the way to New York Harbor. The office and the views take my breath away. This is a long, long way from the Top of the Mark where my mother took us when our family was on vacation in San Francisco all those many years ago. There I gasped with awe when I saw the view of the entire sparkling city, the first big city I'd ever experienced. I wish my mother were alive to see the wonders of New York City spread out before her in the view from the windows of my thirty-sixth-floor office. She would have been thrilled.

Grey gives me an interior design budget to furnish and decorate my office to my taste. I get some help with this. I know I want a light, airy feeling, something that projects confidence and authority, and something that, although not girly looking, doesn't look too masculine. The office turns out beautifully. I have two couches upholstered in a summery looking pale green and white print that face each other across a large brass and glass coffee table, a couple of pull-up chairs and a small bench for meetings, and a beautiful French-looking desk with a complementary armoire. I hang some floral art pieces and bring in a gorgeous large, green leafy tree. I feel like the office projects me—who I am and how I'm different from all my male contemporaries.

Shortly after the announcement of my promotion in the press, I receive a letter from a woman named Amelia Fatt (no relation to Arthur Fatt, one of the founders of Grey). Amelia writes that she's a personal shopper and would like to come in to meet and talk with me. This sounds interesting. I wonder what Amelia has to say. We executives all dress rather formally for work—suits and ties for the men and skirts or pant suits with silk blouses or sweaters for me. I always wear high heels, and always make an effort to look professional and well put together. But going forward, I think I may need to up my game. In my new role, it's important I come across as confident, capable, and authoritative, very much as a woman in charge. Amelia comes in to see me. She tells me how she works, and the more she talks, the more I begin to think she can help me. She tries to get to know me and to understand my taste. It's a good conversation, and we decide to work together. Once I engage Amelia, she comes to my house and goes through my closet, identifying what I have and what I might need to project the look and the attitude I'm shooting for. We agree on what to shop for, and Amelia makes the rounds of Bergdorf's, Saks, and Bloomingdale's, assembling the key elements of my "executive vice president" wardrobe. Amelia has exquisite taste, and she understands color and silhouette very well. These are things I've never thought about consciously before. She's very exacting about fit: jacket sleeves have to be just the right length, jackets cannot bunch over the shoulder blades, trouser legs have to break at exactly the right spot over the instep, and on and on. Slowly, slowly, over time I assemble a very elegant, classic wardrobe, feminine but not frou-frou, in fine fabrics and warm, soft colors: greens, browns, burgundies, navies, pinks, and purples. Primary colors and black are not included. Amelia teaches me that they look too harsh on me. She helps me with handbags, shoes, coats, and even jewelry. Despite the fact that Jim has worked in the cosmetics business and I've worked on the Revlon account at Grey, I don't know much about how to apply makeup; all I wear is a little lipstick, probably a vestige of my "no makeup" intervention with Miss Brooks in high school. Amelia introduces me to a makeup specialist who teaches me what products to use and how to use them. He creates a very soft, natural look for me, and tells me he wants me to look like my best self. He shows me how to apply the makeup myself and emphasizes that everything I use should be in moderation. My newly evolving look makes me feel confident. I feel I can meet with any group of high level executives and project a sense of authority and self-possession.

Many times with clients I am the only woman in the room. One of Grey's newest clients is Mitsubishi, the Japanese company. We're assigned to introduce their cars to the American marketplace. Because Americans know little to nothing about Mitsubishi, its management invites Grey's team to spend a week in Japan, learning about the company's history and visiting several of its facilities around the country. We're greeted by our guide when we arrive at Narita International Airport in Tokyo. Though it's not, this feels like my first visit to Japan; I have no recollection of the time so many years ago that my parents and I were in Tokyo en route to our ship in Yokohama on our escape journey. Our Grey team learns, as we're driving to Mitsubishi's offices in downtown Tokyo, that Mitsubishi accounts for one-eighth the gross national product of Japan. This is a formidable company, involved in many huge and diverse businesses, including banking, infrastructure construction, electronics, and automotive and airplane manufacturing. Mitsubishi has organized our visit to impress our team with the company's might and power. Our first meeting begins in the afternoon. Our Japanese hosts direct us to sit on one side of the table, organizing our seating arrangements very carefully. Although it's not clear to me what the seating protocol is, one of my colleagues who's a very tall, handsome, and authoritative-looking man is placed by our hosts at the center of the table. I, the only woman on our team, am placed at the very end of the table, next to the door to the ladies' room. Once the seating process is completed, we have a rather formal exchange of business cards. Our cards have our names and our titles written in English on one side and in Japanese on the other. When our hosts turn over my card and read my title in Japanese, I hear a great intake of air. My title is the senior-most of our group, and this is a mortifying moment for our hosts, a great breach of protocol. As

I learn, the most important person in the group is supposed to sit at the center of the table. This leads to much scurrying about as plans for additional meetings and seating arrangements are changed. As I think about this, it's one more time when women are not thought to have the same value as men. This time though, the situation is rectified, publicly, and I feel vindicated.

Our Mitsubishi hosts are not really sure what to do with me. This is the land of the "salarymen," men who all wear navy or black suits, come into work early in the morning, work with their heads down all day, and at five o'clock go to their clubs. The clubs feature hostesses who serve the men drinks, and karaoke. Everyone has a favorite American song sung in the style of an American singer: "I Left My Heart in San Francisco" Tony Bennett style, some Frank Sinatra, and even "Y.M.C.A." All of my male teammates plan to go to the clubs; I tell my hosts I'd like to go too, to see what they are like. Once again, I hear an intake of air; they don't know what to do. Because I'm their guest and I am the senior person, they have to take good care of me. But, they whisper, *"She's a woman."* And women do not go to the clubs. Eventually, they figure something out. They assign a special guide to take me to a club, but I'm only allowed to stay for fifteen or twenty minutes, and then I have to leave. This brings back memories of my HBS dinner at the Harvard Club in Boston when I was the only woman guest and was told I was not allowed to enter through the front door; that was for men only. I had to go around to the alley and through the kitchen to get in.

At the club, I expect to see the Japanese hostesses dressed in kimonos with obis and wearing traditional makeup. I'm very surprised to see that's not the way it is at all; the attractive hostesses are dressed in Calvin Klein business suits. They kneel before the salarymen, catering to them and pouring their many, many drinks, and complimenting them on their singing. I leave as planned and go back to my hotel while my teammates stay until the wee hours. The next morning they tell me the salarymen go through this same routine every night, then go home on the subway in the middle of the night and do it all again the next day—day after day.

Maybe I'm moving the needle for women just a bit in one of the most important companies in Japan, being assigned, eventually, the center seat at the table and being taken to a club, even if for only fifteen or twenty minutes.

Mars is one of Grey's most important global clients. It's among the largest privately owned companies in the world; the principal owners are brothers John and Forrest Mars and their sister, Jackie. Mars is well known worldwide for their confectionary brands, like Snickers, M&M's, and Mars bars; it's also a worldwide leader in the pet food business, with brands like Pedigree and Whiskas. The company operates in a very quiet, secretive way; it's not showy or flashy in the least. Mars consistently pushes Grey hard; they are focused on ensuring our very best people do our very best work for them. Grey is assigned a new pet food brand in Europe by Mars and asks our team to come to Windsor, outside London, near their dog food plant, to be briefed. We are housed in a magnificent old mansion boutique hotel, and on our arrival we are invited to join Forrest Mars for dinner in the grand dining room at the hotel. At 8 p.m. we all take our seats at the beautifully appointed dining table, replete with gorgeous linens, crystal, china, silver, and lovely floral arrangements. Forrest Mars, our host, a very stern man who doesn't seem to have much of a sense of humor, starts the meeting. He welcomes us and then says, "We at Mars believe very strongly that the people who work on our dog food business need to own dogs. They need to have a deep understanding of and love for dogs that can only come from owning one. Let's go around the table, and one by one, each of you tell a story about your dog." *Holy cow! What am I going to do? I do not have a dog. I do not want a dog. I know so little about dogs I can't even fake it.* If Forrest realizes I don't own a dog, he'll have me on the next plane out of here, back to New York. This would not be good for me or for Grey. As the dog stories begin, I'm thinking and thinking; I finally decide I have two options. I'm wearing a long string of pearls. I could break my pearls and we could all go crawling around on the floor looking for them. This would create a distraction and would disrupt the dog chronicles. Or I could feign illness and lock myself in the ladies' room for a good long time. I like my pearls and don't want to break them, so I opt for the ladies' room. I run in and stay and stay and stay, what seems to me to be an inordinately long time. I finally peek out and see they seem to be finished discussing the dogs, so I venture back out. *Phew! That was close.* The dog food briefings—and life, go on.

One day at Grey my phone rings. It's the Radcliffe alumnae office. They're doing an edition of their alumnae magazine featuring profiles of alumnae who have been successful in a variety of careers. They'd like to feature me as an H-RPBA alum and business success story. I agree. They send a writer to interview me and a photographer to my office. We go through the interview, and the last question I'm asked is, "What would you advise corporate leaders today as it relates to women in business?" I answer, "Take advantage of the enormous talent pool women represent. After all, women account for half the brain power in America and the world." Several weeks later I receive a copy of the magazine. The story turns out well; there's a full page photo of me at my desk. But the caption under the photo reads, "Barbara Feigin: Half the brains." I can't believe it. I call Radcliffe, home of the most prestigious publishing program in the world, and ask, "How could you?" You'd think the Radcliffe publishing group, of all people, would think not to disparage women in such a blatant way. They have no real answer for this clueless mistake. All they can do is say they are sorry.

It's the mid-'80s and I'm invited to become a Whitman College overseer, a small group of accomplished alumni who contribute talent and/or treasure, as the college states, to the college. It becomes clear to me that Whitman's president and key members of the board know and admire Grey's work in strategic research and planning. Whitman is having enrollment challenges and is looking for strategic guidance in developing a powerful new plan to build student enrollment. I become an overseer and get Ed's approval for Grey to do the first ever research and strategic planning project pro bono for Whitman. We do a solid piece of comprehensive and extremely enlightening research. We learn that there's very little awareness of Whitman among target students, their parents, or their advisers, and those who've heard of Whitman know next to nothing about the college. I consult with the president of the college, who's very enthusiastic about the work and eager to have me present it to the board of trustees as the foundation for developing a new enrollment strategy. I prepare and rehearse my presentation and make my way from New York to Walla Walla to meet with the trustees, nine middle-aged to elderly white men. I present in the most professional way I know how, walking through the data, piece by piece, and moving on to propose implications for action.

As soon as I finish, the chairman of the board, a short, feisty elderly man in his shirtsleeves, stands up. He is very accomplished, an engineer who has had a distinguished career on the Manhattan Project with the Atomic Energy Commission and later with Bechtel Corporation. With his face getting redder and redder, he shouts in a very belligerent tone, "This is complete bullshit. I don't believe any of it." I am stunned. I have presented to many different executives in many different businesses in many countries around the world, and no one has ever spoken to me like this. Everyone in the room freezes. No one knows what to do or say. My sponsor, the president of the college, slumps down in his chair and says nothing. I simply say, "I've presented you with the facts—the data. Of course it's up to you to decide what you might want to do next." The meeting comes to a quick and very awkward close. I think again of Alvin Achenbaum's words: *We propose; you dispose.* Later, I wonder: *Would the chairman ever have dared to speak to me in such a patently belittling way had I been a man?*

My trailblazing life as a "Mad woman," often the only woman, in the fast-paced world of advertising, is exciting, fun, and deeply satisfying. I love the collaboration, the problem-solving orientation, and the creativity. My life as a mad woman intensifies, with much more of the same during these hectic and demanding years as a wife and mom at home.

CHAPTER FOURTEEN

Our Crazy Balancing Act

During these same years, as I'm working hard to build my career and Jim is doing the same, the boys are growing, and every day is a new adventure for us both. From the beginning we decide we'll focus on just two things: family and work. We agree that one of us will always be home; we won't both be away on business at the same time. We also agree that we'll both try to be at the boys' special events, and if we can't both be there, at least one of us definitely will be. Even at that, we're moving at full speed and we're occasionally exhausted, but we're good partners and we love it all.

The first thing we need to deal with is finding a larger apartment and then moving. We buy a big, beautiful, bright apartment on East Eighty-Sixth Street in Manhattan, across the street from Carl Schurz Park and overlooking the East River. As we get ready to move I rush home after an intense day at work, spend the next couple of hours together with Jim, bathing and feeding the three boys, playing with them, and settling them into bed. Then I load our double baby carriage with as many of our belongings as I can jam into it. I walk this mini-moving van the twelve blocks from our current apartment to our new one. I unload the carriage and then go through the whole process a second time. We want to limit what's left for the movers to handle. Our financial situation is tight so we're trying to keep our moving costs as low as possible. When I finally get home, I fall into bed for a few hours of sleep before the hectic routine starts all over again the next morning.

We move in September 1970. One of the best things about the new apartment is that Michael, now four years old, has his own space, space that Peter and Daniel can't invade. Once we settle in, Jim and I are relieved to see how happy Michael is, laughing and dancing gleefully to his favorite Herb Alpert music. We put away the punching clown.

As time goes on, some of the actions of Peter and Daniel leave me speechless, and often lead to both Jim and me locking ourselves in the bathroom and laughing helplessly. One day when they are toddlers, I arrive home after work and our nanny, Sarah, is looking dejected and depleted. She says, "Take a look in their room. See what they did when I put them in for their naps." I do, and I see they have completely dismantled their air conditioner. I can't believe my eyes. It's as if I'm looking at a cartoon. The innards of the air conditioner are spilling out of its frame; it is finished—gone. What do I do? I have no idea. They will just have to do without air conditioning. Not long after this, we have an encore. I get home, and again, Sarah looks dejected—done in. Again she says, "Take a look in their room." I do, and I see that when Sarah thought they were napping they took Peter's crib apart. Neither Jim nor I has the least idea how to put it back together. Luckily, we have a handyman in our building who spends several hours working to reassemble it.

My father and Kate come to visit us again when Peter and Daniel are toddlers. My father is in his element, overjoyed to be a grandfather now of three grandsons, not just one. And once again, Kate hangs back. My father loves giving Peter and Dan and Michael their baths, which they take together in a tub full of bubbles. When the boys get out of their bubbly bath, he dries them very vigorously with a big bath towel and rubs their mops of curls. They all love this ritual and laugh together all the way through it.

One morning when Peter and Daniel are around two, I wake with a start. I think I hear the banging of pots and pans. I leap out of bed and run to the kitchen. I'm horrified to see Peter and Daniel have found our stepladder. Peter is holding it for Dan, and Dan is on his tiptoes on the top step, reaching for our sharpest knives on a pegboard near the ceiling. Both boys are naked and laughing. They're very excited about this latest adventure. Jim and I think they're on the brink of getting into

Daniel, Peter, and Michael, three men in a tub

dangerous trouble. We know we have to do something to prevent any future incidents, so we uneasily decide we'll put a lock on the outside of their bedroom door, and after we put them to bed, we'll lock them in their room. Friends who see the lock look very puzzled and say to us, "Isn't that Peter and Dan's room? Is that a lock on the outside of their door?" We say, "Yes . . . don't ask. You'd never understand."

During these early years Jim and I are becoming more and more attuned to the extraordinary and strange symbiosis of Peter and Daniel. They are profoundly and mysteriously connected in a way that's indescribable. It's as if they are two parts of a single totality. They have a special way of communicating. They use a language we don't understand, although they understand one another completely. When they first begin to talk, they actually answer for one another. At dinner, I ask Peter, "Would you like to have some more beans?" Daniel says, "No." They think as a single unit. The most important implication of their oneness is that it gives them total, complete confidence. This is a double-edged sword. They are never afraid of anything. Each is always and ever deeply, foundationally supported by the other, but theirs is a unit that's very tough for anyone else—like Jim, me, or Michael—to

Peter and Daniel

Peter, Michael, and Daniel, knights in shining armor

penetrate. As Jim and I talk about this strange situation, we begin to understand that the balance of power between us as parents and Peter and Daniel has been turned on its head. Normally, children begin to realize during their teenage years that their parents have feet of clay. With Peter and Dan, Jim and I have feet of clay from the beginning. It's very hard, nearly impossible, for us to punish Peter and Daniel when they misbehave. They simply don't care; they have one another. This is a situation that sometimes leaves Michael in shock. He can't believe that Jim and I have so little control when Peter and Dan act up. For Jim and me, it's a continuing challenge.

From the time they were very young, all three boys have called us "Mom" and "Jim." I'm not sure what brought this about, though everyone calls Jim "Jim"—not just family and friends, but neighbors, the people who work for him, our building staff, and tradespeople in our neighborhood. It must have seemed very natural to the boys, and Jim loves it. People who don't know us probably think Jim is my second husband. But when they see us together, this idea is immediately dispelled. Michael has dark hair and bright, shining brown eyes like we both do. When he's a young boy and the three of us walk down the street together, Michael looks like our little brother. Peter and Dan have red cheeks like mine and laughing brown eyes like Michael's and Jim's. From the time they're very young, it's obvious they're built very much like Jim, and they stand and walk exactly the same way Jim does. When they walk down the street with Jim, they look like mini-Jims. There's no chance that when people see Jim with his sons they'll mistake him for my second husband.

August 8, 1974, is Jim's fortieth birthday. I've planned a surprise party for him, inviting family, friends, and his colleagues. It's all set to be a happy, joyous, fun celebration. But this is not to be. Instead, we learn as we gather to celebrate that Richard Nixon will be resigning as president of the United States later this evening. His resignation comes in the wake of the Watergate scandal—a break-in at the Democratic National Committee headquarters and the subsequent cover-up by the Nixon administration, all masterminded by the president himself. Our party comes to a halt as we huddle around the television set to hear Nixon make his speech. Although this is a shameful moment for our country, all of us at the party are relieved that this scandal is over and Nixon will be gone. We try to get back into party mode as we sing "Happy Birthday" to Jim and he blows out his forty candles, wishing for a better tomorrow.

* * *

Michael is in nursery school, and it's time Peter and Daniel start at Michael's school as well. Jim and I want them to be in separate sections so they can begin to develop some sense of independence. But the only way we can arrange this is for Dan to go to a morning session, and Peter to one in the afternoon.

I've always told my assistants at Grey that they should interrupt me anytime anyone in my family calls. One day my assistant interrupts me in a meeting to say that Peter's teacher is on the phone. His teacher says, in a very troubled sounding voice, "Mrs. Feigin, it's Miss Gobel, Peter's teacher. You need to come to the school right away. Peter is huddled under a table, keening in a very loud voice, and we're unable to get him out." I leave my meeting, race to find a cab, and speed to the school very quickly. I hear the keening before I enter the room. It sounds terrible—like a wounded animal. I crawl under the table where Peter is huddled and try to comfort him and quiet him down. This is the first time he's been separated from Dan, and he doesn't know how to handle it. He's bereft. We leave the school, and for the next several days, I take him to school and stay with him while he gets accustomed to his "new normal."

Another day, when Michael is in second grade, my assistant at Grey interrupts me in another meeting to say that Tom Mansfield, the headmaster of Michael's school, is on the phone and needs to speak with me right away. I can't imagine why he would be calling me. He says, "Hello, Mrs. Feigin. I'm calling you from the doctor's office where I've taken Michael. He fell down when we were ice skating, but he's crying so hard, I don't really think he's hurt." This sounds totally illogical to me. I'm not sure I've heard him correctly, but I say, "I'll be there right away." Again, I race for a cab and speed to the doctor's office. The doctor tells me I need to take Michael to the hospital. He has a spiral fracture the entire length of his leg. I try to comfort Michael while he has a toe-to-hip cast put on, and eventually we find our way home. Another day in the life of a mad woman and her son!

Amid all our craziness, Jim is recruited to become vice president of marketing at Almay, the hypoallergenic cosmetics company. He

Jim, successful executive

excitedly takes on the position; it's a major career step forward for him. At Grey I'm still working on the Revlon business. I tell Ed Meyer about Jim's new job, and as a courtesy Ed informs Sandy Buchsbaum, our senior client at Revlon. Ed hears back from Sandy, "Ed, we love Barbara, but she's going to have to come off our business. This is a clear conflict of interest." Ed argues that Jim and I have great integrity and would never divulge company secrets to one another. Sandy insists, and sadly, although I understand Sandy's point of view, I come off the Revlon account, which had been my first assignment when I started at Grey. Despite all the times the agency has been humiliated and made to grovel, I'll miss working on the Revlon business. Revlon is a company that fully understands the power of advertising. It's been a privilege to work with a client who pushes us hard to do our best work, work we're enormously proud of, and to be the best we can be.

The symbiosis of Peter and Daniel makes life challenging for Michael. He's a supportive older brother, but right from the beginning he understands instinctively that he'll never be as close to them as they are to one another. No one will be. Michael becomes very self-reliant. From the time he's a toddler, he likes to figure things out for himself, and he's very good at it. He never asks for help, and Jim and I usually are not aware of what he's working on until he demonstrates for us his mastery of it. When he's five, he teaches himself to read during Christmas vacation from kindergarten. When he's eight and we're on vacation in California, he teaches himself to swim, working at it doggedly hour after hour, day after day. And when he's in his early teens I hear an odd set of clicking noises outside our kitchen as I'm preparing dinner one evening. I peek out the door, and there is Michael with his phonograph all set up, a book of instructions open, and a set of paper footprints spread out in a pattern along the floor. I watch him for a while and realize he's teaching himself to tap dance. I can't believe it. I can't imagine how he's able to do this on his own, but he is. He becomes a fabulous tap dancer.

Luckily when Michael is in elementary school he discovers theater, and even at this early age he develops a passion for it. Theater gives Michael a world of his own to enter, a world in which he can thrive. Jim and I believe this is vitally important for him. His first big role, when he's in third grade, is as the Cowardly Lion in *The Wizard of Oz*. Then when he's in fourth grade he appears as Fagin, singing and dancing his way through *Oliver*, and receives his first ever standing ovation. He moves on in eighth grade to play Sky Masterson in *Guys and Dolls*.

He's the romantic lead and his girlfriend plays Sarah, the female lead, a situation that causes knowing smiles and laughter all around. In his senior year at Trinity, where Michael goes to high school, he plays the lead in *Anything Goes* and brings the house down with his magnificent singing and dancing. No one at Trinity has been aware of Michael's talents, as he's been a member of a repertory theater group outside the school, the First All Children's Theater, during his earlier high school years. *Anything Goes* is a thrilling success for Michael, and we're absolutely overjoyed for him.

As I was growing up I loved all our family traditions; I think they were very important in creating the bonds that tied us together. I want my family, Jim and the boys, to have those same kinds of traditions, ones they'll look forward to and remember. Starting when the boys are very young, we have a big family Thanksgiving dinner every year—turkey and all the trimmings, candles, flowers, silver, china, the works. Christmas is epic—a fresh tree, stockings full of goodies for everyone on Christmas morning, and gifts galore. Getting ready for the big day takes months of planning. For one of our very first Christmases, early in our marriage, I gave Jim a small marble lion figure to celebrate his being a Leo. He loves that Leo is his astrological sign because Leo symbolizes great strength; he's pleased to be a very physically strong man. He was so happy with this gift, I thought to myself, *I'm going to try to start a lion collection for Jim.* From then on, whenever I traveled I tried to find a "local" lion figure to bring Jim when I returned home, and he began eagerly to anticipate each new lion in his collection.

Whenever anyone in the family has a significant achievement of any kind, we celebrate with a special Carvel ice cream cake inscribed with a message of congratulations. The boys and Jim all love this ritual. And birthdays are important. One year on my birthday Jim and the boys planned a dinner to celebrate. I worked late in my office on the thirty-sixth floor at Grey, planning to meet them all for dinner at a Chinese restaurant a couple of blocks away. There were only a few of us working late, when all at once the fire alarm started to ring. This was scary; we were in a high rise and we needed to get out. I rushed around our floor, herding everyone together to go down the fire stairs. Once I was sure everyone was out, I raced down thirty-six flights of stairs in my high heels, in a mini-panic to get out of the building. When I got to the bottom of the stairs, I was greeted by the firemen; my knees buckled and I collapsed, unable to walk. Two of my male colleagues carried me out to a taxi, injured football player style, and rode with me the two blocks to the restaurant. They went in to get Jim, who came out and carried me in to dinner. My sons, and the restaurant staff, thought I was so drunk I couldn't even walk. It took me a week to recover and walk again.

Michael has done very well in school, and is advised to consider and apply to a handful of topflight colleges. Jim and I take him to visit Princeton, Brown, Tufts, Williams, Carnegie Mellon, and Northwestern. We're bewildered and dismayed that he doesn't seem to like any of them and won't even consider applying. The last college we visit is Wesleyan, and as we pull into the parking lot, Michael announces, "This is where I'm going." I ask him why he says that, what his thoughts are. He has no real answer. His feelings about Wesleyan are purely emotional. He says, "I just feel right here. I feel comfortable." Wesleyan is, in fact, the only college to which Michael applies, a situation that intensifies my crazy mad woman state. He insists that he will handle the application process completely on his own, and will not allow either Jim or me to see his essay or any of the rest of his early decision application materials. Michael keeps telling me not to worry, "I'll get in." I don't think he has a realistic idea of how competitive the admissions process is. On December 7, a week before Wesleyan is due to send out its acceptance letters, I get home from work to find Michael and Jim laughing very excitedly. Michael tells me that when he'd been on the Eighty-Sixth Street crosstown bus, he'd looked out the window as the bus approached First Avenue and seen Jim waving a letter at him with one hand and an envelope with the other. Jim was shouting, "You got in!" I have two reactions. I'm absolutely thrilled for Michael. He wants so much to go to Wesleyan, and now he will. But at the same time I'm appalled that Jim opened Michael's letter and didn't leave it for

Daniel, Michael, and Peter at Michael's graduation from Wesleyan University, 1988

Michael to open himself. I tell Jim privately how upset I am with what I think is his invasion of Michael's privacy. Jim does not want to dwell on this. He wants to move on to a family celebration of Michael's fabulous achievement. Michael goes on to have a great experience during his four years at Wesleyan; he graduates from Wesleyan with honors.

The Day School, Trevor Day School today, where all three boys went through the eighth grade, has a very student-centric attitude. The school focuses on helping each child become the best he or she can be. Music is included in the curriculum, with recorder class, taught by Miss Rhoda Webber, serving as the introduction. Peter and Dan hate recorder class and have only nasty things to say about Miss Rhoda Webber. Jim and I are concerned about their negative attitude and worry that they'll behave badly in class and will get into trouble. We've given up any hope that they'll settle down and get serious about recorder class. One evening, though, we're in the kitchen preparing for dinner and we hear what we think are recorder notes coming from Peter and Dan's bedroom. I say to Jim, happily, "Oh, I'm so glad to know they're finally taking to recorder class." We tiptoe to their bedroom door, open it a crack, and peek in. Each of them is sitting cross-legged on his bed—playing the recorder through his nose! Jim and I rush to the bathroom, lock ourselves in, and gasp with laughter.

At the beginning of Peter's and Dan's eighth-grade year, Jim and I begin to think about where they'll go to high school. We want them to go to a coed school, one that's large enough that they can be in separate sections. After much strategizing, we agree the best options we have are boarding schools. We're not happy about this. We love having the boys at home, going to their games and other events, and opening our home to their friends. But we begin our search. On the day we somewhat unhappily plan to send in our acceptances to Northfield Mount Hermon, a very fine boarding school in Massachusetts, my assistant at Grey tells me I have a call from Terry Ippolito from the Packer Collegiate school in Brooklyn. While I've heard of Packer, I don't know much about it, but I take the call. Ms. Ippolito says, "Mrs. Feigin, we'd like to invite you and Mr. Feigin and Peter and Dan to come to Packer and meet with Peter Esty, our headmaster, and with our basketball coach, Dennis Britton." I tell her we are about to go on vacation, and she asks, "Can you come first thing tomorrow morning?" I say that we'll be there, and immediately call Jim, who knows Packer from his days growing up in Brooklyn and thinks very highly of it. I also call the headmaster of the Day School who very enthusiastically recommends Packer. Although we'd never considered Packer because it's in Brooklyn, it meets all our criteria. It's coed, it's large enough for the boys to be in separate sections, and it has an excellent reputation. I ask the Day School headmaster, "Are the boys being recruited? How could that be?" This is unheard of in New York private schools. He laughs and says "Packer knows the boys from basketball." The two schools had played a championship game; the Day School won; and in their somewhat spooky oneness, Peter and Dan were memorable stars. So Peter and Dan go on to have a wonderful high school experience at Packer that's everything we've hoped for.

We go on many family vacations—to Disneyland, Hershey Park, and Williamsburg. Our favorite is Dorado Beach, Puerto Rico, a beautiful old pineapple plantation developed as a resort by Laurance Rockefeller.

We have wonderful times together—at the beach, the pool, and the tennis courts, and eating delectable meals. It all feels like a wonderful dream, yet another aspect of our charmed lives.

Life at home with my four alpha males, Jim and the boys, is often raucous, rowdy, and rambunctious. I like to have time alone with each of the boys, time for us to talk quietly. I'm very lucky that my business travels take me all over the world, and I'm sometimes able to take one of the boys with me. These are very, very special times for us to have adventures together. Michael goes with me to London for a week, and we go to the theater every night. Peter goes with me to Hong Kong, where he teaches me to negotiate by walking away in Stanley Market. He says, "Just watch, Mom, the salesman will come running after you, ready to make a deal." He's right. Daniel goes with me for ten days to Australia. We snorkel in the Great Barrier Reef. We spend time at a sheep ranch where Daniel, my New York City born-and-bred son, helps with the birthing of a calf. We're amazed to see kangaroos jumping across the roads on our way to the ranch. These moments mean everything to me as I build steel-like bonds with each of my sons.

During Peter's and Dan's high school years, Grey is getting computers for the first time. I'm intimidated by my computer. It's a laptop and I decide to take it home for the weekend so I can work on it and get comfortable using it. I set it up in my home office but the weekend goes by and I never get around to dealing with it. Peter and Dan have friends over to stay for the weekend and we have our usual whirlwind of activities. I bring my computer back to my office on Monday. I'm having a big meeting in my office with six or seven of my colleagues in the room. We're working on a major project, and we've decided on our next steps. We're in the process of setting up our next meeting to get together to share our work and our ideas. I say to the group, "Let me check my calendar on my computer." I push a key on my computer, and a booming voice rings through the room: *"BARBARA FEIGIN, GET YOUR HEAD OUT OF YOUR ASS!"* Every time I push another key, the voice repeats its message. All of my colleagues roar with laughter, and I'm mortified. My darling sons have gotten their hands on my computer over the weekend and worked their devilish magic.

* * *

Jim is once again recruited for a terrific new job: president of Posner Laboratories, a cosmetics and toiletries company making and marketing products especially for African Americans. Posner's spokeswoman is Natalie Cole, the great singer. The boys get to meet her when we're on a family vacation in Los Angeles and go backstage to a concert she gives at the Hollywood Bowl. We're all thrilled that Jim will run his own operation, something he's always wanted to do. So he's off on an amazing new adventure.

During Jim's years at Almay, he had become friendly and worked closely with Dan Nugent, Almay's vice president of sales. When Jim goes to Posner, he brings Dan along with him. Jim and Dan are good partners; they bring complementary skills to their work. They both have an itch, an ambition, to own a company. For a long time they cast about and finally they find a company to buy, a small cosmetics company called Charles V. Their idea is that they will reenergize the company—update its product line, revitalize its branding, and sell the line through Walmart. They are excited about the potential for Charles V and work on their plan enthusiastically. But not for long. Unbeknownst to Jim, Dan is diagnosed with terminal lung cancer. After learning this, Dan commits suicide. Jim is devastated. He continues to go forward on his own, but he is so traumatized emotionally it's slow going. It's a hard and sad time.

During their junior and senior years at Packer, Peter and Daniel spend many hours discussing whether they want to go to the same college or to separate colleges. Every night they talk about this just before dropping off to sleep. Jim and I try to listen at their bedroom door. We feel they should do what they decide they want. This will ensure they have a good experience. They finally tell us they want to go together, to the same college, because they've concluded this will be the last time they'll be able to play ball together. We support their decision, and they are both accepted at Franklin & Marshall, an excellent small liberal arts college, much like Whitman, in Lancaster, Pennsylvania. They leave for college, and Michael returns home for a time after his Wesleyan graduation, another change in family dynamics. Jim and I don't see much of Michael. We're at work during the day, and he's working in theater so is gone in the evenings when we're home. We know he won't be with us long; he's eager to get his own apartment. But it's fun and interesting for us to have this time together with Michael and to get to know him as a smart, funny adult.

CHAPTER FIFTEEN

More about My Father

In October 1979, Jim and I are in Los Angeles on a combination business/vacation trip. One evening our phone rings. It's Kate, saying that my father, who's had a history of heart problems, has had a heart attack. Jim and I pack up and leave immediately for Seattle. We go directly to see him at the University of Washington Medical Center. He's in a semi-seated position in his hospital bed, propped up by many pillows. His mouth is open, and he's struggling mightily for every breath. He is very, very thin; his features are very sharp, almost birdlike. I'm appalled to see how ill he is. No one talks about what his prognosis might be.

I decide to stay in Seattle for a time with Kate, and Jim goes back to New York to be with our boys. After a few days in the hospital, my father is sent to a drab, depressing-looking rehab facility. I go every day to spend time with him, but he's so ill he can barely speak. It's clear to me he's not making progress. After several days the time has come for me to go home. Jim and the boys need me, and I have to get back to work. I go to the rehab facility for a last visit with my father before I leave. When I get there, he's upset because the aides are trying to get him to walk, and he just can't. He can hardly stand up. He has no strength at all, no energy. He's in his skimpy light blue hospital gown which flutters around his knees, and I see he's wearing his brown dress shoes with no socks. He's able to take only a step or two with his walker, and then he falls back into bed. He can't really carry on a conversation, but I spend some time bringing him up to date on the latest exploits of the boys, which brings a smile to his face. Finally the moment comes when I have to tell him I need to go back to New York. I take his hand, kiss him softly on the forehead, and tell him goodbye. As I walk out of his room I look back sadly one last time at my frail, failing father, and head for the airport, thinking this day, October 29, 1979, is probably the last time I'll ever see him.

My flight arrives back in New York in the early afternoon, and I decide to stop at Grey on my way home to check in and pick up my mail. When I get there, I see have a message from the CFO of Posner, Jim's company. An emergency call had come in from Kate and he'd taken the call in Jim's absence. Kate had told him that my father had died that afternoon when I was on my flight home. As I think about it, I come to believe he'd hung on just long enough to say goodbye to me. He simply had no more strength after that. My father was seventy-nine years old.

I go home and tell Jim what's happened. Then I sit down with the boys, who are nine and thirteen, and tell them that my father, their grandfather whom they'd loved so dearly, has died. We are all deeply saddened—crushed. I spend the evening at home and leave the next morning for Seattle. My father, like my mother, had not wanted a funeral. He is cremated, and his ashes are buried next to my mother's.

I spend several days with Kate. We reminisce about my father, eat comfort foods, and reminisce some more. We even laugh together now and then as we remember happy times. Eventually I have to go back to my life in New York with my family and my work.

As I take the long, cross-country flight from Seattle, I think about all the things I've admired and appreciated about my father. Most of all, he had great strength of character. He escaped to America with no money, no English, and no idea how he'd make a life for his family, but he was determined to do so. Because he didn't know where we'd live in America, he'd even brought a tent along on our escape journey so we could live in that, if need be. His grit and perseverance paid off for him. He had a strong work ethic and over the years was able to build a career he was proud of at Sears. He was fiercely devoted to his family. I think about all the years and years of fear and stress and anxiety he experienced, first while getting out of Germany, then during the Holocaust and the executions of his parents in the concentration camps, and finally with my mother's illness. With my mother, he went through years of not knowing—*Is today the day?* Initially she was given only a year to live; then she went into remission; then crisis followed by remission, again and again. It was agonizing, and through it all, my father was a tower of strength and support. He was calm; he was a problem solver; and he never, ever complained.

I remember about a year after my mother died when my father told me he and Kate had decided to get married. I said, "That's fantastic!" I was very happy for him—happy that after all his years of stress and anxiety, he was going to be free—free to relax, to travel, to laugh, to have a good time, all of which came true for him. He and Kate had a very happy fifteen-year marriage.

I think too about all the things I wish I'd asked my father about—things I wish I knew: *What were his parents like? What was his boyhood like? What did he do for fun? What kind of an education did he have? What brought him to Berlin? What was his job at Ford? Did he have it long? Did he like it? How did he happen to become a typewriter repairman? How did he meet and court Mother? How and when did he learn what happened to his parents?* And on and on. There are so many questions—so many things I'll never know.

My plane is about to land. I think about how awed and inspired I am by my father's bravery and courage and by his persistence when searching for solutions to seemingly intractable problems. I'll be very fulfilled if my children see those same traits in me. In tough times, of which there were many, he kept moving forward. There's perhaps no better example of this than his perseverance in getting our family out of Germany. I'm so grateful he knew and loved Jim and our boys. The boys will always remember their happy times with their beloved grandfather.

CHAPTER SIXTEEN

My Charmed Life, No More

It's July 28, 1990, the day my world comes crashing down.

I'm fifty-two years old. Life is good. I've been happily married to Jim for nearly thirty years. We're great partners. We're best friends. We love and respect one another deeply. He still makes me laugh every day, and it still gives me a thrill to hear him refer to me as "my wife." Our sons are doing well. Michael is on a long-planned, postgraduation cross-country road trip and is planning to meet Jim and me next week at the Bel-Air in Los Angeles, our favorite hotel. Peter and Daniel have finished their first year at Franklin & Marshall and are working as counselors at the summer day camp run by their alma mater, Packer. My career is thriving and I'm loving it. I'm gaining national recognition as an authority on consumer trends and am rising through the executive management ranks at Grey, considered a "worldwide powerhouse" in the advertising business by *Fortune* magazine. I'm feeling like I'm in a good place. I'm grateful for our charmed life.

It's Saturday morning. I wake up and see Jim walking into our bedroom, bringing me a cup of coffee in bed as he often does on weekends. But I see he's holding the coffee cup with his arm at a very awkward angle—in a stiff, almost clawlike position. And I see he's dragging his foot. Alarm bells clang in my head. I think: *Oh, my god. Something really bad is happening.* I think Jim may be having a stroke. I jump out of bed, grab the coffee, and help Jim get back into bed. I know I have to find a doctor fast. Jim doesn't have a doctor. And it's Saturday in the summertime in New York, July, when no doctors are around. *What the hell am I supposed to do?* In my panic it doesn't occur to me to take Jim to the emergency room.

I think and think and remember that Daniel has an early morning squash game at the Heights Casino in Brooklyn Heights with his girlfriend, Cat Yatrakis. I remember Dan or Cat once mentioned that Cat has an uncle, George Yatrakis, who's a doctor with an office near our apartment. I reach Dan, and he and Cat call Dr. Yatrakis, who agrees to see Jim as soon as Jim can get to the office. By the time I help Jim get dressed and we make our way downstairs to get a cab, Jim can hardly walk. I have to practically hold him up as we slowly make our way into the office. The minute he sees Jim, Dr. Yatrakis says, "Mr. Feigin, you're having a stroke. You need to get to the emergency room, around the corner at Lenox Hill Hospital, immediately." As we are leaving, Dr. Yatrakis pulls me aside and says to me very quietly, "Your life will never be the same." Truer words were never spoken.

Jim is in the ER for what seems like a very long time. The doctors tell us that Jim is still in the process of having a stroke, and they can't predict how long this will go on or what the aftereffects will be. I'm nearly catatonic with fear, panicked that Jim will die. He is finally moved from the ER to an acute care room in the hospital where the medical staff works to get him stabilized. Jim is pretty severely paralyzed on his right side, but fortunately his mental faculties and his speech are not affected.

Peter and Daniel hurry to Lenox Hill to be with Jim and me during this terrifying time. We are all nearly frozen with fear. We more or less hold one another up and try to stay as calm as possible and not to cry. We don't want Jim to see how profoundly devastated we all are. In the midst of all the chaos, I have to make contact with Michael and tell him what's happening. Since he is on a road trip, there is no way to contact him, but I know he'll soon be at the Bel-Air to meet us. When he gets there and is told that our reservations have been canceled, he thinks there's been a mistake and tries to reach me at my office. I'm at the hospital, so my assistant has to tell Michael what is happening. I feel terrible about this; I'd wanted to tell him myself, but I had no choice. Michael gets in touch with me immediately and we talk through the details of Jim's situation. I say to Michael, "Turn around and head back to New York as soon as possible. But take your time. If you get back here too fast, Jim will think he's dying."

On Jim's birthday, August 8, in Lenox Hill Hospital, he turns fifty-six years old. Jim always looks forward to his birthday and likes us all to pay homage and make a big fuss over him on his Big Day. On this day we all have to fuss over him as he lies there in his paralyzed state, trying to recover. I think this is the first time I've ever seen Jim cry. This breaks my heart.

I continue to be nearly crazed with worry, fear, and concern, not sure during these initial days whether Jim will make it. I feel like I'm on a hamster wheel, perpetually running around in circles and getting nowhere. I go rushing to see Jim at the hospital every morning on my way to work, rushing back at lunchtime and then again after work. I can't stand being in the hospital. I know the exact times Jim is due to receive his medications, and if the nurses are even a few minutes late I get hysterical and chase them through the halls. I feel certain Jim will die if he doesn't receive his meds at exactly the appointed hour. I hate the smells of the hospital—Clorox and disinfectants not fully disguising the terrible food odors and odors of sick people. I cannot stop watching the clock. I feel desperately conflicted; I want and need to be with Jim, but I can't wait to escape.

During all my hours at the hospital, I think back to the time before I realized Jim was having a stroke. I remember that Jim, who's never sick, actually stayed in bed sleeping for two days. This was highly, highly unusual, but Jim told me he thought he might be coming down with the flu and was going to "stay in bed and sleep it off." This had all made sense to me.

Over all the years of our marriage, Jim's refusal to have regular physical exams had created an undercurrent of worry and concern for me, but I could do nothing to deal with the problem. Jim wouldn't even discuss it. It turned out Jim had uncontrolled high blood pressure that could have been controlled had he attended to it. This is what's caused him to have this devastatingly terrible stroke. I know as I sit with Jim in the hospital that his debilitating stroke at the young age of fifty-five will change the course of his life and our family's life forever. This realization stirs many emotions in me: overwhelming sadness, even despair; a sense of powerlessness; and feelings of anger and even outrage. It brings back to me the feelings I had during the terrible time when I was eleven and learned that my mother had terminal cancer and was given only a year to live. I guiltily try to suppress these feelings so I can focus on Jim's condition, hope for his improvement, and try every way I can think of to help him.

I continue to go to work every day and am grateful to be with my longtime Grey colleagues who have become good friends, working together on problems we actually can solve, not like the ones I'm facing with Jim. I'm in a fog most of the time, but my routine helps me to get through each day.

Eventually we need to find a rehab facility for Jim. The Rusk Institute is known to be the best and most advanced stroke rehab facility in the world. But getting admitted is nearly impossible—like getting admitted to Harvard. My boss, Ed Meyer, is on the board of NYU hospital, of which Rusk is a part. Ed pulls some strings and gets Jim admitted.

Rusk, a few blocks away from my office, is a drab, dingy, and depressing place, and Jim becomes quite depressed and uncommunicative. I continue my frantic hamster wheel routine, stopping by to see Jim at lunchtime, often going with him to one of his PT or OT classes, and rushing back after work so I can be with him as he eats his dinner and then tell him good night. Through it all, I am in an ongoing state of high anxiety, stress, and near panic. I can't imagine how our lives will unfold; I can't even imagine what the next day will bring and how I will cope with it. I feel overwhelmed all the time—terrified, panicked, uncertain and unclear about what might happen next. I'm nearly totally alone with my fear and terror. Peter and Dan are in New York, but I don't want to burden them; instead, I feel I need to be there to support them.

Rusk provides each patient with a team of medical specialists, each focused on a different aspect of rehabilitation. Included on the team is a psychologist, Dr. Aaron Strauss, who specializes in counseling the spouses of stroke patients. I'm encouraged to see Dr. Strauss and to talk with him. He is very calming and helpful, clearly understanding what I'm experiencing and feeling. He says, "I know you probably can't even imagine this now, but you *will* smile again."

Jim is in Rusk for about six weeks, working diligently at physical therapy, occupational therapy, and trying to recuperate. He becomes mobile, but limps pretty dramatically, and he is unable to use his right arm and hand.

Michael finally makes it back to New York during Jim's time at Rusk. We all meet in a small garden there. Jim is in his wheelchair, totally uncommunicative. Michael is in shock when he sees Jim. He tries to engage Jim, but Jim will not even make eye contact with Michael, let alone speak with him.

Jim is about to be discharged from Rusk, and my terror intensifies. I am nearly frozen with fear about how we'll manage with his disability. Peter and Dan have returned to Franklin & Marshall for their sophomore year, and Michael is living in his own apartment. I am on my own. I hire Simon, an aide we'd met at Lenox Hill, to come to help Jim during the days when I'm at work. Jim is very clear about how he wants Simon to operate. He does not want anyone hovering over him; he wants help only when he calls for it. One evening I come home from work and find Jim alone. I ask where Simon is, and Jim says, "I fired him. He hovered over me too much and tried to tell me what to do." This means more major panic for me. Jim and I talk, and he tells me he thinks that if I can help him shower, dress, and put on his leg and arm braces in the mornings before I leave for work, he'll be OK on his own, with our longtime housekeeper, Sylvia Spencer, there during the day until I return home. I am nearly beside myself with anxiety about his safety, but I finally agree to give it a try. I wonder if I'll ever be able to get back on an even keel. Will I ever be able to enjoy life again?

Jim and I have never fought in our lives. We disagree about things; we talk about things; and occasionally we have little outbursts, but we never have fights. Now he lashes out at me. And my instinctive reaction is to lash back. We get into awful shouting matches. I don't know what to do. I don't want to live like this; this is terrible. When I tell Dr. Strauss, the psychologist, about it, he says, "Just try leaving the room for a while." I do, and it works. It gives Jim time to settle down and pull himself together.

It really bothers and frustrates Jim when he needs help—getting into and out of a car, or his chair, any kind of help. I think it makes him feel like less of a person. That's profound. He can't do *what* he wants *when* he wants *how* he wants.

Before his stroke, he liked to go for a walk in the evening and smoke a cigar, but now he can't just pick up and go. If he wants to go to the park, someone has to take him to the park. He can't drive. He's always been a very successful crossword puzzle fanatic and he likes very difficult puzzles, the harder the better. He especially likes double acrostics because they are so challenging. He's always done his puzzles in ink and timed himself so he could show us all how quickly he's been able to solve them. When his right hand becomes paralyzed and he has to use his left hand, it becomes more difficult for him to do the puzzles because he can't read what he's written with his clumsy left hand.

Jim had always "aspired" to have a black leather chair, and when we finally got to the point that we could afford to, we bought one, together with a matching ottoman. He was thrilled. But when he becomes disabled he can't sit in his prized chair. He needs to have a different kind of chair that fits his body and on which he can push himself up when he is trying to stand.

One of Jim's doctors has told us it will take a year for his brain injury to heal. Jim ultimately gets through that first terrible year and begins to find some level of stability. The time finally comes when Jim can go downstairs in our apartment building and do his exercises. We have a very long lobby, and he diligently walks back and forth twenty laps in the lobby, limping each step of the way. He sometimes waits for me to come home from work, standing outside the building and chatting with the doorman. This is something he can do on his own. He becomes less overtly angry. He doesn't lash out. But he has to live a circumscribed, very strictly routinized life. And sadly, he never becomes fully independent again, never becomes the man he'd once been.

It's clear Jim cannot go back to work. He has a very limited attention span. He can't possibly make his way to his office and back and be there on his own and deal with the crowds of the city. He's simply not able do what he'd planned and needed to do to build Charles V. We agree that we need to close the business, a crushing decision that ends Jim's dream.

With Jim's stroke come two deaths: the death—or transformation—of Jim from a strong, vital, vibrant, energetic, fun-loving, sociable, and, most important, independent man into an uncertain and dependent person whose world becomes small and who for some time becomes uncommunicative and depressed and loses the sense of humor that has been so much a part of his identity.

The second profound death is the end of a life that I've loved and the end of my vision as to what my future with Jim will bring. My life, and our family's, will forevermore be divided into the time before Jim's stroke and the time after Jim's stroke. This is truly a life-changing transition.

After Jim's stroke, I am crazy for a year, as if I've been hit in the head, absolutely cuckoo. I'm a pretty controlling person, used to having problems and figuring out solutions. But this is an earth-shattering situation, and there is nothing I can do to change it or make it better. I've never been in a position like this in my life. It is just awful. I am in a state of suspended animation for quite a long time trying to figure out how to deal with the day-to-day, minute-to-minute responsibilities of caring for Jim, who can't be the man he was, no matter how hard he tries, no matter how much he wants to be.

During this time when I'm in my cuckoo-like trance, I actually buy the same car twice. When Michael was about to graduate from Wesleyan, shortly before Jim had his stroke, he'd told Jim and me about the cross-country car trip he wanted to take with a friend after graduation. He'd asked whether we would consider buying him a used car for the trip as a graduation gift. Jim and I talked it over. We'd agreed that we'd like to buy the car, a used Dodge Caravan, for Michael. Michael has never asked us for much, and we were happy to buy him such an important gift for such an important occasion. After Jim's stroke when Michael has returned from his trip, he's living in New York and has no real need for the car. He discusses this with Peter and Daniel, who have returned to Franklin & Marshall for their sophomore year. Peter and Dan call me one day and say, "Mom, we've talked with Michael, and we'd like to buy the Caravan from him. He doesn't really have any need for it now, and if we had it, we could drive home regularly to visit Jim.

What do you think?" I tell them I think this is a great win-win idea, and they say, "Well, Mom, we don't have the money to buy the car right now. Do you think you could loan us the money so we can pay Michael?" I say, "Yes," immediately, and they buy the car, paying Michael with the money I've loaned them (having a pretty clear idea it would never be paid back) for the car we'd bought Michael! As I slowly emerge from my stupor, many, many months later, it dawns on me what I've done. I've bought the same car twice. Amid all our trauma, I have to laugh.

For a long time, in my zombielike state, I try to avoid thinking about the monumental life changes I'm facing. I try to take one day, one hour at a time. Shortly after Jim's stroke, I have dinner with a friend. I tell her about what Dr. Yatrakis said to me, "Your life will never be the same." She asks me, "What are you going to do? Are you going to leave?" And I am shocked. I say, "Of course not. I have no choice." She says, "You always have a choice."

I'm devoted to Jim, but I come to understand that for us to go on I have to find a way to adjust completely to a new way of life and a new kind of relationship with a changed person. I'm determined to try to rebuild our lives and to help Jim rebuild as best he can his sense of self. From the very beginning we've been strong partners—in making our life decisions, in raising our sons, in loving one another totally and completely. But now I have to take the lead—managing our lives, our household, Jim's medical care, and our finances, including becoming our family's sole support, much as my mother had had to do when my father was no longer allowed by the Nazis to work. I've now become the person in charge rather than part of a partnership. It is a massive change. Fortunately, though, I feel competent to do what I have to do, and slowly I take over.

Clearly it's a vastly different world, not just for Jim but for me as well. Over time, Jim and I do find our way again. It's different from what it had been; it's a new kind of equilibrium. But as Dr. Strauss, the Rusk psychologist, had told me, I *do* smile again.

CHAPTER SEVENTEEN

Mad Woman Redux

As I try to come to grips with my life after Jim's stroke, I begin to recognize that I am Jim's caregiver-in-chief, and I grow to understand how deep and all-encompassing, even a little overwhelming, this role is. I am fully in charge of ensuring Jim's health, his safety, and his well-being. This responsibility is always at the forefront of my mind. Whatever decisions I make, whether it's having dinner with a friend, going on a business trip, or spending time with the boys, I think it through in the context of my caregiver role.

At the same time, I'm on the cusp of taking on a more prominent role at Grey and beyond in the business world. I'm very conscious of wanting to pursue my business opportunities, first because they're interesting and exciting, and I feel that with hard work I can have some success. But also I'm becoming increasingly aware that I need to build this part of my life to provide a balance with my caregiver role. I recognize that being Jim's caregiver could become all-consuming and even depressing if I let it.

And, of course, the boys continue to need nurture and TLC as they try to recover from the shock of Jim's stroke and become adults who begin to make life-defining decisions about careers, marriage, and family.

So there's a lot going on. I juggle mightily and am determined to concentrate my full energy on each part of my evolving life. I have very little time for anything other than my caregiving role, my work, and my time with the boys. I try to walk a few miles every day for exercise and I see friends for lunch from time to time, but that's about it during these early terrifying days. I focus on helping Jim to be safe and comfortable and to feel deeply loved. I want to achieve important and satisfying career goals. And I want the boys to feel secure and loved and supported by deepening family bonds.

I start and end my days helping Jim—helping him shower, dress, put on his arm and leg braces, walk into the kitchen for breakfast, and later doing the backward version to help him get ready for bed. Every single day, when I help Jim with his braces, it brings back memories of my dreaded job helping my grandmother with her ugly iron brace those many years ago. It's all very depressing. I buy and organize Jim's medicines, set up his medical appointments, and deal with his insurance claims. Our housekeeper, Sylvia, is at home with Jim every day. But generally, when I'm home, I'm at his beck and call, running to him as fast as I can when he shouts out my name, "Baaahhhbra." It is a sad and endless routine. I look forward to the times the boys come to visit Jim. They can always make him laugh; I love the sound of his laughter. We often have a glass of wine together on Friday evenings to welcome the weekend—a nice ritual in our "new normal" life.

At the same time, my challenges and responsibilities are increasing exponentially at work. I help lead the way in updating Grey's branding philosophy, moving from focusing on a product's benefits and attributes to focusing on the "who" of the brand, the intangible character traits that enable the brand to connect emotionally with the consumer. For Jif peanut butter, for example, we've always featured the brand's "peanuttier taste and smell," but we now go on to stress the emotional payoff: because of this Jif is the brand that "choosier mothers choose." My job entails crystallizing and articulating our "Brand Character" philosophy, educating our own people about it both in the US and around the world, designing and implementing new research tools and techniques to help develop Brand Character strategies, and leveraging this pioneering point of view in Grey's new business efforts. I write and speak about this to the business community outside of Grey as part of Grey's prospecting activities.

Because of my leadership role in developing and disseminating our Brand Character point of view, Ed Meyer expects me to be a key player in Grey's new business efforts. Although Ed is generally very businesslike, respectful, and charming in his dealings with me, I also know he can change on a dime and try to instill fear in me if that's what he thinks it will take to get me to do his bidding. There are certainly times of stress when dealing with Ed, especially in new business activities which are vitally important to him. Ed, who always seems to find me when I'm away from the office, calls me when I'm speaking at a conference in Tucson. I'm planning to spend a few days afterward at the Canyon Ranch spa. I've been looking forward to this brief respite for a long time. Ed says, "Barbara, you'll have to come back to New York immediately." I tell Ed I can't do that. I have long-standing reservations at a very expensive spa and have paid a significant deposit. He says, "You'll have to switch your reservation to their facility in the Berkshires. I've called them and they will make the switch. I need you to come back right away. We have an opportunity to pitch CoverGirl and you're essential to the pitch." I'm dumbfounded that Ed has taken it upon himself to call the Canyon Ranch spa and discuss switching my reservations. He's in intimidating mode. There is no room for discussion or disagreement. I change my plans and make my way back to New York. Procter & Gamble, Grey's most important client for whom we do advertising of many brands, has just acquired the CoverGirl cosmetics business. Ed is determined that we win the account, which will be massive and very visible. We kill ourselves, working nights and weekends, to put together a stunning presentation about how we see the consumer opportunity for building the CoverGirl brand, how we'd define CoverGirl's brand character, and how our creative work would be driven by the casually beautiful look and feel of the brand, expressed in the line, "Easy, breezy, beautiful CoverGirl." P&G's CoverGirl team is mesmerized as they hear our plan and see our creative ideas. After a short caucus at the conclusion of our presentation, they award Grey this highly coveted piece of business. This is a tremendous triumph for Grey and for our team. Ed is beside himself with excitement and satisfaction. And afterward, I do go to Canyon Ranch—in the Berkshires.

* * *

Multinational companies are beginning to explore the potential for developing global points of view for their brands—for efficiency and effectiveness, ideally expressed in global advertising, sometimes with a local touch. We are working with 3M on their Scotch Videotape brand. The 3M company is committed to developing a global advertising campaign for the brand, but the company's local marketers in various countries around the world are all fighting with one another about who has the best idea for advertising. Our key client contact at 3M is Don Rushin. Don is frustrated with all the fighting going on and unsure how to develop a common point of view that all the countries can buy into. I take the lead for our team, telling Don, "We definitely can help." We develop a piece of global strategic consumer research to explore the viability of all the ideas being considered. When the research is complete, we use the data to demonstrate to clients in all 3M countries the commonalities they share, which will form the strategic foundation for an advertising plan. This leads to the development of an award-winning global ad campaign for 3M: "The world watches Scotch," which is supported by extolling the sharp images and rich colors achieved with Scotch Videotape. Together with Don, our team travels around the world presenting the results of the research and the advertising strategy developed based on these results. We go to Copenhagen, Stockholm, Paris, Dusseldorf, London, and to Hong Kong, Tokyo, and Seoul, and slowly, based on our data, we build consensus. We're in Hong Kong on my birthday, and the 3M Hong Kong people surprise me with a fantastic birthday banquet, complete with singing, endless numbers of toasts, and many, many courses of delicious foods all served on an elegant lazy Susan table. I never in my wildest dreams imagined celebrating my birthday at a Chinese banquet in Hong Kong. Truly a celebration to remember. And, in Hong Kong, I find a beautiful green jade lion to bring home to Jim for his collection.

The 3M experience is an important success story not only for 3M but also for Grey. As the marketing world becomes more global, Grey's ambitions are to become an important player in this bigger, wider world. Working with 3M, we've expanded our tool kit. We now not only have offices around the world, but we have tools and techniques and a model to implement with other clients as they too want to go global. The world is beginning to take notice: *Fortune* magazine continues referring frequently to Grey as a "global powerhouse" in the advertising business.

When our team goes to Dusseldorf for 3M, and for many other client meetings I've attended in Dusseldorf, I've made it a rule never to stay overnight—I fly in early in the morning, fly out in the evening, and if necessary fly back the next morning. I've always had a deep antipathy, even a fear, of staying overnight and handing my passport over to the hotel registration people as is the custom in Germany. I've never tried to analyze my feelings, though I'm sure they're vestiges of my family's fear of and long-ago escape from the Nazis. I can imagine the terror on my mother's face when she had to hand over our documents for examination by the guards and soldiers at our many stops on the train as we escaped, and I don't want to relive that by handing over my own passport.

In 1987, I'd received a call from Bill Pike, Jim's HBS classmate and our good friend. Bill was vice chairman of Morgan Guaranty Trust and a longtime member of the board of directors of the VF Corporation, a company high up on the list of the Fortune 500. Bill wanted to explore my interest in becoming a corporate director of VF, the nation's leader in producing and selling jeans. Bill told me the board needed to move from being a production and sales company to becoming a marketing company, from being a domestic company to becoming a global company, and from being a jeans company to becoming a company with a portfolio of brands in a number of different categories. The board also wanted to bring a woman into its ranks. Bill knew of my Grey experience and thought I'd be well suited to fill the bill. He said that if I was interested he'd like to recommend me. I was thrilled with this opportunity. Since this directorship would be extracurricular to my work at Grey and would involve several days of commitment each year, my first step was to discuss it with Ed. He was very enthusiastic about my becoming a VF director. He thought it spoke well not only of me personally, but also of Grey. And so I became a director of a New York Stock Exchange company. It's well understood in the business world that a directorship on a NYSE company board is the pinnacle of business success. Directorships come with compensation—both cash and stock options. Although this is not why I join the VF board, the added compensation is, of course, welcome especially when I become our family's sole breadwinner. If only my mother and father were alive. They would be so thrilled and so proud.

The board's job is to hire, and if necessary fire, the CEO, to oversee the financial health of the company, and to counsel and advise on the company's strategic direction. It takes me a while to find my footing with the board. I learn very quickly that although VF's CEO is very friendly and polite, he definitely runs the show and does not expect anyone to question him. The company has its roots in the South, and many of the directors are southern men. They all enjoy their roast beef dinners and cigars, laughing and joking together after the board's business meetings. I'm the only woman and by far the youngest person at the table. They are not quite sure what to do with me. Eventually, as the company begins to get more and more serious about transitioning its mission to global marketing, my voice is heard, and I have some important things to say.

During the time after Jim's stroke, I am named chair of one of the most important committees of the VF board, the Nominating and Governance Committee, responsible for shaping the board and recruiting new directors. I feel quite certain the CEO has asked me to chair this committee because he thinks that as a woman I'm a weak link and will be a rubber stamp for all his decisions. I surprise him, not really happily, by taking a strong, professional lead in reshaping the board, recruiting directors from premier global consumer marketing companies like Procter & Gamble, General Mills, Darden Restaurants, and Yum! Brands, among others. Our committee has agreed that their combined experience will help enable VF to achieve its transition objectives. At one point the CEO calls me and Bill Pike, who was one of my committee chair predecessors, into his office and tells us he and another director have played golf with the head of an elevator company and approached him about joining the board. I am very surprised. I remind the CEO that we have a process. The Nominating Committee needs to meet and vet any candidates, needs to ensure they support our criteria which at this point include global marketing experience, and then needs to present them to the board for election. I say we really cannot support his plan, and Bill Pike echoes my point of view. The CEO is furious. As he nears retirement, he never really gets over the fact that a "weak girl" has stood up to him.

During my time on the VF board I'm in Hawaii on a short stopover from a 3M trip to China. Jim had never wanted to go to Hawaii. He thinks it's too long a trip from New York, and if we wanted an island vacation, we could go to the Caribbean. So I take advantage of my trip and decide to spend a few days enjoying Hawaii. Once again, Ed finds me. He calls and asks, "What are you doing in Hawaii?" I tell him, "I'm on my way home from a 3M trip to Asia, Ed. I'll be back in a couple of days." He says, "No, no, no, no. We have an opportunity to pitch the VF intimate apparel business and you're on the VF board. I want you to be sure that business is assigned to us." Ed is adamant: "I need to get that account into Grey." I say, "Ed, I can't do that. That's such a conflict of interest. I absolutely cannot do that." Ed says, angrily, "I want you to understand, Barbara, where your loyalties have to lie. You are a senior executive of Grey and your first loyalty needs to be to Grey." I tell him, "Ed, I am fiercely loyal to Grey. I've been loyal to Grey for years and years. My first loyalty is to Grey. So if I have to resign from the board of VF in connection with this, I will do that. But I cannot do what you're asking me." Our phone call is nerve-wracking. I stay in Hawaii for a couple more days wondering what will happen when I return, but by the time I get back Ed has gone onto something else. It's very unusual, almost unheard of, for any of Ed's executive team to say no to him. While my stance angers him, I think he also respects me for it.

In this same period, I'm named chairwoman of the Advertising Research Foundation (ARF), an industry association comprised of hundreds of representatives from advertising agencies, corporations, research suppliers, and media companies. The ARF was founded in 1936 to share knowledge about advertising and media effectiveness. I'm just the second woman in its history to become chair. This is a big and important industry job, also extracurricular to my work at Grey; I'm honored and excited to take it on. Again, Ed is very supportive; again he believes this is important not just for me but for Grey as well.

The ARF has a huge conference every year, with luncheons on successive days in the New York Hilton ballroom, the largest in New York. Hundreds and hundreds crowd in to hear the featured speakers. One of my jobs as chair is to recruit the speakers and introduce them to the audiences. I go to my friend and Grey colleague, Alec Gerster, the head of our media operation, to strategize about whom we can persuade to speak. We need two real draws to build attendance at our conference. I'm very excited when Alec tells me he's wrangled two fantastic personalities for me: Katharine Graham, who has just taken over leadership of the *Washington Post*, and Peter Jennings, the very attractive and popular anchor of ABC's evening news program, the most watched on television. When I meet Katharine Graham on the first day, I see she's not at all happy to be speaking. I try to engage her in conversation to make her feel more at ease, but she's nervous and a bit cold and unfriendly. She does a great job, however, and wows our audience. The next day, a Wednesday, those being seated on the dais for lunch gather in the anteroom to line up. There's no Peter Jennings. I go into mini-panic mode, trying to think of what I'll do if he's a no-show, when he comes running into the room, red-faced and sweating. It's the day after the Super Tuesday elections, and Peter has dashed in directly from the airport. We sit next to one another on the dais; Peter looks extremely uncomfortable, actually a little sick. He's not eating a thing. I ask him if he's OK, and he says, "No. Look at all these people. What am I going to do?" I begin to realize he's both frightened and unprepared, not a good combination. I say, "Peter, you're going to be fine. You speak to millions of people every night." He says, "No, I don't. I speak only to the camera. What am I going to talk about?" I say, "Peter, just talk for a few minutes about the reporting you did last night for Super Tuesday, and then we'll move to a Q&A." He says, "What if no one asks me anything?" I really can't believe I'm having this conversation with the great icon, Peter Jennings. I tell him, "I'm sure plenty of people will have questions for you, and if need be I can get things started." When he finally gets going, Peter is a great hit with the crowd. They're fascinated with what he has to say about the elections. He wraps up, I thank him profusely, he breathes a huge sigh of happy relief, and I finally exhale.

Back at Grey, starting in the late 1980s and into the '90s, I spearhead a series of studies geared toward understanding consumer social megatrends. Our sense is that knowing the consumer zeitgeist is becoming more and more important to our clients as a backdrop for their advertising. We do a major study identifying America's UltraConsumer, who values the finer things and experiences in life: everything from imported chocolates and fragrances to high-end designer goods to adventure travel. For the UltraConsumer, we learn that enough is never enough.

We publish our work in a revamped version of Grey's longtime newsletter, *Grey Matter*. Our clients are excited that we're continuing to plow new ground in consumer learning, and this work becomes another important door opener in Grey's new business prospecting work.

More broadly, this study strikes a nerve. It generates enormous amounts of publicity. I'm interviewed by the *Wall Street Journal*, the *New York Times*, *Fortune*, and *Time* magazine, all of whom are intrigued by the UltraConsumer. I'm invited to my first television appearance on *Good Morning America*, the nation's most highly rated morning show, cohosted by Joan Lunden and Charlie Gibson. Grey brings in a consultant to give me some media training; she teaches me how to "bridge," or pivot from the question being asked to the point I want to make, a very helpful piece of learning. At *GMA* Joan is friendly, but Charlie, who comes across as jolly and avuncular on television, starts giving me a very hard time. He disparages the research, suggesting it's not really believable. I'm taken aback, astonished, that Charlie would try to sabotage me on his show. But I try to stay cool—and not to let on to Charlie that he's unnerved me. I bridge, as I've been taught by the media trainers, to the points I want to make, calmly but forcefully reporting the facts we learned from the American public and showing the data that prove my points. This has been another powerful learning experience for me. Although I didn't fully realize or appreciate it during the course of my training session, the trainers have taught me how to take control of a situation and how to stay in control of it. But afterward I do wonder if this has been just one more example of sexist behavior by a powerful man.

All the publicity about the UltraConsumer reinforces the reputation I've begun to establish as a "nationally recognized authority" on the mores and societal norms of the American people. Ed, of course, is thrilled, as this helps to further build Grey's reputation as the expert on consumers. And my son, Michael, laughs. He thinks it's ironic that a little refugee girl who spoke only German and who grew up in a peculiar little refugee family in Chehalis is now recognized as an authority on the American consumer.

Shortly after Jim Collins's bestseller, *Good to Great*, is published extolling Circuit City Stores as one of the nation's most amazing business success stories, I get a call from Alan Wurtzel, the company's longtime chairman and CEO. Circuit City, a New York Stock Exchange company, is a national retail electronics chain. Circuit City was the first to introduce no-haggle pricing for electronics, a breakthrough innovation in its day, conceptualized and spearheaded by Alan. The company is headquartered in Richmond, Virginia.

Alan asks if I can get together with him to talk about potentially becoming a Circuit City board member. He says I've been highly recommended by Catalyst, the national nonprofit advocacy organization focused on enhancing the role of women in business, on whose board of advisers I sit. I tell Alan I'm intrigued and that I'd like to think it over for a day or two and then get back to him. I'm very excited about this opportunity and rush home to talk it over with Jim. Jim is excited too, and encourages me to go forward. We talk about the fact that travel to Richmond, Virginia, will be involved, and he says, "Don't worry; we'll figure it out." And because this assignment too would be extracurricular to my work at Grey, I talk to Ed Meyer, who's thrilled about the opportunity for me. He definitely thinks my association with Circuit City would be good for Grey. I call Alan, and we arrange to meet at the very elegant Cosmos Club in Washington, DC. Alan and I have a good rapport; he's easy to talk with and makes me feel comfortable. He tells me about the history of Circuit City, which his father had founded, and how he views the company's threats and opportunities. Circuit City is at a challenging crossroads. For many years, the company had been thriving without much competition. But Best Buy has stormed into the electronics market with much more attractive real estate locations than Circuit City's, and Amazon is becoming a major factor in the competitive landscape. Circuit City is being squeezed and needs to determine a strategic path forward to survive and thrive. Alan grills me closely about my own background and experiences. At the end of our lunch, Alan tells me he'd like to recommend that I be elected a director, and I enthusiastically agree.

I go to my first board meeting in Richmond, not quite sure what to expect, once again the only woman in the room. Whenever I try to speak, the men on the board simply talk over me and don't pay any attention to what I have to say. I quickly begin to raise my voice louder than its usual pitch, and keep at it until I'm heard. The Circuit City staff who support the board are not used to working with a woman director. When we take a break mid-meeting, I ask the receptionist outside the boardroom to direct me to the restroom. She points down the hall; I follow her direction. I open the door to the restroom and to my horror, there's the chairman of the board sitting on the toilet, trousers puddled around his ankles. What a mortifying way to launch my tenure as a Circuit City director. It takes a while, but Alan and I are finally able to make eye contact again.

My whirlwind life continues. While I'm hard at work, making my way up the executive management ladder at Grey, things have stabilized at home and settled into a routine. Jim has rebuilt some of his strength and stamina. Even though he's still paralyzed on his right side, he's mobile and continues to walk back and forth for twenty laps of the block-long lobby in our building every day. His sense of humor is back, thank goodness. It's such a vital part of who he is and what I love about him.

One day when I get home from work and go into our TV room to greet Jim, he very excitedly says, "Look at this!" He hands me a brochure from the Cornell Alumni Association describing a trip they're sponsoring on the rivers of Russia. I'm in a state of stunned disbelief when Jim says, "Barbara, I think we should do this." I say, "Wow! That sounds great! But are you up for it? Do you think you can do it?" We have done no traveling together at all since Jim's stroke. This is a very ambitious trip; it would be a major undertaking for Jim. Jim very enthusiastically says, "Yes, I'm ready. Let's do it!"

I am thrilled that Jim, in his disabled state, wants to do the trip. This is a major milestone for him, both physically and psychologically. At the same time, in my caregiver-in-chief role, I'm a little unsettled about how we're going to accomplish it, but I resolve to do everything in my power to help make this adventure a success for Jim. I'm relieved the trip is a river tour. We'll be mainly on a riverboat, but will take several short land excursions as well. Among the many other things Jim knows about, he's been an avid student of Russian history. He's deeply knowledgeable and intrigued about all things Russian. Maybe his interest in Russia is a function of his family's roots there. He's determined he'll master whatever it takes to go on this trip. I can't wait for Jim to experience in person all that he's read and studied about over the years.

And so we're off—first stop Paris. I've arranged for a car and driver to meet us at Charles de Gaulle airport and drive us to our hotel. I wrangle our luggage, driving the cart with one hand and taking Jim's arm with the other to help him keep his balance as we lumber through the airport, find our driver, and go to the car. My heart sinks when I see it's an immense SUV with a very high step. I know there's no way Jim will be able to climb into that car. I try to explain the situation to the driver, but he speaks no English and I speak no French. I resort to pantomiming to him what the problem is. He finally nods that he understands. He gets down on one knee, puts his hands together stirrup fashion, and motions Jim to climb into the stirrup and into the car. Jim is a big man; the driver is a very slight little fellow. It's clear there's no way this will work. It will only lead to disaster. I have a nightmare worry that if he tries this, Jim will fall and break some bones. The driver eventually understands that we need another plan. He runs off and returns with a box Jim is able to use as a step stool. Together, the driver and I are able to boost Jim into the SUV. A stressful way to start our adventure, but we make it.

We arrive at our very elegant hotel, the Bristol, in the middle of Paris. Jim has always believed that vacations should be nicer than home, so we celebrate with a luxurious supper in our room: scrambled eggs with truffles, smoked salmon, wine, and delectable French pastries.

Our next stop is Moscow, which couldn't be more different from Paris. Moscow is very gray and dreary looking, and its people are as well. The fall of Communism and dissolution of the Soviet Union have taken place recently. I'd expected the Russian people to be happy to be free, but they seem very much as my father had found them on our escape journey—grim and passive; they don't seem to know what to do without being told. Our living quarters are on our boat, which is moored in the Volga River. Although I'd been to the Volga before, when I was two-and-a-half and in Moscow with my parents, I have no recollection of it at all. The boat is rather primitive. When we go to our cabin, I check out the bathroom and am startled to see there is no shower. We call for help, and the Russian steward shows us that we have to attach a frayed-looking, faded, rust-colored hose to the faucet in the bathroom sink and spray ourselves while we stand over a drain, a hole in the middle of the floor. Quite an unnerving experience for Jim, whose balance is on the shaky side, and for me, responsible for making sure he doesn't fall over.

We spend a few unforgettable days in Moscow, touring the Kremlin, Red Square, and the Pushkin Museum, where we see glorious Impressionist art. It all seems like a breathtaking fairy tale, actually being among the buildings until now we've seen only in pictures—onion domes in a riot of colors and patterns: red, green, blue, yellow, and white stripes, zigzags, squiggles. Jim is very, very slow as we go on our walking tours. We always bring up the rear, but we trudge on, determined to take everything in. Despite the challenge, Jim is very happy to be here. He's excited to be experiencing the history that until now he's only studied.

We leave Moscow on our boat, traveling first on the Volga, then through several sets of locks onto the Neva, passing very ancient and primitive-looking villages en route, and eventually arriving in St.

Petersburg, which is nothing at all like Moscow. It's very European in appearance, a bit like a run-down version of Venice, with many canals, some of which we tour. The city is preparing for a major anniversary celebration. As we tour, we pass what appear to be very elegant, freshly painted mansions, like beautiful palazzos in Venice. But as our boat turns the corners we see that the backs of these mansions are dilapidated and falling apart.

On our last night in St. Petersburg, we are invited to go to a dinner and ballet performance at a beautiful and historically significant palace. Jim is excited, because this is the same palace in which Rasputin had been rolled up in a rug and thrown out the window from the second floor into the river below. Jim is determined to see the exact window where this took place. The problem is that we are on the first floor, and the only way to get to the second floor is on a very narrow spiral staircase. I say, "Jim, you cannot do this. You cannot go up this tiny little spiral staircase. It's too dangerous." He is adamant: "I am going up," he states, essentially telling me to back off. I'm terrified, thinking, *If he does make it up to the second floor, how in the world will I get him back down?* So, Jim starts up the stairs, dragging his paralyzed leg step by step. The others in our group are aghast. After he's gone a few steps up the staircase, he realizes that this is not going to work, and he makes his way back down. He's crushed, because he's been so intent on seeing this spot that he's read so much about over the years. I'm very sad, but at the same time much relieved.

All in all, our trip is a huge success. It's the first time Jim has felt he really could venture forth as his new self. I'm thrilled for him, and really for both of us.

While all this is going on, important things are happening on the home front. After graduating from Franklin & Marshall, Peter begins his career with a job in corporate sales at Six Flags Great Adventure theme park. Peter is assigned the Northeast Corridor, from Boston to Washington, DC. He gets no training at all; it's as if he's thrown into the deep end of the ocean. He's expected to jump in and figure things out for himself. I give him what I think is one important piece

Daniel, Michael, and Peter at Daniel and Peter's graduation from Franklin & Marshall College, 1992

of advice: "Fish where the fish are." I tell him to target big clients with big budgets. Small ones will take just as much time and energy to cultivate as the big ones, and the payoff will be much less. Jim is able to travel with Peter on some of his selling trips. Peter learns an enormous amount from Jim in their conversations in the car, and Jim absolutely loves spending this time with Peter and mentoring him in this early part of his career. I'm sure this must make Jim feel good; he's being helpful to Peter in a vitally important way.

Eventually, Six Flags, with Peter deeply involved, starts a search for an advertising agency, and Grey is on their list of contenders for the business. I stay completely out of this solicitation, not wanting to get near a conflict of interest situation. Grey works very hard to figure out the strategy for the Six Flags brand and traffic-building efforts and develops an exciting advertising campaign to do the job. Once the competition ends, Grey is awarded the account. I'm both thrilled and amused; Peter is a client of my agency, and my mentee, Doreen Massin, works on his account. Small world.

Daniel is elated to have landed exactly where he's wanted to be since he was in elementary school. He's a coach and an English teacher at his and his brothers' alma mater, Trevor Day School. I think Dan is the kind of teacher I always hoped my boys would have; he seems to have a real calling. He focuses with laser sharpness on his students' welfare, getting to know and understand each one as an individual, helping them all to learn, and, most important of all, working to build their confidence. Seeing Dan in action fills me with pride.

Michael works in various aspects of theater, his great love since he was a child. He does some acting, very far off-Broadway, and works behind the scenes in theater production as much as he can. Trying to make a life in theater is a very precarious proposition. Luck plays a big role in finding steady work. To earn money between theater gigs, Michael works as a personal trainer. He develops an excellent reputation, becomes well known in the field, and builds a significant clientele.

On September 22, 1995, Michael marries Lawson Harris, a fellow actor he met in acting class. They have a beautiful wedding at a spectacular spot, the Loeb Boathouse in Central Park, alongside a gorgeous lake. As Jim and I watch the ceremony and reception unfold, we wish together for all that's good in life for our firstborn son. And something wonderful happens on February 23, 1997. Erica, Michael and Lawson's beautiful daughter, is born. We are captivated by Erica, our first grandchild, and overjoyed to welcome her into the world. The next generation begins.

CHAPTER EIGHTEEN

The Ties That Bind

Even as we weather tumultuous times with Jim's precarious health situation and my dramatically changing professional life, wonderful things are happening with our family.

After they both graduate from college, Peter reconnects with Natalia Mendez, a high school classmate, at their friend Paul Asencio's wedding. They hadn't dated in high school, but Natalia had had a big crush on Peter. She'd even drawn a big pink heart around his picture in the Packer yearbook. Peter spies Natalia at Paul's wedding and switches place cards so he and Natalia will be seated together at the reception. The rest is history. They're together from that moment on and are married on July 30, 1999. Jim and I have known Natalia for years, since high school, and we're delighted that Peter and she are married. It's a happy, happy time. And the happy times continue. Peter and Natalia have a daughter, Alexandra, on February 27, 2001, and their son, Thomas, is born on April 19, 2003.

One afternoon in the fall of 2000 our phone rings. It's Stephanie Verhoeff, Daniel's longtime love, who asks, "May I come over?" I say, "Sure, when would you like to come?" She says, "Right now. I'm on the bus a couple of blocks from your building." Dan and Stephanie were introduced by a mutual friend some years ago and have been together for quite a long time. Dan has been eager to marry Stephanie, but until

Peter and Natalia's wedding, July 29, 1999

now Stephanie hasn't felt ready. I say to Jim, "I hope she's not coming over to tell us she's breaking up with Dan." The doorbell rings. It's Stephanie with her arms full of flowers. She seems to be hyperventilating, and when I take the flowers, she shakes her arms up and down. I tell her I'll put the flowers in the kitchen and will meet her in the TV room where Jim is waiting. When I get there, Stephanie is having trouble catching her breath. I can't imagine what she's going to say. Finally, she gulps and says, "I want to ask Dan to marry me." I'm ecstatic and say, "That's wonderful. What does Dan say?" Steph says, "I haven't asked him yet; I came here today to ask your permission first. I plan to get him a Carvel cake inscribed with the question 'Will you marry me?'" Jim and I are thrilled and delighted. We've wanted this for Dan

Daniel and Stephanie's wedding, March 24, 2002

for a long time; we think they're a perfect couple. Daniel and Stephanie are married at the Boathouse in Central Park on March 24, 2001. Their son, Jackson, is born on July 22, 2003, and Dylan, their daughter, comes along a little later, on September 4, 2007.

Elle, Michael and Lawson's second daughter, is born on April 28, 2002.

Jim and I love having all these grandchildren. We are very lucky they live nearby; we see them often. I'm happy they're able to spend time with Jim. When they're with him, they always make him laugh—his hearty wonderful laugh. As the kids get older, they try to imitate Jim's laugh, "ho . . . ho . . . ho . . ." And they love playing with Jim's lion collection, the one I've assembled for him over the years on all my travels. In addition to the jade lion I brought him from Hong Kong, there's now a steel one from Venice, a crystal one from the Czech Republic, a carved wooden one from China, a brass one from East Hampton, a soapstone one from India, and many others, including a couple Erica has given him for Christmas. He keeps the collection on our desk. Whenever they arrive, the kids make a beeline for the lions and sit for hours, making lion families, lion parades, lion circus performances, and on and on.

As I learned from my mother, rituals are important in building strong family bonds. We continue to have epic Thanksgiving dinners with exactly the same menu every year. One year I decide to surprise everyone with homemade cranberry sauce. This is a big mistake. There is a hue and cry from all our sons: "Mom, what's wrong with the cranberry sauce? There are no rings around it." They miss the indentations from the can.

Christmas continues to be a huge event every year. We have a Christmas brunch around noon, and again the exact same menu every year. This is followed by the opening of what seems like a million gifts spread under the tree. These times are very loud and boisterous, and very much fun.

Because my alpha-male sons all have such strong, almost overpowering personalities, they tend to suck all the air out of the room when the family gets together. I decide that for me to get to really know their wives, and for their wives to get to know one another, I will start a ritual of taking them all out to dinner once a month at an elegant New York City restaurant. I'm not sure how, or even if, this is going to work.

Jim with his boys—Daniel, Michael, and Peter—at Key Biscayne, 2006

For our first dinner, I have an icebreaker question ready: "What's the most important decision you ever made?" This is a magical conversation starter. Everyone tells her story; we're all absorbed as we listen to one another. At one point, as the conversation goes on, I look up to see the waitstaff sweeping the floor and piling chairs on top of tables. We're actually closing the restaurant. This is the first of many, many more dinners. Our bond is strengthening.

Every Christmas I give each of our grandchildren "an experience of your choice with G'ma." When Dylan is around seven, she is mesmerized by cosmetics and how to apply makeup. She spends a lot of her free time watching makeup tutorials on her computer. For her experience, she wants to go for lunch to Alice's Tea Cup—Alice in Wonderland themed—and then shopping at Ulta, the cosmetics store that to Dylan is a true wonderland. We wander through all the aisles of this huge store. She knows she's too young for these cosmetics, but she's fascinated by seeing them all. When she's finished looking around, I tell her we can buy one thing for her, a neutral toned lip gloss. She's thrilled. Next stop: manicures for us both. The next day I receive a letter from Dylan: "Dear Grandma, Thank you so much for the perfect day. It was the best day of my entire life. Love, Dylan." Our bond, too, is strengthening.

Another Christmas when Alexandra is around eight, she flips the experience gift on me. She gives me a hand-drawn and colored card picturing a store window with the name "Claire's" on the awning. I ask Alex to tell me about the picture, and she says, "Grandma, I'm going to take you to have your ears pierced." I'm a little taken aback; I say, "I don't think I can do that. I'm afraid to have holes put in my body." Alex says, "Don't worry, Grandma. I'll come to pick you up in a cab and take you to Claire's, and I'll hold your hand while the lady pierces your ears." And that's what we do. My eight-year-old granddaughter brings me into the modern world of pierced ears.

One of our important family traditions continues to be taking everyone to a beach resort for a family getaway every year. We think it's a wonderful way for the family, including all the cousins, to bond, relax, and have fun. High on our list of favorite places is the Ritz-Carlton at Key Biscayne in Florida. It's very family oriented, and, importantly, a place we can navigate with Jim in his wheelchair. By now Peter is working for Marquis Jet, the private aviation company. He's very excited because he's able to get access to a private jet to take us to Florida and back. This is terrific—no need to slog through the airport with Jim. We fail to think about how Jim is actually going to get into the plane.

There is no Jetway, just a small flight of very steep and narrow stairs. *Oh my god,* I wonder, *what are we going to do?* There's no way Jim can make it up those stairs. Natalia, Peter's wife, says, "Barbara, you have to go into the restroom and you can't come out until I come to get you. Because your sons are going to carry Jim into the plane." I don't even want to think about this, and I certainly don't want to watch it. Jim is a big guy, and Michael, Peter, and Daniel are going to lift him and carry him into the plane. It's too ghastly to contemplate . . . really terrifying. But they do it. And we get there and go through the same thing again going home. This is just one example of how our sons do anything and everything to support Jim and to ensure that our family traditions can continue.

Jim is very happy for our family to have this special time together in such a beautiful place. Key Biscayne is idyllic for us: great beaches, wonderful pools, tennis, rolling grass so the kids can play, and outdoor movie nights, all such a far cry from my early days as part of a refugee family in Chehalis with very little money and few to no indulgences. Our granddaughter Erica's favorite time of day at Key Biscayne is midafternoon when she joins us in our room while Jim is resting. Jim

Me with Jim and grandchildren, Key Biscayne, 2007

Jim's 75th birthday, August 8, 2009

orders her a big bowl of ice cream. The room service waiter comes and serves it to her as she sits cross-legged in the middle of the bed. She devours the ice cream with a huge smile on her face. She loves being the firstborn grandchild in the family and treasures the special attention she gets from Jim.

I always try to arrange to have family pictures taken when we're on a Family Fling trip. We all wear matching tee shirts. After much complaining about this, the fun begins as the photographer tries to wrangle all fourteen of us. Jim quickly loses patience, followed by his sons and grandsons. The scene gets a little wild and woolly; the photographer begins to sweat a bit, but I'm determined to finish the photo shoot as planned. We finally get all the shots we want. The following Christmas, every family receives a photo album to remind them of a perfect family time together.

When Jim was a boy, I don't think his family paid much attention to his birthday. Since we've been married, I've always made a big fuss over him on his special day. I wake him up by singing "Happy Birthday." He gets gifts and cards and keeps track of his phone calls.

He loves his birthday. When Jim is seventy-five, on August 8, 2009, our sons and I decide to have a blowout surprise celebration for him. We take over the dining room of Primavera, his favorite, very elegant Italian restaurant and plan a delectable meal with wonderful wines. We invite our extended family and friends from every chapter of Jim's life: his boyhood friends, college friends, Army friends, friends from HBS, and the friends he's made throughout his business career. They live in all corners of the country. And to our shock and delight nearly all of them come. Our sons have made a video of the highlights of Jim's life, which everyone enjoys seeing and reminiscing about. When everyone is gathered, Peter wheels Jim into the dining room in his wheelchair. Jim is flabbergasted—totally surprised and overcome with emotion. It's a truly joyous moment. We enjoy our dinner, and then there are many toasts and speeches, some very touching and some hilariously funny. Dan's toast is last. He says, "The best thing I'd like to say about Jim is that he taught us all how to be good fathers." I think to myself, *This is as good as it gets. What more could a father ever ask?*

CHAPTER NINETEEN

Turning Points

February 1, 1999, is the day I retire from Grey. It's been thirty years since I began my exciting and richly satisfying Grey career in the tiny office next to the broom closet. I've loved my time at Grey. I'm proud of my role in building Grey's competitive edge with tools and techniques to understand the consumer more deeply than our competitors are able to, and in turn building Grey's business to previously unimagined heights. It's been an exhilarating and rewarding run.

Yet, over time, it's become clear to me that Ed Meyer is starting to feel that Grey's approach, of which I've been a major part, has begun to be passé. Grey for years has been ahead of the pack, and now the pack has begun to catch up. Advertising has always been a business of young people, and I'm now sixty-two years old. Although Ed has never explicitly talked to me about this, I think he feels the need for a new direction with fresh thinking and a more youthful sensibility. As I begin to understand and internalize what's happening, I decide the time has come for me to move on. I'm overwhelmed with a swirl of emotions—great pride in what I've accomplished, sorrow to be severing such a vital part of my identity, and vulnerability in that I have no idea what might come next for me. I arrange a six-month consultancy with Grey to help me come to grips with my transition, and Grey continues to provide me with office space.

Me with Ed Meyer at my Grey retirement dinner, 1999

Ed hosts an elegant retirement dinner for me with my closest colleagues and friends in a private dining room at the Park Avenue Café, one of my favorite restaurants. The room looks beautiful, with gorgeous flowers, candles, silver, and china. It's all deeply affecting; I'm seeing a significant part of my life pass before my eyes. There are many toasts and speeches, with much laughter and a few tears. When it's my turn, I thank these friends with whom I've worked so closely, including many nights and weekends, and with whom I've struggled and laughed over the years. I tell them how much their friendship and our work together have meant to me, and I wish them all great success in the future. Ed concludes the festivities by presenting me with a pair of dazzling diamond and gold anemone-shaped earrings. Their beauty leaves me breathless.

Sometime later I'm going up in the elevator to the office I still have at Grey. The elevator is completely full. A young man turns around, looks closely at me, and says, "Hey . . . didn't you used to be someone?" I burst out laughing, as does the entire elevator full of people. How quickly they forget.

I'm spending a day or two a week at Grey in my consulting capacity and continue to work on the VF and Circuit City boards. But for the first time since I was ten and working in the strawberry patch, I have time available to focus on things that interest me other than work. I know for sure I want to spend more time with Jim. We plan a riverboat trip up the Rhine to celebrate my retirement.

We start in Istanbul, exotic, chaotic, magical—unlike any place I've ever been. One of the women who'd worked with me at Grey is Turkish, and her father and family have a rug business in Istanbul. She arranges an introduction for Jim and me and an appointment for us to visit their showroom. We've decided we'd like to buy each of our sons a Turkish rug which we'll give them for Christmas. I am armed with measurements for each one's apartment, and Jim and I are off to the rug merchant. Things start very slowly, with some friendly conversation and a rather formal tea service. Then the fun begins. We're shown a dizzying array of rugs, each one more ravishing than the next. As the afternoon passes on, we choose an exquisite rug for each of our sons and arrange to have them all shipped to New York. As we're preparing to leave, my colleague's father says, "But you haven't picked out anything for yourselves." I look at Jim and he looks at me, and we agree we'll take a look, although this would be an extravagance we hadn't planned on. After seeing several rugs, my colleague's father says, "I have just one more you need to see." He shows us a gorgeous small prayer rug in beautiful jewel tones of dark reds, greens, blues, and cream. I gasp, and Jim says, "We'll take it." I'm deeply touched that Jim knew instinctively how much I loved this beautiful rug. We'll have a magnificent treasure from this fascinating trip.

* * *

I'm enjoying this relatively relaxed time, though I do have a little underlying anxiety about what I will do next. I haven't yet figured this out. Meantime though, I've taken up yoga, spent much more time investing in my relationships with my women friends, and enjoyed the cultural wonders of New York—theater, ballet, concerts, museums—that I've never had time for before.

In December, during the week between Christmas and New Year's, I go to an afternoon movie, another luxury I've never before had time for. When I get home, I go in to talk with Jim. He doesn't sound right to me; he seems to be slurring his words. I think, shocked, *This cannot be happening again. He can't be having another stroke.* I get Peter on the phone and ask him to talk with Jim so he can tell me what he thinks. He says, "Mom, he's definitely slurring his words. He's having a stroke. Get him to the hospital immediately. Michael, Dan, and I will meet you there." I'm heartsick, terrified, and incredulous that this horrific nightmare is repeating itself. Only this time, it's even worse than before. The stroke is in exactly the same part of his brain as the earlier one was. All the physical manifestations he had from his first stroke are exacerbated. He's even more paralyzed on his right side, and his balance is severely affected.

We know what we have to do. We have to get Jim into Rusk again for rehab, which is easier this time because he has a doctor there and has been there before. Jim spends several weeks at Rusk, and I feel like I'm back on my hamster wheel, rushing there for lunch, and then to my office, and then back again for dinner and to say good night. This brings back all my feelings of sadness and loss from before. Our sons are very supportive, but in many ways I feel alone.

It's clear when Jim gets home from rehab that he'll need help with everything. For the previous ten years, he's been able to go downstairs and go walking on his own. He hasn't been able to go very far, but he's at least been able to do that. He's needed help before for showering and dressing, but now he needs help for standing up, sitting down, walking—everything. This situation essentially robs him of the last bit of independence he's had. It's a huge jolt to the psyche—both Jim's and mine.

While he's in Rusk, Jim becomes friendly with Lorna Evans, one of the aides who works with him. Lorna tells Jim that if he needs help when he gets home, she'd like him to consider her for that position. Lorna comes to work with us. She puts together a team of her colleagues and friends from Rusk and together they work out a schedule that gives us 24/7 coverage. Lorna is Jamaican, and every Monday morning when she arrives, she brings her groceries, including her goat meat. She likes to prepare her Jamaican goat dishes for herself and her crew.

Both Jim and I feel confident with our caregivers. They've been very well trained at Rusk and clearly know how to work with Jim and his limitations. Jim and I are both devastated with this latest ghastly event, but from our past experience we know we'll be able to figure out yet another "new normal."

We settle into our somewhat hectic new life at home with Lorna and her team and our longtime housekeeper, Sylvia Spencer. We're all buzzing around the house, focusing anxiously on caring for Jim and keeping him safe. As the routine solidifies, I realize I need to find a new opportunity outside of home in which I can invest myself and make a difference. I know I don't want to do the same thing I've been doing for the past thirty years. I need a new challenge, a chance to learn new things and to work with smart people whom I respect. What will this be? I have lunch one day with Jon Lynch, a friend of Peter and Dan's who is a partner at Chase Capital Partners, later to become JPMorgan Partners, the private equity arm of JPMorgan. Jon tells me about their portfolio of companies, which includes a number in the consumer marketing business. Jon says he and his partners don't really know too much about consumer marketing. He asks, "Why don't you consider joining us as a senior adviser and representing us on the boards of some of those companies?" I think this sounds perfect; it will be new and interesting, and I'll have something of value to bring to the table.

I sit on the boards of three of their portfolio companies, including Vitamin Shoppe. As is always the case, the work I'm able to do is as good as what the client allows me to do. Vitamin Shoppe is very open to learning about and using marketing communications strategically to build its business. I think I make a very positive difference in helping to energize their brand, build traffic at their stores and their website, and boost their revenue. I learn that serving on the boards of private companies is very different from working on public boards. It involves playing much more of an operating role and making introductions to those who can bring needed expertise to the company.

I work with JPMorgan Partners until the market crash of 2008, at which point they decide they no longer can justify having any senior advisers. Once again, I float off into the ether, wondering, what am I going to do next? I'm flummoxed as I try to figure out a path forward. I love working with boards. I love working with smart people on challenging issues for companies I respect. As chair of VF's Nominating and Governance Committee, I'd instituted a very effective comprehensive board self-evaluation process focused on assessing the board's past performance and providing guideposts for future action. Maybe this is a business idea; maybe I can start a boutique board consultancy specializing in this kind of work. I have no idea whether this idea would take hold in the marketplace.

I talk with Jim about it. Always optimistic and practical, he says, "Give it a try. It's an experiment. If it works, fine, and if it doesn't, you will have tried it." This is some of the best advice I've ever received.

I start my boutique consultancy, Feigin Associates, LLC. My associates are Jim and my sons. By now, Peter is president of Marquis Jet. He assembles a small team of his marketing people who moonlight to help me put together my marketing and branding materials, all of which are strong, motivating, and look very elegant and professional. But I don't get very far. No matter how hard I try, my selling efforts gain no real traction—no significant response. This is very disappointing; it's nearly a total bust. I've enjoyed putting my business plan and materials together, and I continue to do occasional strategic marketing projects, but all in all this has been an experiment that hasn't worked.

While this part of my business life is faltering, I get a call from Dawn Lesh, a former client at Bank of America. Dawn tells me I've been selected for the Market Research Council Hall of Fame, joining the prestigious icons of the profession whom I've long admired and who have inspired me for all my career. The luncheon at which I'm installed is an opportunity for me in my acceptance remarks to thank some of the people who helped me along the way, making a difference in shaping my career and my life.

Tom Dunkerton is at the lunch, and I tell him how thankful I am that he took a chance on me all those many years ago and hired me as a marketing research trainee at Vick Chemical. And Val Appel is there too. I tell Val that like Larry Brown, the famous Detroit Pistons basketball coach, he believed in doing the right things the right way, and learning this from Val has been an invaluable lesson for me. And I also thank Val for going to bat for me and helping me to get the first ever maternity leave at Benton & Bowles, something that was vitally important to me at an early stage of my career. (Val tells me after the lunch that he has no memory of this at all.)

Three of my Grey colleagues whom I want to recognize are not at the lunch, but I talk about what each has meant to me as I've built my career. Al Achenbaum, who was head of Marketing and Research at Grey, inspired me to want to work with him in pioneering the use of research and the resulting foundation of facts as a catalyst for strategic planning. I thank Al for teaching me about the business leverage of research and the powerful role research can play in the strategic marketing process.

I thank my longtime mentor at Grey and friend, Shirley Young, who taught me to zero in on the big things that matter. From Shirley I learned a lot about the importance of focus and concentration, energy and determination, and perseverance and teamwork. As I observed Shirley at work, I learned much about how to be an effective leader. And finally, I thank Ed Meyer, chairman and CEO of Grey and my longtime boss, who taught me so much about how to build a business, how to make and sell powerful advertising, and how to inspire teams to work together to make things happen, and who gave me the opportunity to do work that I loved for thirty years.

Peter and Dan represent our family at the luncheon, and I thank them and the rest of my family for putting up with many years of my late nights and weekends of work and my many out-of-town trips, for always encouraging me, always being interested, and always making me laugh.

* * *

On September 11, 2001, it's a beautiful morning in New York City—not a cloud in the crystal clear blue sky. But Jim isn't feeling well, and I call Dr. David Miller, his longtime physician. Dr. Miller asks me, "Do you have your TV on?" What an odd question. I tell him, "No." He says I should turn on the TV. The first plane has just hit the Twin Towers. Dr. Miller says that things at the hospital are frenetic; everyone is preparing for the victims. Jim begins to feel a little better, and the two of us stay glued to the TV. A second plane hits the Twin Towers, and both these beautiful iconic New York City landmarks crumble before our eyes. And then there's another crash into the Pentagon, and another in a field in Pennsylvania. The unimaginable has happened. The US and New York City have been attacked by terrorists. More than two thousand people have died in the attack on the Twin Towers alone. New Yorkers are rushing madly from the Wall Street area where the attacks happened, covered with ashes and dust and looking wild-eyed. They wander the streets, frantically looking for their loved ones. As time passes, every surface—every building wall, every mailbox, every tree trunk, is covered with xeroxed sheets, each one with a photo and a plea: "Have you seen [fill in the name]? Please call [fill in the phone number]." New Yorkers are shocked, numbed, traumatized, in a trance-like state of disbelief. I wonder, *What is happening to our country?* It's a time of intense fear of what the future will bring, no doubt similar to the terrible fear my parents must have felt in their last days in Nazi Germany.

Jim's and my fortieth wedding anniversary is on September 17, and we've planned a party with family and friends on September 14 to celebrate. We wonder whether we should call the party off, but our instinct is to go ahead with it, thinking this a time when people who care about each other should come together and support and comfort one another. I call each of our guests to talk about this, and all agree. We should definitely go ahead. Although many of our out-of-town friends won't be able to make it, all who live in the city plan to.

All over New York, buildings are flying American flags in a gesture of profound patriotism. I want us to have a small flag at our front door when our guests arrive, but I need to find one. I run all over our neighborhood on the Upper East Side and finally find one at a card store. I'm amazed, three days after the attack, to still see huge plumes of smoke rising from the spot on Wall Street where the Twin Towers had stood, nearly eight miles away. This is a nightmare scene; it's hard to believe it's real.

Our guests arrive, comforted to be together. We all share our stories and our impressions, our sorrow and our fury, our vulnerability and sense of loss. This is not the celebration we'd planned. It's more like a devastatingly sad wake.

CHAPTER TWENTY

Exploring My Roots

I've always felt a strong emotional resistance to going to Germany. I know it's not rational, but I have very strong feelings of avoidance. I've known about our family's escape, though until my sister shared my father's journal with me I'd never known any of the details about what brought it about, how it was planned, and what the escape itself was actually like. I've known too about the execution of my father's parents in the concentration camps during the Holocaust, although this was never discussed with me. But even when I was very young I'd sensed my parents had experienced terrible trauma, though they didn't speak to me about it and I never asked. Throughout our marriage Jim has told me from time to time that I've let out bloodcurdling screams in the middle of the night. He's always said he thought I was escaping from the Nazis in my nightmares. I never had any recollections of the screams or the nightmares. But I'm sure it's these buried feelings about long-ago traumas that are expressed in my middle-of-the-night terrors.

On my seventieth birthday, Jim and our sons and their wives hold a big surprise party for me. I've just returned from a VF board meeting in Lugano, Switzerland, and Milan. Afterward I went by myself for a few days to Venice, which was like a magical dream. Around every corner was a vision even lovelier than the one before. I went everywhere, hungry to take everything in—the canals, St. Mark's Square, Peggy

Guggenheim's palazzo and museum, and La Scala, the opera house. I tell my friends at the party how much I loved this trip, and one asks, "Where are you going next?" I shock myself when "Berlin" pops out of my mouth. Somehow, it now feels like the time is right for me to go.

My longtime friend, Nancy Baker, who's surprised me by coming to the party from Los Angeles, immediately says, "I'll go with you." Nancy and I have been good friends for over fifty years. Our husbands were classmates at HBS, and Jim was in Bill and Nancy's wedding in Henderson, a small town in North Carolina. When Nancy and Bill started their married life in New York and later when we both began to have children, our families became close. We'd both gone through good times and hard times. Bill and Nancy moved to Los Angeles. When they were living in LA, when he was about eleven, their older son, Garrett, fell down one morning on his way to school. He had a severe brain injury and died shortly thereafter, a tragic, devastating loss for Nancy and Bill. They were divorced some years later, and Nancy worked to regain her equilibrium and rebuild her life, a situation I could clearly relate to.

Although we don't see one another often, we try to take a trip together every year. We've spent a week at Wrightsville Beach in North Carolina at Nancy's brother's home; another time we went on a fascinating road trip from Natchez, Mississippi, to Baton Rouge, Louisiana, learning much about the history of the area as we went along. We've also gone together to Savannah, Sanibel Island, and Santa Fe. Whenever we're together, we talk about everything—our families, our children, our worries and concerns, and our hopes for the future. We're both curious and we like to laugh. We always pick up our conversations right where we left off the last time we talked. Nancy is beautiful, intelligent, warm, and one of the most generous-spirited people I know. I love having her as a friend.

Jim thinks it's a great idea for me to go to Berlin. He thinks it's important that I explore my roots; he'd found his own time in Berlin during his Army years fascinating. So Nancy and I make plans and set forth.

German is my native language; I spoke only German at home until my parents learned to speak English. When my grandmother came to live with us, she spoke no English, so I had to speak German to her. At

Whitman I studied German and worked for Herr Santler, the German professor, correcting papers. But in all the years since, I haven't heard German, spoken German, or even thought about speaking German. As the trip approaches, I think that I'd probably be able to understand a little bit, but hopefully the people in Berlin will understand and speak enough English to help me get by.

When we arrive in Berlin, Nancy and I leave the airport and get a taxi to our hotel. I tell the cab driver, in German, where we want to go and ask him some questions in German about what we see as we make the drive. I'm astonished to be able to speak German fluently, even idiomatically, the entire time we're in Berlin. We go to a museum and I ask the tour guide a question in German. She asks where we're from. Nancy says, "Los Angeles," and I say, "New York." The guide says, in German, "Oh my goodness. You speak German really beautifully." I'm amazed to be able to speak German so easily and well. It's all been repressed—buried somewhere deep inside my brain all these years.

Nancy and I find Berlin to be a very exciting city, vibrant and energetic, with a lively cultural scene. We go to the beautiful Tiergarten, Berlin's inner-city park, see dramatic architecture, and visit topflight museums. At one, we see the famous Nefertiti sculpture—imposing yet serene; it's simply beautiful. We take a boat ride on the River Spree, we go to the ballet, and we hear wonderful music. Jim had been to Checkpoint Charlie when he was in the Army and often told me about how the German officers checked the undersides of cars there. We go to see it, and go to the Brandenburg Gate and the Reichstag, where we ascend to the roof and look out over the city. I'm uneasy as we go to Hitler's bunker, where he and his officers hid and did their planning for the war. And we go to the relatively new Jewish Museum Berlin. The entire bottom floor is filled with floor to ceiling photographs of concentration camps with skeletal looking prisoners wearing their striped uniforms. These prisoners could have included my grandparents. The photographs are horrific. They shock me and make me feel so physically sick I have to leave the museum. I run out the door as fast as I can, trying to escape from the knowledge that it could have been me in those photographs if my parents hadn't rushed me away to freedom. This is too much for me to take in.

One cold and rainy morning Nancy goes with me to explore my roots. We walk on Unter den Linden, an elegant boulevard in the center of the city. It's lined with linden trees down its center median. My mother had spoken many times about how she'd loved this boulevard, strolling and stopping at a café for a coffee. We then go to the railroad station where my parents and I had caught the train out of Berlin and started our long and terrifying trip to escape Nazi persecution. We go to the city hall where my parents were married. Finally we start to look for the apartment where my parents lived when I was born, at Bülowstrasse 58. By this time it's raining harder and getting quite cold. Nancy decides she'll wait for me in the lobby of a neighborhood bank. I walk on alone, determined to find the apartment. At last I get there, and though I don't expect to be, I'm overwhelmed with emotion. It's a compact, red brick building—nondescript, although its significance moves me deeply. I see the small churchyard across the street from the apartment where my father took me to play, where Jews were forced to wear a yellow star and to sit only on public benches painted yellow. I imagine my young father, refusing to sit on the yellow bench but sitting on a chair he brought down from our apartment when I played in the churchyard.

The trip to Berlin has been interesting, uplifting, and devastating, as I made my way to see all the places I'd heard my parents speak about. I'd never grappled with any of these feelings until now; I'd simply repressed everything. But with my trip to Berlin and all that I experienced there, I feel like some of the missing pieces of the puzzle of my life have begun to come together. I know more now about where I've come from and what's made me who I am.

CHAPTER TWENTY-ONE

The Long Goodbye

For several years, I've rented a house for the summer in East Hampton, a Long Island beach community that I love. Jim has never liked the beach very much, and for years, when he was able to stay alone, I went out for long weekends by myself, often joined by our sons and their friends, and he stayed in the city. But when he's no longer able to stay alone, he reluctantly agrees to come with me. We usually go out on Thursday and return to New York on Monday morning. Our longtime driver, Jim Federico, takes us back and forth. Our caregivers usually do not join us in East Hampton. I am in charge. I help Jim shower, a scary proposition because the bathroom is not configured for someone with Jim's disabilities. Then I help Jim dress. He's exhausted from all this stressful activity and needs to take a nap. While Jim is napping, I rush out to take my three-mile walk to the store to buy the *New York Times*. He always times me—today it's fifty-one minutes, fifty-two minutes, fifty-three minutes. Then we sit together on the deck. Jim does the crossword puzzle, very awkwardly forming rough looking letters with his left hand; I read the paper and we chat. We have lunch, and Jim naps again.

Then I race to the beach to meet my longtime friends, Pat and Bernie Siskind, who own a home in East Hampton. We meet nearly every day at beautiful, serene Wiborg Beach, one of my absolutely favorite places in the world. This is a peaceful interlude for me. I sit back in my beach chair, sigh deeply, and relax. Over the years, I've met and become friends with a number of Pat and Bernie's friends: Joan Kallman, Lois Freeman, and Doris Nathan, who often gather with us at Wiborg. We chat, telling stories, discussing politics, talking about the latest books we've read and movies we've seen, relating updates about our kids, gossiping, laughing, as all the while I'm furtively glancing at my watch. When exactly an hour has passed, I run to the parking lot, jump into my car, and quickly drive back home.

In the middle of one night when we're in East Hampton, I wake up to a whistling, teakettle-like sound. I have no idea what this could be. As I come more fully awake, I realize it's Jim, trying to catch his breath. Jim whispers that he thinks he has allergies. He tries to sit up and he can't breathe; he tries to lie down and he can't breathe. He continues to lie down, sit up, lie down, and he can't catch his breath. I don't know what's wrong. This is very scary, and I begin to feel panicky. I'm not sure what to do. So finally I call 911, and they send the local volunteer ambulance, which arrives very quickly. The EMTs immediately give him oxygen, which seems to help a bit, and they move very efficiently to load him into their ambulance and drive him with sirens blaring to Southampton Hospital, twelve miles away. I follow in my car, and once Jim is in the ER we learn that he has a severe case of pneumonia. I think he was close to dying, and I'd had no idea. Jim is in the hospital for several days until he gets over the infection, and then I take him back to East Hampton in his weakened state for more recuperation.

When Jim begins to feel better, I begin going back to the beach again for my hour stay. One day when I get home I go the bedroom to see how Jim is doing. He's not on the bed. I'm terrified. I say, "Jim! Jim!" He's lying on the floor alongside the bed. I'm scared and I feel guilty. He'd tried to get up to pee and he'd slid down the side of the bed. He says, "I'm not hurt." But he's been lying there on the floor. I can't pick him up. I have to call the police who come very quickly and help him back onto the bed.

Jim says, "I can't come here anymore." I say, "You're right. We have to go home and figure out another plan. I don't want you ever to have to go through anything like this again. This was just awful."

At home we talk it over. Jim tells me he thinks I should go to East Hampton for long weekends as we've been doing. He knows how much I love it. And he will stay home with Lorna and her crew looking after him. I have very mixed emotions about this plan: a combination of guilt and relief. I reluctantly agree to give it a try. It's definitely not perfect, but it works for us.

Jim's health begins to fail very seriously. He begins to have heart, respiratory, and lung-related issues, all of which eventually devolve into congestive heart failure. A congestive heart failure episode can bring on pneumonia, as he'd experienced in East Hampton, or pneumonia can bring on an episode of congestive heart failure. These episodes are terrifying; they're like drowning and not being able to breathe. So this leads us to a period when Jim is stable for a while, and then he has another terrible episode. I call the ambulance; he's rushed to the hospital; his lungs are drained; he's put on oxygen; and he recoups for a few days. This happens many times. But he's never able to recoup to the same level he'd been before the episode. It's agonizing for me because I'm unable to do anything to stop it or to be helpful in any way as he steadily declines. All I can do is observe. I feel massive anxiety and stress. This takes me back to thoughts of my father and the constant worry and agony he must have felt as my mother went through her seemingly endless rounds of crisis and remission, the times between the two becoming shorter and shorter with each experience.

In the midst of all the stress associated with Jim's perilous health situation, other important events are happening to me and to our family. I decide that, after fourteen years, I need to resign from the Circuit City board. The company is going through some difficult times and the board needs to meet much more often than usual, for long periods of time. With Jim's health so precarious, I can't commit to being in Richmond for these frequent and protracted meetings. I need to be accessible to Jim when he needs me. Reluctantly, I tell the board my situation, and my time as a Circuit City director comes to an end.

Another big change is about to happen. Michael, whose marriage has not been going well for some time, tells Jim and me that he's decided to get divorced. He wants to look forward to a happy time for the next half of his life. Jim and I are very supportive of Michael's decision, though we understand he'll go through some rocky times in the short term. We want all that's good for him, and our sense is that if Michael thinks this is the right thing to do we are behind him all the way.

April 26, 2010, is the day I retire from the VF board, having reached the board's designated retirement age. This is a significant occasion for me. I've been on the board for twenty-three years and have loved every minute of my association with this magnificent company, whose portfolio of brands now includes The North Face, Vans, Timberland, JanSport, Lee and Wrangler jeans, and many, many more. I am the only woman on the board when I join and the only director with marketing and brand-building experience. I'm very proud of the work I helped lead to transform the company from a premier domestic manufacturing company to a global marketing powerhouse with a portfolio of exciting lifestyle brands. As longtime chair of the Nominating and Governance Committee, I worked to build and reshape the company's board so that it aligned with the strategic mission and goals of the company. CEO Eric Wiseman hosts a lovely retirement dinner for me in Greensboro, North Carolina, where VF is headquartered. My family is invited, and Peter and Daniel accompany me. After a delicious dinner and wonderful wine, many of the directors with whom I've worked and who have become friends give heartwarming speeches and toasts. When it's my turn, I look around the table and am enormously gratified that I helped recruit most of the directors who make up our outstanding, first-class board. I thank everyone for the opportunity we've had to work together to profoundly transform VF's mission and culture and to make it an even better company. And I thank them all for their friendship and for the fun we've had together over the years. To end the evening, Eric presents me with a breathtakingly beautiful gold dahlia pin sprinkled with sapphires and diamonds, and with a pair of gold and diamond earrings. I'm overwhelmed. I know I'm going to miss working with my director colleagues on all the challenging and interesting issues VF faces. But it's been a good run, and it's time for me to move on.

September 17, 2011, is our fiftieth wedding anniversary. Jim, though clearly weakened, feels well enough for us to have a party to celebrate this amazing milestone. We have cocktails and dinner for our extended family, including all our grandchildren, at a restaurant we've always enjoyed, Maloney & Porcelli. Peter helps me organize a sumptuous meal with wonderful wines. Throughout the evening a piano player plays a lot of the Cole Porter and Gershwin music we love. A photographer takes candid photos during the entire event,

Me with Jim and family, 50th wedding anniversary, September 17, 2011

Celebrating our 50th wedding anniversary with Daniel, Peter, and Michael, September 17, 2011

Me with grandchildren, 50th wedding anniversary, September 17, 2011

getting many shots of our family and of all our guests. There are many toasts and speeches. Michael, who has a wonderful voice, sings "Summer Wind" and brings the house down. Each of our grandchildren performs, some with speeches, some with songs, and Dylan even does a dance. I wrap things up by saying, as Lou Gehrig did, "I feel like the luckiest person on the face of the earth. I've spent fifty years married to the love of my life, and he's filled every day of our fifty years together with love and laughter." Though Jim doesn't have much energy, he's able to enjoy our celebration. It's a bittersweet moment when the party draws to a close. We both understand this is likely to be the last event we'll be able to celebrate together. By the end of the evening, we each have tears in our eyes.

It's January 2014. Jim continues his roller-coaster life with more and more frequent congestive heart failure episodes, each one more serious than the last. He's weakened by each episode. His decline is more and more severe. On a freezing cold day in mid-January, I bring Jim home from the hospital after his most recent horrific episode, during which he'd been gasping desperately, unable to breathe. The EMTs who bring Jim home get him settled back into bed. When they leave, Jim begins almost immediately to have another episode, gasping and struggling mightily for each breath. I call Jim's longtime doctor, Dr. Miller, explain the situation to him, and ask if he thinks it's time we bring in hospice. Dr. Miller says, "Yes, I'll make arrangements immediately."

I call our sons, who know by this time to anticipate emergencies with Jim. Peter and Dan and their wives and Michael come to our apartment immediately. We all gather in our bedroom which is crowded with Jim's medical equipment: his hospital bed, wheelchair, oxygen tanks, and more. I crawl up next to Jim on my bed, which I'd pushed alongside his hospital bed, and our sons and daughters-in-law huddle around the bed along with Lorna and our longtime weekend helper, Yvonne Adams. We are all very quiet and very somber, agonizing as we listen and watch Jim struggle, gasping and wheezing with an eerie whistling sound accompanying each tiny breath, unable to do

Me with Jim and family, Thanksgiving 2013

anything to ease his torture. I feel totally helpless, only able to watch and wonder what the next terrible moment will bring.

A major blizzard has begun by now. We feel we've been waiting forever as Jim struggles for every breath, but finally the doorbell rings. It's two hospice nurses whose first words are, "Where are the drugs?" I have no idea what they're talking about, so they explain that hospice was to have delivered a boxful of drugs wrapped in plain brown paper that we were to put in our refrigerator. One of the nurses examines Jim, who continues to gasp and struggle, while the other gets on the phone to try to locate the drugs. It turns out the delivery person is stuck in the blizzard. The hospice nurse asks if any of us has any drugs around, and initially we say we don't. Then Stephanie remembers she has some Percocet left from the time she was recuperating from her caesarian. The nurses ask her to please bring it over as quickly as possible, as Jim can barely breathe. They feel that this will help calm his system. Stephanie pulls on her boots and rushes home through the blinding snow to retrieve the Percocet, which the nurses administer immediately. Shortly after that, Jim finally catches his breath, and he is able to go to sleep. The drugs finally arrive—morphine and antianxiety drugs, all to calm Jim and make him comfortable.

Me with Jim and grandchildren, Thanksgiving 2013

Soon, the hospice doctor, a very personable and professional young man, arrives. He asks us all to step out while he examines Jim. My daughters-in-law have gone home to look after their children, and Michael, Peter, and Daniel and I wait in the TV room without speaking, all of us dreading to hear what we think the doctor is about to tell us. He finally comes in to join us. He sits down and asks, "Have you made arrangements?" His question is a shock to all of us despite our knowing what dire shape Jim is in. I say that we haven't and ask the doctor how much time he thinks we have. He responds, "I'd say a maximum of six hours." We're speechless. He asks us what kind of arrangements we think we want, and I tell him a very simple cremation and no funeral service. He then asks if we have a funeral home we can call, and I tell him the only one I know is Frank Campbell's. He says, "Don't go there; it's way too expensive for what you want." He recommends a place in Greenwich Village called Crestwood. Everyone swings into action. Dan calls Crestwood and makes preliminary plans. Michael and Peter work on drafting an obituary. And I sit—in a foggy stupor.

We are all in a state of suspended animation, knowing that the end can come at any moment. The hospice doctor and nurses instruct us as to how and when to administer the various drugs, the key goal being to keep Jim comfortable and calm. They also make it very clear that when Jim dies we should call them immediately and not call 911 or anyone else. They instruct Jim's helpers in no uncertain terms to that effect and tape a reminder note on the refrigerator. They explain to us that they will facilitate the arrangements with the funeral home, and this will help us avoid a lot of bureaucratic red tape.

The real shock is that the end does not come that evening, in a "maximum of six hours." Jim, who like my mother loves life and fights fiercely to hang on to every precious moment, lives for nearly six more months. During these months, our sons come regularly to spend time with Jim. He is usually heavily medicated, sleeps a lot, and fades in and out of awareness. He barely speaks. When he does talk, he hallucinates some about his happy Army days at the Philadelphia Quartermaster Depot, remembering being responsible for buying all the toilet paper for the US Armed Forces. He reminisces about the long walks around New York City he used to love to take, and he regales our sons with the corny jokes he used to tell them when they were little boys. In a strange and somewhat twisted way, this is a warm and very loving time for all of us.

Jim has very little strength or energy and is so heavily drugged he doesn't have much of an attention span. He becomes weaker and weaker, but his aides make sure to wheel him into the kitchen for breakfast every day. I go into our room several times throughout the day to check on him, and last thing before I go to sleep and first thing when I wake up I put my hand on his chest to check whether he is still breathing.

It is heartbreaking to watch Jim suffer and fade away. During the dire time of Jim's decline, as he moves closer and closer to death, I just want it to be over. I wonder how long this is going to go on. I just can't stand it. It's like *The Perils of Pauline*. I feel like the train is going to run over us any second. These thoughts make me feel very guilty.

We've been invited to Portola Valley, California, to attend a celebration early in June for Don Yates's eightieth birthday. Our families have been dear friends for well over fifty years, since Don and Jim were roommates at HBS. I tell Jim I think it would be a good thing for me to go to represent our family, if he thinks it's OK. I'm not sure if Jim hears me, let alone understands me. When the day arrives, I say to Jim,

"This is the day I'm going to Don and Jane's for Don's birthday party. I'll only be gone a couple of days." I kiss Jim goodbye; he is not responsive. He's not conscious of very much. I don't realize this is the last time I'll see him. Any time can be the last time I see him. Lorna, who is very religious and very driven by her Jamaican traditions, and who has had a lot of experience dealing with patients in very critical condition, has long told me that Jim would not die when I was home. He'd wait until I was away. I am astonished that she is right.

On the morning of June 12, 2014, when I'm on the West Coast, my phone rings. It's Dan, telling me Jim died at 10:30 this morning. Vivia Martin, one of his aides, was helping him get ready for the day. She'd gone to the bathroom to get something, and when she returned to the bedroom, Jim was gone.

I quickly organize myself and get the next flight home. Our sons are in my kitchen waiting for me when I arrive. They've followed hospice instructions, and Jim's body has been taken to Crestwood. I go with Michael the next day to see Jim. Peter and Daniel do not want to go; they cannot look. Though I've been extremely nervous and uneasy about seeing Jim's body, I'm happy and relieved that I've done so. I kiss Jim's cheek. At long, long last, Jim looks at peace.

CHAPTER TWENTY-TWO

The Aftermath

Michael and I go back to Crestwood after Jim's cremation to pick up his ashes. The funeral director, a friendly young woman, hands me a navy blue canvas tote bag. Inside is a small box wrapped in plain brown paper and carefully taped closed. It all seems very surreal to me. Michael asks me if I'd like to have lunch with him. It happens that Crestwood is around the corner from the Minetta Tavern, the restaurant where Jim had "proposed" to me over dinner those many years ago. Michael suggests we go there. I love this idea, so I put the navy tote bag over my shoulder and off we go. We have a very nostalgic lunch; I regale Michael once again with the story of my proposal—how I spilled my drink over the table when Jim casually said, "When we get married . . ." After lunch, once again I grab the navy tote and jump on the subway to go home. Our sons and I aren't sure what we'll ultimately do with Jim's ashes, so until we figure it out I put the navy bag with the small brown box in my china cabinet for safekeeping.

None of us wants to have a funeral service for Jim. Rather, we decide to have a celebration of his life. We do this at the Vinegar Factory, in an event space above a local market Jim loved. We serve drinks and plenty of delicious hors d'oeuvres, show the fabulous video of all the stages of Jim's life our sons had made for his seventy-fifth birthday celebration, and put posters of other photos up throughout the room. We keep the feeling very informal and, to the extent we can, celebratory. More than two hundred people attend, which I find astonishing. They include family, friends from out of town, people from all stages of Jim's life, colleagues of mine from Grey, and many friends of our sons whom Jim had known over the years. Jim's medical team is there—Dr. Miller and all the hospice doctors and nurses; all of Jim's helpers, Lorna and her team, are there as well. I have a chance to talk with Dr. Miller and to thank him for all the years he's taken such good care of Jim. I tell him the hospice doctor had told us in January that Jim had a maximum of six hours to live, and here we are in June, nearly six months later, celebrating his life. Dr. Miller throws back his head and chuckles, "He did not know Jim Feigin. Jim was going to die when he good and well felt like it. He was not going to rush things."

Each of our sons speaks, as do I, all of us celebrating Jim's wonderful qualities as a husband, father, and grandfather. We talk about his decency, his honesty, his fundamental integrity and, of course, his sly sense of humor and his wonderful booming laugh. There are laughter, some tears, many memories, and some funny stories. One of my friends says, "Barbara, that was a combination of a shiva and an Irish wake. It was fabulous. I've never been to anything quite like it." I wish Jim could have been at this party. He'd have loved it.

I want our sons to have Jim's personal items. I lay them all out on the bed: his monogrammed wallet, his briefcase, also monogrammed, his watch, studs for his tuxedo shirt, and more. For our twenty-fifth anniversary I'd given Jim a silver key ring and fob, which I'd had engraved, "25 years of love and laughter." Jim had many colorful polo shirts that are still in good shape, and a huge collection of baseball caps in every color, each with the name of the team or company he was rooting for: Whitman, the University of Washington, Marquis Jet, and Trevor, among many others. He'd enjoyed wearing these caps and matching them to the color of the polo shirt he was wearing. I'd given Jim his favorite tie, a Ferragamo with a Leo the lion print, and that was on the bed with all the rest of Jim's treasures. I ask Michael, Peter, and Daniel to come over and take whatever they like. I leave them in the bedroom to decide among themselves who will take what. They are in

Daniel, me, Peter, and Michael planting Jim's tree, June 2015

there for quite a while and come out, each with his selections in hand. I'm not exactly sure who's taken what or how they've decided, but they seem happy with their choices.

Months go by, and my sons and I have still not decided what we'll do with Jim's ashes. Michael comes up with a fantastic idea; we should plant a tree in Jim's memory—a pink dogwood in Carl Schurz Park, across the street from our apartment. Daniel is on the board of the Carl Schurz Park Conservancy and is very friendly with the head botanist there. Although the park usually does not allow the planting of trees, he persuades her to make an exception. I meet with her and we walk the park to pick out a place to plant the tree. We decide on the perfect spot, alongside the walkway between Eighty-Fourth and Eighty-Sixth Streets, just behind the bench Jim used to sit on when he took the boys to the playground when they were young.

On the designated afternoon of the planting, we come from all directions for the occasion, Michael and family from Brooklyn, Dan and family from their schools, and Peter flying in from Milwaukee where he's now working as the president of the Milwaukee Bucks NBA basketball team. Natalia and their kids come from Trevor.

The park's arborist has chosen and planted the tree and has left a trench around it so each of us can put a shovelful of dirt into the trench. In advance, I tell the head of the park conservancy that we want this to be a private get-together. I know she would object to our spreading Jim's ashes as we plant the tree so we want to do this without her observing us.

I bring my navy tote bag with the brown box to the tree. I open it up once everyone is gathered. It is very carefully wrapped and the wrapping is glued together very tightly. I finally get the box open as everyone is waiting, somewhat impatiently, for us to start the planting and spreading of the ashes. But inside the box, I find a very thick gauge plastic baggie with Jim's ashes. The baggie is closed with a metal fastener that's impossible to open. And I haven't brought a knife or scissors with me. I know if I go back to my apartment everyone will disappear, especially Peter and Daniel, who find it very upsetting to be involved in our ceremony. So I have to move fast; I run to the corner about a block away to the hot dog cart and say to the man in charge, "Would you mind loaning me a knife for a few minutes? I'll bring it right back to you." He loans me the knife; I run back to our group and cut a small hole in the baggie with Jim's ashes; and I run back to the hot dog man to return the knife.

Each of us, including the children, then puts a shovelful of dirt around the tree. But only Michael and I, and eventually Dylan, strew Jim's ashes around the planting. Dylan, who is six, keeps saying, "I want to put in more powder." Peter and Dan turn their backs to us during the whole process, finding it all very distressing. I have expected to feel very sad on this day, but actually I feel joyful, even elated. I think Jim would be pleased with what we've done. It feels right.

CHAPTER TWENTY-THREE

New Beginnings

I am in something of a daze during the early weeks after Jim's death. I have been totally focused on caring for Jim and dealing with his roller-coaster episodes of desperate failure followed by some recuperation, over and over again, each time being worse than the last. It seems very strange to me not to be totally consumed by this as I have been 24/7 for so long. But I have much that I need to do.

First, I have to arrange for Jim's team of dedicated caregivers, the ones who've been so devoted to him day and night for so many years, to leave us. We have many tearful conversations, sharing happy, funny, and sad memories. But soon they take their leave. We promise to stay in touch with one another. Then I have to arrange to give away all our medical equipment, of which we have a houseful: wheelchairs, a hospital bed, canes, special commodes, shower benches, grab bars, and on and on. I'm eager to donate all this very expensive equipment to charity, but to my great and unhappy surprise, no charity seems to want to take it. At long last, with the help of one of my doctors, I connect with someone who arranges for it to be donated.

I'm the executor of Jim's estate. Jim and I had worked closely with our attorney, Bob Schneps, and our financial planner, Ed Markman, to get our affairs in good order before Jim died, but a lot of work is involved in executing Jim's wishes. I find it all very exacting. I feel that it's taking me forever to accomplish. Bob Schneps tells me, though, as we're wrapping things up, that he's never had a client who'd been able to accomplish so much so quickly.

All of these tasks keep me very busy, but I'm well aware, as I complete them, that I need to think about creating a new beginning for myself. As I think back, I'm sure my parents must have had similar feelings as they disembarked from the *Hikawa Maru* in Seattle. I need to create a new life chapter, very different from the past. I need to think about how to do that in a way I'll find interesting, fun, and deeply rewarding. Quite a tall order, but one full of opportunities and challenges.

As I begin to empty our apartment of Jim's hospital equipment I see how banged up it's become. After many years of scrapes and bumps from Jim's wheelchair and hard wear and tear resulting from so many of us—Jim, me, and all his helpers, living in such close quarters, the apartment clearly needs to be refreshed. I think about what I might want to do. I begin to realize I want to do a major reset. I understand that this will be a metaphor for a reset for my life.

I bring together a very talented contractor, Constantine Rigas, who has done two renovations for our son, Peter, and his wife, Natalia, and my longtime interior designer, Kyle Wells, who's helped me with small-scale interior design projects over the years. I tell them I want to do a full gut renovation and that I want them to work collaboratively, which seems to be a new approach for them.

My experience at Grey has taught me that all the players on creative projects need to be involved up front, in the strategic planning phase, rather than sequentially, as contractors normally work with designers. This is the model I adapt for my renovation, and it's a fabulous success. We gather around my dining table and brainstorm together over the course of a few planning sessions, poring through magazines for pictures, making sketches, looking at photographs of Kyle's and Constantine's other projects, all to help define the look and feel and attitude we're shooting for. Then everyone gets to work. I want something light, bright, airy, and fresh. Together Constantine and Kyle develop exactly that for me. I need to empty the apartment completely. I do a major purge, discarding, donating, and even selling a few things. Everything else goes into storage or into Kyle's workrooms to be refreshed along the lines of the strategy we're implementing.

I need to move out of my apartment for a year while the work goes on. I do some research to figure out where to go and find an extended-stay hotel/apartment, the Marmara, on East Ninety-Fourth Street, around the corner from Trevor. I ask Peter to come with me to look at what's available and to help me negotiate an arrangement if I decide Marmara is right for my needs. I tell Peter all I need is a studio, and he says, "Oh, no, Mom. You can't be living in a studio at this stage of your life." So we decide on a one-bedroom apartment, and Peter makes a very attractive deal for me. Even after all these years, I think men who negotiate prefer to do so with other men, rather than with women. Some things are slow to change.

At long last my renovation is completed. The end result is stunning—far beyond anything I could have imagined or hoped for. The colors are soft, the sensibility is relaxed serenity, and the apartment has an indoor-outdoor feeling, with windows and the terrace overlooking the park. I have a Grand Opening bash for my family and friends and for Constantine and Kyle, so all are able to see and enjoy my simply beautiful apartment. The apartment is filled with pink peonies; the lights are low; the wine is flowing; the food is mouthwatering; soft music is playing. It's a lovely, elegant experience. Bringing my "new" apartment into being is by far the most indulgent thing I've ever done for myself. It makes me happy every day. The entire creation is very much a symbol of my new beginning.

I'm now in what's clearly a new and different stage of my life. I have time for myself, which I've never really had before. This takes some getting used to. I think about all the things I've wanted to do, just for myself, over the years, for which I simply haven't had the time.

I get started. I continue with yoga at the small studio in the Village Michael recommended. I love the serenity of my yoga time. I've heard about Pilates; it sounds like a lovely, "dancerly," stretchy practice. I'm introduced to Jo d'Agostino, a fantastic Pilates trainer with whom I make an instant connection. I love working with Jo, and as I spend more and more time with her on Pilates, I feel that my balance and my strength are improving.

I take a film class and a class in modern art. My longtime friend Pat Siskind also has time now. She and I have similar cultural interests and tastes, and we see and do all the wonderful things New York has to offer—things I haven't had time for since the period after I retired but before Jim had his second stroke. We go to museums, concerts, theater, movies, and we always have three or four more interesting things to look forward to on our to-do list. For the first time in a long time, I have lots of time to read, which I love.

I spend much more time at my East Hampton rental in the summers, no longer feeling torn about needing to rush home to Jim in New York City every Sunday evening or having to constantly, nervously check my watch when I'm at the beach. East Hampton has a very lively arts scene—art, music, lectures, theater—and now I'm able to enjoy them all with my beach friends. We also meet frequently for lunches and dinners at various excellent Hamptons restaurants. My family comes regularly to stay with me, and we have a ball. We go to the beach, play in the pool, and the kids play soccer and badminton. There's also plenty of time just to hang out and talk together. Dinner is a major highlight of each day. We grill chicken, hamburgers, or fresh, delicious local fish and vegetables every night, and I make my signature tomato salad with fat, juicy local tomatoes, red onion, freshly picked corn, basil, blue cheese, and balsamic dressing. Everyone clamors for it; it's definitely a family favorite. We also have a family ice cream tradition which everyone, child and adult, looks forward to. We put six or seven half-gallon tubs of ice cream, all different flavors, on the table. Everyone has a spoon. We pass the ice cream around the table, and each person takes his or her spoon, digs in, and passes the ice cream to the next person. We go round and round until the tubs are nearly empty. This is the best!

People ask me during these times, "Aren't you depressed? Aren't you lonely?" I had expected maybe I would be. Of course I miss Jim—his companionship, his wit, his twinkling brown eyes, and his wonderful booming laugh. But I'm really not depressed or lonely. All in all, I'm finding this chapter fun, relaxing, and stress free, a massive change in my lifestyle from recent years. Actually, as I adapt more and more, I'm enjoying life very much.

CHAPTER TWENTY-FOUR

Whitman Revisited

When Jim and I were putting our affairs in order we decided to make a significant financial gift to Whitman College. The gift established the Barbara Sommer Feigin Distinguished Student Scholarship and Internship Endowment. The scholarships and internships are earmarked for people like me: refugees or immigrants, or the children of refugees or immigrants, who are highly qualified but don't have the financial wherewithal to attend Whitman and who want to go into the business world. This is our way of thanking Whitman for making it possible for me to attend and in turn changing the trajectory of my life.

We were invited to Whitman in November 2013, to a very elegant dinner with the president, the senior staff, and the board of trustees to honor us and celebrate our gift. Jim was not able to go, so I represented us both. The dinner was held in a beautiful wine-tasting room—honey-colored woods that gave the room a warm glow, twinkling chandeliers, long rough-hewn farm tables with striking candelabras at intervals down the length of each table. I met many of the trustees, who were welcoming and friendly. I stood up to speak, and as I told my story, starting with our family's escape from Nazi Germany, the room became perfectly still. When I finished, the room erupted with applause. A line formed next to my chair as many people, including

Peter van Oppen, the board chair, came to introduce themselves and tell me how profoundly moved they've been by hearing my story and how thankful they were for our gift.

A few weeks later, around Thanksgiving time, I got a call from Peter van Oppen, who was coming to New York; he invited me to breakfast. We had a long, friendly, getting-to-know-you conversation, and Peter told me a little about the issues currently confronting Whitman. I liked Peter very much; we had an easy rapport. I was completely surprised a few weeks later when Peter called and asked if I would consider becoming a Whitman trustee. This had not entered my mind. I told him I was very interested, but because of Jim's critical condition I needed a little time before I could commit. He understood, and we agreed to stay in touch.

In May, shortly before Jim dies, I am elected a trustee of Whitman College. I feel honored and privileged to be selected. Since Whitman has been so transformational in my life, it's exciting to think about how I might be able to make a positive difference for the college going forward.

I go to my first board meeting in May and find Walla Walla completely changed. When I was in college, it was a small farming town surrounded by wheat fields. Now it's known as "the Napa of the north," with over 120 wineries. It's become a destination, a charming small town featuring wonderful restaurants and a main street replete with many tasting rooms. The Whitman campus is gorgeous; there are beautiful trees and lovely plantings along with striking pieces of sculpture placed throughout.

I know immediately that my new role at Whitman will be a very good one for me, one I can really sink my teeth into. I find the other trustees to be very interesting; they're smart and highly accomplished people whom I feel I'll enjoy getting to know and working with. And Whitman is at an important crossroads. George Bridges, the current president, is set to retire, and the board is about to launch a presidential search. The new president will be expected to develop a strategic plan—essentially a road map geared toward ensuring the college continues to be relevant and vibrant in the years ahead. Strategic planning is what I've spent my career doing; I'm excited to come onto the board when I can contribute to planning for change.

At one of my first board meetings one of my trustee colleagues, David Nierenberg, asks me to join him at an informal dinner with a group of first-generation students he's put together. David finds my story as a refugee who had a transformational experience at Whitman inspiring and thinks it would be valuable for today's first-generation students to hear about it. We meet at a Chinese restaurant on the outskirts of Walla Walla and start by going around the table, each introducing ourselves, each telling our own story. David and I are shaken to learn how badly these students are struggling. They feel isolated; they have serious financial troubles that make their full participation in what Whitman has to offer nearly impossible; and, worst of all, despite the fact that Whitman offers a raft of support services, they have no idea where to turn for help. David and I report to the board about what we have learned and agree to prepare a paper for the Student Affairs staff with suggestions for action. This effort results in a highly successful initiative for first-year, first-generation students: Whitman's Summer Fly-In Program. Students in the program are flown to campus for a week in the summer before they matriculate. They are assigned mentors, participate in detailed orientation activities, learn about all of Whitman's support services and how to tap into them for help, and engage in many activities geared toward giving them a feeling of belonging to the Whitman community. This program has become an ongoing part of the Whitman experience. It's a program that makes a vital difference in first-generation students' lives, putting them on a path to success. I'm very gratified to have helped catalyze this effort.

I've had a good deal of governance experience chairing the VF Nominating and Governance Committee; the leadership of the Whitman board was eager to tap into this experience. I am named chair of the Governance Committee of the Whitman board and a member of the Executive Committee. Whitman's new president, Kathleen Murray, launches her tenure by initiating the development of a strategic plan, and I am named to her planning committee. One of my most important accomplishments on the Whitman board comes with another assignment. I am asked to spearhead a committee to review and revamp Whitman's entire board governance structure and operating practices, something that hasn't been done for more than twenty years. This is a major project; it takes nearly a year to complete.

We have a superb committee that works very diligently and collaboratively. We develop a full set of organizational and operational recommendations that are adopted in their entirety by the board. They are implemented with great effectiveness immediately thereafter.

The Whitman board meets three times a year in Walla Walla. To get there, I fly from New York to Seattle, stay overnight at an airport hotel, and fly to Walla Walla the next morning. One of the wonderful bonuses of my time in Seattle is that it gives me a chance to reconnect with two of my dearest Whitman friends, Maggie Iversen Johnson and Judy McClane Slattery.

Maggie, the first person I'd met at Whitman, and her husband, Max, who'd been in my class at Whitman and has also become my good friend over the years, live near the shore of Lake Washington in Yarrow Point. I often go to their home for lunch, and we catch up on each other's news. Max, who'd been on the Whitman board some years ago, also, amazingly, had been Grey's client in our LA office when he'd been a marketing executive at US West Direct. Maggie and Max have visited us in New York and know our sons, and I know their two daughters. Even though we don't see each other often, we always have lots to talk about—old times, old friends, our families, and the goings-on at Whitman. Their home is lovely, and Maggie keeps it up beautifully. I always tease her when I visit, telling her, "I love my time in Shangri-La!"

Judy Slattery was my roommate for a time in the Tri Delt section of Prentiss Hall, the girls' dorm where all the sororities were housed. Judy lived in California for many years after our Whitman graduation and only recently moved back to the Northwest. Judy's husband, Frank, died a few years before Jim did. She has a daughter, Anne, who's Michael's age. Although we hadn't seen one another for many years until I started traveling to Walla Walla, we'd always stayed in close touch. I'd always considered Judy a close friend, and I'm thrilled we're able to get together in person again. We spend many long lunches talking about everything—politics, what it's like adjusting to being a widow, our families. Judy is a talented writer. She encouraged me to write a memoir. Others have suggested this from time to time, but I never took their suggestions seriously. I think maybe I was a little intimidated at the prospect of trying to do a piece of creative writing. This is completely alien territory for me. But Judy said, "Barbara, you have to do this. Your story is so rich. It's so fascinating and so important. It needs to be told." It's Judy's support that gave me the courage to try writing my story. And she continues to support and encourage me every step of the way.

As I've learned so often throughout the course of my life, luck and timing affect everything. Until I actually joined the Whitman board, I would never have been able to contemplate doing so. My time was in very short supply, initially with my high-level and high-pressure job that required round-the-world travel, and more recently with the demanding circumstances of Jim's failing health. And since Whitman is across the country from New York, attending meetings requires several days, including travel. But now I suddenly have time and intellectual bandwidth available. I also have deep feelings for Whitman and the role the college played in my life. My relationship with Whitman at this time enables me to come full circle and becomes an important part of my new beginning.

CHAPTER TWENTY-FIVE

Travels with Nancy

I've always loved to travel—to see new places, learn about history, and experience different cultures. Jim had been a wonderful travel companion and guide. He was very well educated and had endless curiosity and boundless energy. We'd been to many places in Europe together, and I'd always hoped we'd be able to travel more when I retired, but this was not to be.

I do want to continue to travel, and happily, my friend Nancy Baker and I travel well together. We're both high energy and deeply curious. We like to see and do everything. After Jim's death we travel a lot and see a good part of the world.

One of our best trips ever is to Morocco. Morocco is a feast for the senses; it looks, feels, sounds, and smells like no place I've ever been before. We land in Casablanca and travel to beautiful Rabat, the capital city. There we wander through mazelike souks filled with tiny stalls lined up tightly next to one another, each one selling something different—everything from shoes to meats to spices to fabrics and much, much more. As we walk, we have to move out of the way of donkeys laden high with animal skins as they are led to tanneries inside the souks. We visit a tannery and are overwhelmed by a terrible rotten stench coming from the work areas. We are greeted at the door of the viewing room by a woman who gives us sprigs of mint to hold

Me with Nancy Baker in Italy, October 18, 2018

under our noses to help mask the odor. We watch the tannery workers go through the very primitive tanning process. We then wander further and watch snake charmers and street performers. From Rabat we go to Fez, where we dine in an ancient medina, an old-world residence that's simply exquisite. Then we take a long bus trip over the Atlas Mountains. As we're riding along treacherous, winding mountain roads, none of which have guardrails, all of a sudden apes start

Me riding a camel in India, February 2, 2013

swinging from the trees and into the road in front of our bus. We have to stop while the apes make their way across the road. I've never seen anything like this. Our next stop is the amazing Sahara Desert, which is like an ocean—undulating mountains of golden sand that go on forever. We ride camels into the desert, a slightly scary experience, hoping to be able to watch a spectacular sunset. But instead, we're trapped in a fierce sandstorm. Even though our guide has wrapped my head and my face in a purple scarf so completely I can hardly see, I still get so much sand in my hair and my ears that it takes weeks to get it all out. This must have been what my parents experienced while traveling across the Gobi Desert on our escape journey. We move on to the fascinating city of Marrakesh, which has a much more European feeling than any of the other places we've been. The hotels have gorgeous European-looking gardens, and our food is mainly French. Finally we go back to Casablanca where we visit one of the world's biggest mosques, which is awe inspiring, and we have our farewell dinner at Sam's, the restaurant and nightclub from the movie *Casablanca*. There's actually a piano player there playing "As Time Goes By" during our dinner hour. Our whole visit to Morocco is mind-opening—a whole new world I've never before experienced. I've absolutely loved it.

Nancy and I go on many other trips together. They're all pretty unforgettable, but one of the most spectacular is to India, where we ride elephants, go on a wild game safari, sit on the "Princess Diana" bench in front of the magnificent Taj Mahal, and see funeral pyres in the inky darkness of night alongside the Ganges River in Varanasi. On some of our other adventures we walk on Omaha Beach in Normandy and through the imposing American cemetery where nearly ten thousand American servicemen who lost their lives in World War II are buried. In southern Italy we stroll the streets of ancient Pompeii and hike on Mount Etna. We go to Amsterdam, and there I climb up to the tiny attic room in which Anne Frank and her family hid from the Nazis. I'm very aware that this could have been me. We go on a barge trip through the canals of Holland, marveling at the glorious gardens and the amazing feats of water management engineering. We go to Prague where we listen to pickup groups play beautiful chamber music at vespers, and visit Budapest, Croatia, and Barcelona. We love our trips, and whenever we're on one we're busy planning the next. I feel very lucky to be able to travel the world with Nancy, who's such a good friend and compatible travel companion.

CHAPTER TWENTY-SIX

My Proudest Accomplishment

By far the proudest accomplishment of my life is being the mom of Michael, Peter, and Daniel, and with Jim raising them and watching them grow and develop into honorable men with high values. They are devoted husbands, fantastic fathers, and caring sons. They excel at the professions they've chosen. Most of all, they are *there* through good times and tough times. I love them dearly. Our sons have been the light of Jim's and my life from the time they were born; we've been totally devoted to them and their well-being. I know that now, wherever he may be, Jim is smiling down at them and bursting with joy.

I observe with pride and amazement as each of my sons enthusiastically tackles new challenges and opportunities. Dan has been named head of Trevor, the school where he's worked all his adult life. This is a perfect role for him and he's thriving.

Dan took on an enormous project for Trevor, spearheading the financing, design, and construction of a magnificent new high-rise building for the school. The school was designed in a very innovative manner, with a "people first" perspective. Much time and effort were spent in the strategic planning stage working with teachers, staff, and students to learn how ideally they would like to use the facility, and the design was developed along those dimensions. Maya Lin, the famous Vietnam Veterans Memorial designer, is a Trevor parent. She designed

Peter, Fiserv Forum groundbreaking, June 18, 2016

and placed a striking interactive installation on the open-air roof. The entire project is a spectacular success.

In October 2014, Peter became president of the Milwaukee Bucks NBA basketball team. He commutes between New York and Milwaukee; he's usually in Milwaukee for the work week and back in New York with his family for the weekend. He was put in charge of reenergizing the Bucks brand and rebuilding the team's business, which had been suffering badly for many years, but first he was tasked with raising $250 million from the state, the county, and the city to be used in a public-private partnership to build a new arena for the Bucks. At the time, I couldn't imagine how Peter was going to accomplish this.

He's a New Yorker who'd never even been to Wisconsin before joining the Bucks and didn't know a soul in the entire state. I wondered, *How in the world will he be able to do this?* But he did. I'm amazed. I asked him what he learned in the process. He ran his fingers across his closed lips and said, "To keep my mouth shut." He's an impatient guy, but he forced himself to sit quietly listening to each legislator until he was able to understand his or her wants, needs, and concerns. He was then able to formulate a plan to accomplish his goal.

Peter then led the design effort, the development, and the construction of the Fiserv Forum, the Bucks' new state-of-the art arena. After the arena opened to great fanfare, Peter was interviewed on a radio show. The host of the show said, "Peter, the arena is fantastic. It's just beautiful. You must have had a lot of construction experience." After a long pause, Peter said, "Well, I did Legos . . . and I did Lincoln Logs." Peter has had great success rebranding the Bucks and building the business of the franchise to never-before-achieved heights. He has become a very forceful and energetic leader in the Milwaukee community and a very vocal and action-oriented champion of social justice and anti-racism. In recognition of all these achievements, Peter has been awarded two honorary degrees: a doctor of humane letters from his alma mater, Franklin & Marshall, and a doctor of business from the University of Wisconsin–Milwaukee.

In the beginning no one in Milwaukee knew Peter was a twin. Peter always wears a business suit to Bucks games. One of the first times Daniel came to visit him, he wore Bucks gear—sweats and a hoodie—to the game. One of the fans shouted out to Dan, "Hey Peter, glad to see you're loosening up." This case of mistaken identity brings to mind another one from the time Peter was still working at Marquis Jet, which had recently been acquired by NetJets. Peter was at an executive meeting at NetJets headquarters in Columbus, Ohio, around Christmastime. The weather was bad. He was stuck in a snowstorm, unable to get back to New York. He called Dan and asked, "What are you doing for lunch?" Dan said, "I'm free. Why?" Peter told him, "I'm hosting our annual Christmas party for our customers and prospects at noon today at P.J. Clarke's. I'm not going to be able to make it. Can you do it for me?" Dan said, "Sure," and off he went to P.J. Clarke's. He knew a lot from Peter about the Marquis Jet business and about the

VIP guests—top-level business executives, sports stars, political players, and people from the entertainment world. Posing as Peter, Dan welcomed them all, hobnobbed with them and engaged in conversation, and wished them all a happy holiday. I asked Dan whether anyone knew, and he said, "No. Only one young woman who works for Peter was on the brink of figuring it out. She kept following me around and trying to talk with me about a project she was doing for Peter." I told her, "We can't talk about this now. This is a Christmas party. We'll talk about it back in the office." Mission accomplished.

In the summer of 2014, after Jim's death, Michael floored me by telling me one morning when we were at my house in East Hampton, "I want to write." I wasn't sure what he was talking about, so he explained that he wanted to write short stories. He began that very morning to write every day. He's very serious about pursuing fiction writing and sticks with it religiously. I wonder to myself whether Jim's death has in some way unleashed a powerful creative force in Michael.

After working on his own for some months, Michael decided he needed some formal training. He applied to several nonresidential writing programs and eventually earned a master's in fiction writing from Warren Wilson College in Asheville, North Carolina. I've spent my entire professional career in a creative business and have never ceased to be awed by the creative imagination—making something beautiful, inspiring, and moving where nothing before existed. I'm astonished by Michael's creative prowess. Along with pursuing his creative writing projects, Michael works as managing editor and chief content officer at an online health-care start-up focused on providing a holistic care regimen to sufferers of Crohn's and related diseases.

Our family has always been close-knit. Although we've gone through profound change with Jim's death, I think it's especially important in this new chapter of our lives that we continue to celebrate our familiar longtime family rituals. I want to continue to nurture our family bonds and keep them strong.

So our epic Thanksgiving dinners continue with the exact same menu we've had every year. Early in the week before Thanksgiving, in

Family Thanksgiving, 2019

Me with my grandchildren, Thanksgiving 2019

2014, shortly after Jim died, Dan calls me and says, "Mom, I have an important question to ask you." I'm a little nervous, not knowing what to expect, but I say, "Sure." He asks, "Would it be OK with you if I make the turkey this year?" I laugh and say, "That would be terrific!" Dan brines the turkey and roasts it in the oven at Trevor. It's absolutely delicious; we all love it. And Dan now has a continuing assignment for all Thanksgivings to come. As we gather for dinner that first

Dylan, the Christmas elf, 2019

Thanksgiving without Jim, Michael takes the chair at the head of the table, the chair that had been Jim's. He announces, "I'm now the patriarch." This touches my heart. All of our grandchildren understand that their ticket to Thanksgiving dinner is their Christmas list. They're all very earnest about putting their lists together, and all present their lists to me as they come into my apartment for dinner.

Christmas continues to be the massive celebration we all look forward to. Dan and Jackson buy my tree on the street, carry it home for me and set it up. I decorate it. Many of the decorations are from my childhood. We still gather for brunch around noon on Christmas Day; then Michael, wearing Jim's Santa hat, and Dylan, his elf, are in charge of distributing the gifts. Our rule is one at a time, so we can all oooohhh and aaaahhh over one another's gifts. The party usually degenerates into a rowdy, raucous laugh-fest.

Alexandra, Peter, Natalia, and Thomas

Jackson, Stephanie, Daniel, and Dylan

Our grandchildren continue to thrive and to delight me. I keep alive our Christmas ritual of giving each of my grandchildren "an experience of your choice with G'ma." Elle's favorite is for us to meet for brunch at Norma's, a very sophisticated restaurant, and then to go together to an elegant spa for facials. I love this experience with Elle at least as much as she does. Thomas's and Jackson's choice every year is a weekend in Milwaukee to visit Peter, work out in the Bucks training facility, and go to a Bucks game or two. We always go to great restaurants for breakfast and dinner. The boys can't wait for this weekend each year. They love it, and we have a fun time together. One year when they are around thirteen, as we get ready to board our flight to Milwaukee, my row is called before theirs is. I walk down the Jetway, stow my bag, and settle in. I keep an eye out for the boys but haven't yet seen them board. All of a sudden my phone beeps and I get a text from the boys, "Grandma, Delta announced they would give $500 to anyone who would give up their seat and take a later flight. We decided to do this, so see you later in Milwaukee." I leap out of my seat thinking, their parents will kill me. I grab my bag and sprint down the aisle as fast as I can. Midway down, I see my two little darlings, hunched down in their seats and laughing their heads off. They say, "Grandma, we got you; we pranked you!" The memory of their fathers pranking me by installing *"BARBARA FEIGIN, GET YOUR HEAD OUT OF YOUR ASS!"* on my first computer at Grey all those many years ago flashes through my mind. I start laughing with them and we head off for our weekend in Milwaukee.

Michael has been in a relationship for several years with Annelise Strigel, a lovely young woman who was born in New Orleans and raised in Mississippi but has lived for some time in New York. Our family has come to know Annelise, who has joined us at family gatherings over the years. Jim too had met Annelise. I think at first she was a bit overwhelmed by the energy and noise level of our get-togethers, but over time she's become more comfortable. Annelise is a producer for a firm that creates and executes major multimedia presentations for blue-chip clients around the world.

She had a client presentation in Barcelona, and Michael decided to meet her there for a short vacation. He told me he planned to surprise Annelise by proposing to her in Barcelona. I was overjoyed and excited for him. He told Annelise's parents his plan and got their blessing. Annelise inherited her grandmother's engagement ring, and Michael knew she'd always wanted to wear it as her own when she got engaged. He found the ring in Annelise's hiding place and took it with him to Barcelona. He and Annelise went for a hike high up in the hills overlooking the city. He got down on one knee and asked her to marry him. Annelise shouted, "Yes! I want to be a Feigin," and they began to plan their wedding.

June 23, 2018, was Michael and Annelise's wedding day. They were married at the Brooklyn Winery, a working winery with a rustic feel and an informal vibe. The winery is constructed with woods reclaimed from Hurricane Katrina, a charmed coincidence, since Annelise was born in New Orleans. Michael's daughters, Erica and Elle, were his "best persons," Peter, Daniel, Thomas, and Jackson were ushers, Dylan was the ring bearer, and Michael and I walked one another down the aisle. The men looked handsome in their tuxedos and the girls looked beautiful in their formal long black crepe jump suits. When all were in place, the curtain opened in the back of the atrium where the ceremony was being conducted. Annelise, radiant in her elegant bridal gown, was on her father's arm. Michael awaited her with a huge smile on his face, and she actually began to dance down the aisle. They beamed at one another as they recited their vows and when they finished, Annelise shouted with joy, "I'm a Feigin!" All at the wedding broke into applause and laughed with the bride and groom. This was truly one of the happiest weddings with which I've ever been involved. I'm elated for Michael, elated he's found his new beginning. I know Jim is smiling down at the newly married couple, maybe even laughing . . . "ho . . . ho . . . ho!" We wanted so much for Michael to find happiness, and with Annelise he has.

On August 20, 2022, Michael and Annelise's son, Charles James "Charlie" Feigin, is born. I'm enchanted with my seventh grandchild, and our entire family is overjoyed with this wonderful new life, new joy, new love.

The family at Michael and Annelise's rehearsal dinner, June 22, 2018

Michael and Annelise's wedding, June 23, 2018

Peter, Michael, and Daniel at Michael's wedding, June 23, 2018

Erica, Michael, Annelise, and Elle

Charlie, May 2023

CHAPTER TWENTY-SEVEN

Legendary Pioneer

Grey's centennial anniversary is in August 2017, one hundred years from the time Larry Valenstein launched his small agency and hired Arthur Fatt as his office boy. Larry and Arthur soon became partners and built a clientele in the retail and garment industries. They thought they needed a name for the agency that was shorter and easier to remember than "Valenstein and Fatt," so they named it Grey, after the color of the walls in their office. Larry and Arthur's partnership lasted for their lifetimes; together they paved the way for Grey to become one of the largest and most successful advertising agencies in the world, a "global powerhouse," as *Fortune* magazine dubbed it those many years ago.

During the year Grey celebrates its centennial anniversary, a milestone rarely achieved in the advertising world, the agency publishes a beautiful coffee-table book highlighting Grey's work over the years, its history, and the evolution of the philosophy that guided its efforts. A handful of Grey's "famously effective people" are featured with full-page photographs and interviews recapping what each has brought to the agency's success. I am deeply honored to be among them as, "Barbara Feigin, Master Strategist."

In the spring of 2018, Grey hosts a gala dinner to celebrate the centennial in Madison Park, across the street from the agency's offices. Grey's executives from around the world attend. When I arrive I run

MY AMERICAN DREAM   245

Me in the Grey centennial book, 2017

into Mary Ghiorsi, who'd worked with me on my speeches over many years. She says, "Come across the street to the office with me. I want to show you something." We walk into the lobby of Grey's office building where I see a wall of floor-to-ceiling billboards, each featuring the photo and story of one of Grey's eight "legendary pioneers" of the last century. Looking left to right across the wall I see Larry Valenstein and Arthur Fatt, the founders; Herb Strauss, the CEO who followed them; Ed Meyer, my longtime boss, who built Grey into a worldwide megaforce; Al Achenbaum, who originally inspired me to want to come to Grey; Shirley Young, my mentor and friend; myself; and Carolyn Carter, who led our European operations. To find myself among this group of storied pioneers, icons of the advertising world, is one of the true thrills of my life. It's an American's dream come true—a young refugee girl rising from literally nothing but the clothes on my back and accomplishing this. I know how proud my parents would be. And I know Jim is smiling down at me from wherever he may be.

CHAPTER TWENTY-EIGHT

We Are the Champions

It's July 20, 2021, and I'm sitting courtside in the Milwaukee Bucks Fiserv Forum, rapt as I watch the Bucks play the Phoenix Suns in the crucial game six of the NBA championship playoffs. I'm riveted, holding my breath, crossing my fingers and toes, wishing, hoping, praying for a Bucks victory. The entire game has been fiercely fought, with the lead bouncing back and forth throughout. As it comes to the closing few seconds, I can't breathe at all. When at last the final buzzer sounds, the Bucks have won the game 105 to 98. To the shock and surprise of much of the basketball world they have risen from a small-market doormat to become the NBA champions! The entire arena erupts with screams and shouts of joy. I'm caught up in the euphoria, laughing and crying and screaming, rushing to hug Peter who's played such an important role in making this dream come true.

Together with my family I watch as Peter joins the players, the coaches, and the owners of the Bucks at the center of the floor for the ceremonial presentation of the championship trophy. As Adam Silver, the commissioner of the NBA, presents the trophy, pandemonium reigns in Fiserv Forum. The capacity crowd of 17,000 rabid Bucks fans inside the arena, plus 65,000 more in the Deer District, a huge plaza outside the arena ringed with giant television screens on which they'd watched the game, is ecstatic. Along with my family and masses of

Family with NBA championship trophy

fans, I run out to the center of the floor, all of us slipping and sliding on the confetti raining from the ceiling and on the puddles of champagne the players have been spraying on one another to celebrate this incredible victory. Music blasts throughout the arena and outside a magnificent fireworks display lights up the sky. Fans are unable to tear themselves away; they want this magic moment of joy and glory to go on forever.

Eventually Peter grabs me and the rest of our family and rushes us to a private room off the floor where the trophy has been moved and a photographer is waiting to take pictures of Peter and the rest of us, each cradling the trophy. First Peter is photographed, then he together with his wife and kids, then his brothers, and finally he tells me it's my turn. It's an amazing, almost otherworldly, moment. I think Peter knows instinctively how much my being there with him means to me. The golden trophy is big—about half as tall as I am, and very heavy, much heavier than I expected. When I first pick it up it feels like I'm holding a two-year-old. I nearly lose my balance and I'm afraid I might drop it, but I hang on and the photo shoot continues. I think to myself, *This beautiful golden trophy is a lasting*

Peter with NBA championship trophy

symbol of Peter's seven-year dream actually becoming a reality. I'm overwhelmed with pride and love for Peter.

This grand achievement all started in May 2014, when Marc Lasry and Wes Edens took over ownership of the Milwaukee Bucks from the longtime owner, Senator Herb Kohl. Shortly thereafter, Jamie Dinan and Mike Fascitelli joined the ownership group. The team was an also-ran, playing in a run-down arena with a small and unenthusiastic fan base. The new owners hired Peter as president in October 2014, and together they created a vision, a dream, of winning the NBA championship and in the process building a committed, enthusiastic fan base. The hope was to leverage that championship to help change the culture of Milwaukee from segregated, divisive, and downbeat to inclusive and optimistic.

Since 2014, Peter has worked as part of this passionate leadership group to make the dream come true. Peter helped lead the effort to build the Fiserv Forum, the Bucks' much-admired, state-of-the-art arena, and he led the way in reenergizing the Bucks brand and fan base. Most importantly, the Bucks built a powerful team with a strong work ethic led by superstar Giannis Antetokounmpo, known as the "Greek Freak" and guided by a disciplined, talented coach, Mike Budenholzer, "Coach Bud." The Bucks mantra is to "get better every day," and they work tirelessly to do that. The fans in Milwaukee and all over Wisconsin, and around the world, have grown to love the Bucks. Peter, together with the owners, has become an outspoken community leader, always working to reach out and to bring Milwaukeeans together. And now the long-nurtured dream has become reality: the Bucks are the champions!

Two days after the championship game, the Bucks are honored with a ticker tape parade that wends its way through the city. The team, the owners, and key executives ride on the upper decks of bright red double-decker buses, waving and shouting to the cheering crowd of more than 100,000, all wearing Bucks gear, who have come out to celebrate. Our family is on Peter's bus, thrilled we're all able to share in this joyous experience. As Peter waves to the crowds on the right side of the bus, many of those we pass shout out to him, "Thank you, Peter." They know what a significant role Peter has played in making this glorious day happen. Although most Milwaukeeans know who Peter is, many still don't realize he's a twin. So Daniel stands on the left side of the bus, waving to the crowds, many of whom shout out to him, "Thank you, Peter." It's a wonderful, triumphant day for all of us. I wish Jim could have been with us for the win and the celebration. He would have relished all of it, laughing and bursting with pride for what Peter has helped accomplish. And my father would have been amazed at the distance his family has come from the days when he, my mother, and

I fled the Nazis. Once again, he would have been "tickled pink," as he used to say, with what his grandson has helped bring about.

The victory is an important catalyst in bringing the city of Milwaukee together. Milwaukee is a small market, with just the fortieth largest metro population in the US; it sees itself as an underdog, unlike the big, glitzy, flashy places like New York, Los Angeles, and Miami. Small-market underdogs don't usually become NBA champions. "The Bucks victory can profoundly resonate for the city," Peter says when he is interviewed after the game. In the heart of one of the nation's most racially segregated cities, night after night, the exuberant, diverse crowds in the Deer District, shown on TV sets around the world, projected a hopeful vision of what a more inclusive future could look like. As Peter said watching the parade, "you see the most diverse, the most optimistic, most celebrating crowd you've ever seen in your whole life. If you didn't know any better, you'd say this is the most diverse, vibrant city, all rooting for the same thing."

I and all our family are tremendously proud of Peter for helping to conceive a big, important dream and working tirelessly with grit and determination to turn that dream into reality. This is a magnificent accomplishment. My mother was right: big dreams really can come true.

EPILOGUE

A Letter to My Sons, My Grandchildren, and Future Generations

Now that you've read my story, let me tell you why I want you to have it. I want you all to know what came before you. That's important; it's part of the foundation of your lives, of what makes you who you are. I wanted you to know my parents—how brave and courageous they were when they took me, their two-and-a-half-year-old, and escaped in terror from certain death in Nazi Germany. And how grateful they were to be in America, the land of the free, where anyone with education and hard work can make his or her dreams come true. You've learned about my early days and about how eager I was to become an authentic American.

You've read my father's story, told in his own words, and learned who he was and how he navigated our family through seemingly insurmountable hardships and challenges in an epic, historically fraught time. This is all part of your own history.

It's also important for you to know how I managed to have a pioneering career in a time when very few women had careers and even fewer had both a family and a career. This was a time when women were clearly thought to have less value than men. I first became conscious of this gender inequity when I attended the women-only, one-year Harvard-Radcliffe Program in Business Administration and learned that not only was it separate from the Harvard Business

School's two-year MBA program to which women were not admitted, but it was in many ways *unequal*. In that time, women simply were not considered worth the investment of a second year of study. The thinking was that women wouldn't work in the kinds of important jobs men did, and in any event they wouldn't spend much time in the workforce at all before quitting to get married and have babies.

I wanted to go into marketing when I graduated from the Program, but again I learned that women were not valued as equals to men. Line marketing jobs with profit and loss responsibility, the stepping-stone jobs for career path advancement, were completely closed to women. Once again, women were not thought to be worth the investment of training and professional development since, just as at HBS, the prevailing notion was that they'd work only a short time before leaving to be married and have children.

This was the societal norm of the times. No one, not the business schools, not corporate America, not the public at large even contemplated that married women with children could have and excel at careers. I was certainly sensitive to the unfairness I and other women experienced. But it didn't occur to me in those days to object or rebel in any way. This was simply the way the world was. I moved on, went through the back door into marketing via market research, and did the best I could.

I went on to blaze some trails during my long business career, often the first woman in a particular position and often the only woman in the room. As I worked my way up the ladder, in nearly all the situations I faced I had no role model. I had to forge my own path as best I could. It sometimes took me a while to find my footing, and I sometimes stumbled and made mistakes. But over time I not only found my own way but helped to pave the way for other women who followed. And I learned what it means to work with colleagues who care for one another; to work collaboratively together, striving for excellence; to form lifelong relationships; and always to look for ways to make a difference. All this took hard work, long hours, focus, and concentration over many years. And you know what a whirlwind our family life was.

We could never have managed it all had Jim and I not had such a strong love for one another, such a mutually supportive partnership, and such a fierce dedication to our family. You all know how deeply loved by both of us each of you has been from the time you were born. For us, it has always been family first. But how does a strong family get forged? How does the family unit grow strong, and how does each individual build his or her own strengths? I learned much about this from my own parents, who modeled qualities throughout our lives together that I've tried to pass along to you. High values and a strong character were vital to my parents as principles for living; their determination, can-do mindset, and resilience helped them to build the future in America that meant so much to them; and their tenacious work ethic made it all possible.

Finally, I want you to know how important it is to create and nurture strong family bonds throughout all of life. Especially after Jim's stroke and its devastating effect on all of us, our steel-like bonds held us all together. We all showed Jim our love and support, trying to ensure he'd have the best life possible. And we've loved and supported one another, especially as we've each gone through times of vulnerability. These bonds are what has made our family a powerful, loving, enduring force.

As I reflect back over my many years, I'm thankful to have had a life that's been rich and full and rewarding beyond my dreams. Through all of its joys and its sorrows, its triumphs and its struggles, its good times and its tough times, I've tried to focus on being an optimistic problem solver, enthusiastic and resilient. I am forever and always grateful to be an American, because only in America could the life I dreamed about and more become a reality. As my mother taught me so long ago, as all of life evolves and reveals itself, dream big; work hard; and never, ever quit.

Let this be a guiding principle of your own lives as it has been of mine. And just one final thought: have fun and laugh every day. It will do your heart good.

I love you all very much,
Mom/G'ma
October 2021

ACKNOWLEDGMENTS

Reading my father's journal and learning for the first time about life-changing aspects of my family's history I'd never before known inspired me to write about my own life. I wanted to ensure my children, grandchildren, and generations to come would never be ignorant of what came before them. Since I'd never before written a book, I needed and received much help along the way, for which I'm enormously grateful. I thank my sister, Carolyn Granger, who shared with me memories of our childhood and of her conversations with our mother about the escape and our family's early days in America, and who organized the translations of my parents' letters to their parents and assembled supportive documentation. Thanks to my son Michael, who pushed and prodded me to stop procrastinating and to write, who brainstormed with me, and who gave me wise and practical counsel throughout. Keith Meatto became my coach, leading me through the generative phase of the work and teaching me much about writing along the way. Judy McClane Slattery, my longtime and dear Whitman friend and a brilliant writer herself, encouraged and supported me from the time I started to think about writing my story. Judy gave me courage to go forward and to keep at it, and she provided insightful and creative editorial feedback throughout the process. Candace Walsh, a friend of my son Michael and his classmate in the MFA program at Warren Wilson College, was my developmental editor, giving me invaluable help with organizing the manuscript and fleshing out my story. My Chehalis High School friends, Dixie Gillingham Sturza and Don Rhodes, encouraged me from the beginning and shared many memories of our days in Chehalis and at Chehalis High. And Doreen Massin, my friend and former Grey colleague, also urged me on, sharing many stories of our time together at Grey. My granddaughter, Alexandra Feigin, and my brother-in-law, Jim Granger, read my manuscript at an early stage and gave me their reactions and feedback, and Joshua Granger, my nephew, helped me by providing dramatic images to include with my story. Finally, my team at Girl Friday Productions, led by Karen Upson and Sara Addicott, together with G. Elizabeth Kretchmer, Laura Dailey, Georgie Hockett, and Rachel Marek worked tirelessly to turn this book into a reality beyond anything I could have imagined. To all who encouraged me and helped me in countless ways, I thank you with all my heart.

ABOUT THE AUTHOR

As a young German-speaking refugee who fled with her parents from Nazi Germany in 1940 at the onset of World War II, Barbara Sommer Feigin spent her childhood and teenage years in tiny Chehalis, Washington, yearning to become an "authentic" American girl.

Feigin's parents impressed upon her the power of education to open doors to opportunity. With the help of scholarships and work grants, she attended Whitman College, where she earned a Bachelor of Arts degree in political science. She then completed a graduate program in business run jointly by Harvard Business School and Radcliffe Graduate School at a time when women were not admitted to the Harvard Business School.

Encouraged by her parents' admonition to "dream big, work hard, and never quit," Feigin became a pioneering executive who found success in a completely male-dominated business—advertising—when career-building opportunities for women were virtually nonexistent. In her illustrious thirty-year career at Grey Advertising (now the Grey Global Group), she solidified her reputation as a visionary thinker. In all her years as a senior advertising executive and a corporate director, she was more often than not the only woman in the room. In 2017, Feigin was named one of the century's Legendary Pioneers by Grey.

Feigin and her husband, Jim, built a strong, loving family of three sons, including identical twins. Their lives were shattered when Jim had two very serious strokes when he was quite young. For the next twenty-five years, she was Jim's caregiver-in-chief. The family's strong bonds and great love for Jim helped them navigate this traumatic time.

Feigin currently lives in New York City.

Printed in the USA
CPSIA information can be obtained
at www.ICGtesting.com
JSHW082111310724
67312JS00004B/136